Goodison Glory

Goodison Glory

Everton's Millennium Giants Edition

by Ken Rogers

The Breedon Books
Publishing Company

First published in Great Britain by
The Breedon Books Publishing Company Limited
Breedon House, 3 The Parker Centre, Derby, DE21 4SZ.
2000

ISBN 1 85983 218 0

Printed and finished by Butler & Tanner Ltd., Selwood Printing Works, Caxton
Road, Frome, Somerset.

Jacket separations and printing by GreenShires, Leicester

Contents

New Millennium, New Owner, New Challenge - And More Debate About The Venue Of Royal Blue Legends

WHEN I was asked to research and write the official history of Goodison Park as part of the famous stadium's 1992 Centenary celebrations, it was not so much a chore as a pleasure.

My father lifted me over the Goodison turnstiles as a toddler to watch my first Everton game as a new decade dawned at the start of the 1950s.

He was obviously taking no chances. Even though I still could not walk or talk, he was inducting me as an Evertonian – son following father in the great tradition of Merseyside football. What he could not have predicted at that moment in time is that I would become so steeped in the history of the famous stadium that I would ultimately research and write its proud history, leading to the third re-print that is *Goodison Glory – The Millennium Giants Edition*.

When I completed the second re-write in 1998, the story ended with Howard Kendall still in charge during his third managerial reign and with chairman Johnson clinging on defiantly, albeit from his new base in Jersey. The great debate about a possible move from the Stadium Of Royal Blue Legends had reached fever pitch and then abated.

Since then, so much has happened that it was inevitable that the Goodison story would have to be brought up to date to reflect what has been an Everton revolution going into a new and challenging century.

Kendall, the greatest and most successful Everton manager of all time, had to suffer the indignity of reading in the press that his Goodison days were finally over in the summer of '98. He would press on with the Sword of Damocles, or rather the Sword of Johnson, hanging over his head. Kendall must have been under immense personal pressure in those final days. He deserved better, having accepted a poison chalice in many respects after a successful spell at Sheffield United, but the call had once again proved irresistible.

Blues' fans now had to show their remarkable loyalty once again – but not to the chairman who was becoming increasingly reclusive. The arrival of Walter Smith in time for the 1998-99 campaign was a major boost following weeks of speculation. First former player Brian Kidd was tipped for a return to Goodison Park after proving such an influential coach under Manchester United's Alex Ferguson. Then Leicester's Martin O'Neill stepped into the frame, only to step back out again with an improved contract at Filbert Street.

Managerless Sheffield Wednesday had been courting Smith. Johnson, realising that the former Glasgow Rangers boss was on the brink of a Hillsborough move, finally made the phone call that would bring this vastly experienced Scot to Merseyside.

It was progress, but more controversy was just around the corner. There would be major signings, the Duncan Ferguson calamity, the chairman's own exit, the decade's second marathon takeover battle and a True Blue triumph in the shape of Bill Kenwright.

Goodison Park, one of the wonders of Victorian England, had witnessed much change and challenge throughout the 20th century. One thing has not changed and that is the loyalty of the royal blue army.

The fans have turned up in their thousands at Goodison through good times and bad. These are no fair-weather supporters, but people who are steeped in Everton tradition and who deserve to see a major revival. I dedicate this book, not only to the players who have graced the legendary Goodison turf, but also those fans who have certainly graced the mighty stands and terraces for a century and more.

"Nil Satis Nisi Optimum" – Only The Best Is Good Enough for these remarkable supporters.

I went to Major Lester County Primary School in Everton Valley and played all my early football in Stanley Park, the original home of St Domingo FC and then Everton. Perhaps it was inevitable that I would follow the fortunes of the Blues. Incredibly, while I was immersed in the final stages of completing the first edition of *Goodison Glory* in 1992, I found myself playing on the famous pitch for the very first time, at the age of 43.

As I said to one of my teammates in a 'businessman's game' prior to Andy King's benefit match: "Magnificent, but 25 years too late!"

Perhaps it was because my head was full of names like Edgar Chadwick, Jack Southworth, Sandy Young, Harry Makepeace, Dixie Dean, Tommy Lawton and the rest, that the experience was extra-special.

It was a wonderful feeling to be treading in the footsteps of the greats whose feats I had been researching and whose deeds I was more than happy to recall. At the Gwladys Street End I even scored a penalty that Roy Vernon would have been proud of.

I would like to thank a number of people for their invaluable co-operation and support as I worked on both the first draft of *Goodison Glory* and this updated version which features a series of new chapters and new photographs. Firstly, the *Liverpool Echo* and its editor Mark Dickinson for co-operating with this new project and once again granting permission for me to use the newspaper's historic photographic archive. To chief photographer Stephen Shakeshaft and his team, plus all the former *Daily Post* and *Echo* photographers whose work at Goodison Park has clearly stood the test of time.

The *Echo's* chief Librarian Colin Hunt, Les Rawlinson and other members of the library team deserve a special mention. Their assistance was invaluable. My thanks go to Everton Football Club for encouraging me to once again bring this work up to date.

My appreciation goes to everybody who had an in-put into this publication, not least all the writers and reporters who chronicle football, week in, week out, effectively compiling match reports, but in real terms writing the history books of tomorrow.

Everton's Millennium Giants panel (left to right): Ian Macdonald (Everton Independent Supporters), Jim King (Everton Supporters, Goodison), Sir Philip Carter, Bill Kenwright, Brian Labone, Ken Rogers, Alan Myers (Everton Communications Manager), Dave Hickson, David Prentice (Echo Everton correspondent).

Goodison Giants – Walking Proudly In The Everton Hall Of Fame

AS Everton played out the final months of the 21st century, with a glorious past stretching out behind them, there was clearly one very important challenge remaining.

The club had decided to honour the Giants who had played their part in a history-making century and who would soon be taking their place in the club's first official Hall Of Fame.

I was proud to be asked to chair the panel which would ultimately, with the help of the fans, select the ten players deemed to be Everton's greatest – one from each decade.

It would have been easier to climb Mount Everest without oxygen. The challenge was almost impossible. For instance, how could you separate Ted Sagar, Tommy Lawton and Joe Mercer in the 1930s? What criteria would you use to assess the merits of heroes like Dave Hickson and Peter Farrell in the 1950s? How could we prevent one meeting from stretching out from midday until midnight as we debated the credentials of a Golden Vision and a World Cup winner, Alex Young and Alan Ball?

Could we make a case for Ball in the 1970s or would that have been ducking the issue and undermining the obvious claims of Bob Latchford in that era. The other burning issue concerned the most successful Everton team of all time – the heroes of the 1980s. How could you select just one from Neville Southall, Peter Reid, Andy Gray, Graeme Sharp and the rest ? Tricky? You better believe it. It was fortunate we had the definitive judge on that score playing a key role as a VIP panel member – manager Howard Kendall.

My challenge was to research appearances and honours won, decade by decade, providing a working list for the panel that would keep us busy in the Goodison Park boardroom over a three-month period. The panel itself was truly representative, taking account of the views of the board, famous playing personnel covering a number of key eras, the media – and, of course, the fans. Sir Philip Carter and Bill Kenwright agreed to play their part along with former playing

heroes Dave Hickson, Brian Labone, Howard Kendall and Graeme Sharp. The media link was provided by myself and the Echo's Everton correspondent David Prentice. Jim King of the Everton Supporters (Goodison) Club and Ian Macdonald of the Everton Independent Supporters completed the group.

Naturally, those panel members who were former players could not vote for themselves in a given decade although they could join in the the debate which was fascinating, not least when the ex-professionals gave a behind-the-scenes insight into many of the leading candidates from the second half of the century. The plan was to select the ten Millennium Giants by the end of October 1999 and then invoke a major fans' poll to see if it deviated in any significant way from the previous list. If this had been the case, it would have been back to the drawing board for one final debate.

The panel ultimately came to a consensus on every issue – except

Giants on parade… Duncan McKenzie (representing Bob Latchford), Howard Kendall, Alex and Nancy Young, Tom Watson (representing father Dave), Gordon West (representing Neville Southall), Dave and Pat Hickson, Bill Kenwright, Brian Labone (representing T. G. Jones), Keith Chedgzoy (representing Sammy Chedgzoy), Sir Philip Carter, Mrs Dolly Sagar and grandson James Potter (representing Ted Sagar), Melanie Walker and son Daniel Dean Haslam (representing Dixie Dean), Roy Chedgzoy (also representing Sammy), Philip and David Dunkley (representing Jack Sharp).

Fifties giant Dave Hickson and his wife Pat with Bill Kenwright and Sir Philip Carter.

one. Young or Ball for the 1960s. Brian Labone summed up the dilemma when he said: "There is no way you can leave Alan Ball out, but Young is a legend!"

Labone was clearly leaning towards Ball in the various meetings, but then he would try to persuade himself the other way. I can remember him saying: "Bally was a great player and the most consistent. Then again, Alex brought so much skill to the great side he played in. He had a lovely touch and was idolised by the fans. I kicked him in training one time and word got out. The following Saturday the fans booed me, even though I'd been at the club for years!"

Labby's humour could not hide the fact that we were split on the Young-Ball issue. My vote was for Young. Jim King, one of the panel members from the terraces, was a Ball fan. Jim, a respected voice amongst supporters, said: "Ball was an inspiration to the fans through his commitment. While Alex was a brilliant player, you had to question his commitment away from home."

We sat back, intrigued to see which way the supporters would lean. In the poll, Ball's vote was split between two decades, the 1960s and the 1970s. Brian Labone actually gained more votes than

him in the 1960s, but Young came out on top.

Two panel members had not been at the final meeting when the vote was split down the middle. In the final reckoning, they too edged it towards Young and so the die was cast. It was a good, healthy sign that the debate had been so fierce. It highlighted the fact that Everton is a giant of a club, full of legends and super heroes. Here are a full list of the final candidates in each decade with the actual Millennium Giant in capitals . . .

1900-1910: **JACK SHARP,** Alex "Sandy" Young, Jack Taylor.
1910-1920: **SAM CHEDGZOY,** Harold Makepeace.
1920-1930: **WILLIAM RALPH "DIXIE" DEAN,** Warney Cresswell, Alex Troup.
1930-1940: **TED SAGAR,** Joe Mercer, Tommy Lawton.
1940-1950: **T. G. JONES,** Wally Fielding, Alex Stevenson.
1950-1960: **DAVE HICKSON,** Peter Farrell, Bobby Collins.
1960-1970: **ALEX YOUNG,** Brian Labone, Alan Ball.
1970-1980: **BOB LATCHFORD,** Alan Ball, Howard Kendall.
1980-1990: **NEVILLE SOUTHALL,** Graeme Sharp, Peter Reid.
1990-2000: **DAVE WATSON,** Duncan Ferguson.

The life story of each Millennium Giant is featured throughout this new edition of Goodison Glory. The book had previously majored on significant matches at Goodison Park which in itself brought out the star quality of the club's greatest players. Now those individuals have their own place in a Hall Of Fame that will grow year by year.

The Finest And Most Complete Ground In The Whole Kingdom

*B*EHOLD *Goodison Park! No single picture could take in the entire scene the ground presents, it is so magnificently large, for it rivals the greater American baseball pitches. On three sides of the field of play there are tall covered stands, and on the fourth side the ground has been so well banked up with thousands of loads of cinders that a complete view of the game can be held from any position.*

The spectators are divided from the playing piece by a neat, low hoarding, and the touch line is far enough from it to prevent those accidents which used to be predicted at Anfield Road, but never happened. Taking it altogether, it appears to be one of the finest and most complete grounds in the whole kingdom, and it is to be hoped that the public will liberally support the promoters.

Out of Doors publication,
October 1892.

(Top) This is possibly the first image of Goodison Park, a very rough sketch of 'the new Everton football ground' published in the *Liverpool Football Echo* on 13 August 1892. It is clearly not to scale with the palings on the right (the Goodison Road side) too close to the pitch. A cinder bank sloped back on this side. But is nevertheless a fascinating insight into England's first major football stadium.

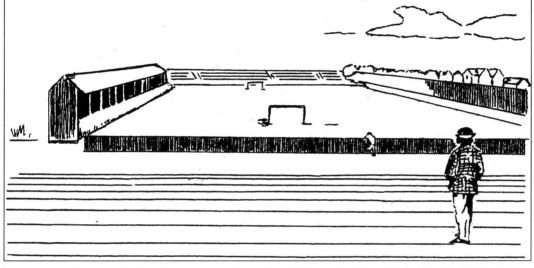

(Bottom) Blueprint for the New Goodison, revealed by chairman Peter Johnson in May, 1997. It is in stark contrast to that first image of Goodison Park, published in the *Football Echo* in 1892, and reflects the football stadia revolution of the 1990s with many of football's oldest clubs either moving home or contemplating an historic switch. One thing is for certain. Everton Football Club will live up to its famous motto going into the 21st century. Nil Satis Nisi Optimum — Only The Best Is Good Enough.

Goodison Park in November 1892, when the Blues entertained Heart of Midlothian. This drawing was published in the *Out of Doors Magazine*. The original church of St Luke the Evangelist is clearly visible. This was a temporary structure that was eventually re-sited in Blowick, near Southport, making way for the present church in 1901.

Goodison Park as it looked from 1938 when the Gwladys Street Stand was completed in time for a Royal visit. The stadium then changed very little until 1971 when the magnificent 1909 Main Stand made way for today's equally magnificent structure.

How an artist envisaged the breathtaking tripledecker Main Stand that was finally completed in 1971.

Introduction

GOODISON GLORY does not aspire to be the definitive history of Everton Football Club. The birth of the Blues has already been dealt with in previous publications, not least in the *History of Everton, 1878-1929* by Thomas Keates and the *Official Centenary History* by John Roberts, published in 1978.

When I first set about writing *One Hundred Years Of Goodison Glory* back in 1992, it was to mark the centenary of one of the most famous grounds in the world by recalling the great games played at this historic venue. In its time, Goodison Park has entertained kings and queens, hosted FA Cup Finals, staged major World Cup matches and been the scene of a thousand and one dramatic Football League and Premiership battles.

Goodison Park is the home of football legends and the eventful careers and feats of many of those giants of yesteryear are captured in words and pictures in the pages that follow. The author makes no apology for repeating the story of the famous 'split' that inspired Everton to leave Anfield and cross Stanley Park for pastures new. No book about Goodison Park would be complete without a clear assessment of the arguments and counter-arguments leading to the club's historic change of venue in 1892. It was a bold decision that would lead to the formation of Liverpool Football Club and the beginning of a rivalry that continues to amaze outsiders.

It is intriguing that, 106 years after the 'emigration' from Anfield to Goodison, the moving debate is back on the agenda in a big way. The vision for the 21st century is dealt with in a new chapter of *Goodison Glory*, but it is the glorious past that still fires the imagination of an army of fans.

My original research for this book revealed a host of new angles. The handwritten club 'minute' books of 1892 were gathering dust in an old vault when I came across them. They brought alive the characters and pioneers of the last century who were brave enough to plot a new beginning. This book salutes their initiative. It also provides a fascinating insight into the training methods of the last century and compares them with modern requirements. There is an insight into the Goodison Park turnstile frauds of 1895 and the Goodison Park Riot which took place the same year.

But the main body of this book is tied up with match action with the emphasis solely on Goodison Park. The first-ever League game; the first League win; the first FA Cup success; the first European game and so on. How did the fans react on those rare relegation days? What was it like at Goodison the day seven goals were scored before half-time? What was it like the day the immortal Dixie Dean made, not only his debut, but his final appearance? Historic matches, golden moments and also days of total despair. Over 50 very special games come under the microscope, spanning over 108 years of *Goodison Glory*.

Hopefully, your favourite encounter is featured amongst these pages. Even if it is not, there will almost certainly be reference to stars and personalities you particularly associate with.

This book could not have been written without the help of the 'Goodison watchers' who have gone before, not least my predecessors on the *Liverpool Echo*, *Football Echo* and *Liverpool Daily Post* whose reports and observations I have drawn on heavily during the compilation of this book. I speak particularly about the likes of Ernest Edwards ('Bee'), Bob Prole ('Ranger'), Leslie Edwards and in more recent years, men like Michael Charters and Charles Lambert. The present *Echo Blue Watch* continues to include David Prentice whose reports of today are the history pages of tomorrow.

A complete bibliography appears elsewhere, but first and foremost, I would like to thank the *Liverpool Echo* for allowing me access to their archive, as well as granting permission for the use of the vast majority of photographs in this publication.

Indeed, the first 'image' of Goodison comes from a rough sketch that appeared in the *Football Echo* on 13 August 1892 – 11 days before the official opening. It is clearly not to scale in as much as the palings down the right (the Goodison Road side) are far too near the pitch, but it is nevertheless a fascinating insight into the thinking of the day. What was futuristic and spectacular to them, might seem plain and distinctly average to the fans of the late 20th century. But one should not overlook the fact that Goodison Park was the first major soccer ground to be developed in this country. Everton took the lead and the rest followed.

The *Football Echo* carrying the sketch also described the ground in considerable detail. The 'prestige' covered stand, on what is now the Bullens Road side of the ground, accommodated the changing rooms and the various offices. The paper asked its readers to consider the achievement of the 'Young Everton party' in transforming the Mere Green Field into an exciting football venue in such a short space of time.

The report said: *The place has been transformed from a morass into one of the best appointed enclosures it is possible to clap eyes on; and all this has been done in the space which has elapsed since the last football season ended. That the committee of the Everton Club were put on their mettle in effecting such a change can be well understood by those who saw the wilderness at Goodison Road before the magic wand of Mr Kelly, the contractor, was passed over it.* [Ben Kelly would eventually become a club director].

The utmost credit is due to this gentleman for his work. He entered heart and soul into the undertaking and appeared inspired along with the committee of the club, in letting the cynics see what could be achieved.

The writer now compared the new venue to the former Anfield headquarters, declaring: *The ground is very extensive, perhaps too much so, and an ordinary crowd will almost get lost in it. It is capable of accommodating a couple of the old Anfield enclosures and then allowing room for knocking about. There is a stand (now Bullens Road) that goes nearly the full length of the field and is capable of seating, so Mr Kelly informs us, over 5,000 people. It is built gallery fashion so that every person who goes on it might have a comfortable and obstructless view of the game. They will also be well-sheltered from the biting east winds that are so prevalent during the football season. At the rear of this will be found a training track for the players which the 'sprinters' of the party will find very useful. Underneath the stand, all sorts of accommodating offices have been built. Here*

will be found well-appointed bathrooms, dressing-rooms, W.C., storerooms, offices for the secretary and a private room for referees, access to the latter being made from the field of play. The players will not have to parade themselves through the public street, as was the case at Anfield Road, in all their 'War paint' and, what is of more importance, visiting teams will not have to 'run the gauntlet' through a crowd of incensed partisans whom they might probably have displeased in some manner on the field.

Here also will be found a telephonic apparatus, connecting the 'Football Echo' offices with the ground which will enable us to give the results of matches, as we did at Anfield, immediately the game finishes.

Prior to telephone contact, newspapers used carrier pigeons to get match information back to base.

The paper now described the goal ends, reporting: *At either end of the ground, strong, well-built galleries have been erected, computed to accommodate at least 10,000 persons and the Goodison Road side has been banked up in such a manner that from 15,000 to 18,000 people can arrange themselves along it in the face of the ornate stand opposite.*

In the centre of the Goodison Road cinder bank, set back against the walling of the ground, secretary Molyneux had another office. It was said that he sat here in his easy chair, writing cheques or keeping an eye on the extent of his vast domain. Chairman Mahon's seat on match days was directly opposite, on the far side of the pitch in the East Stand (Bullens Road). It was situated above the door and passageway that led to the changing rooms. There was standing accommodation in front of the East Stand.

The new pitch was said to be in top-class condition and ready to meet the hard work to which it would soon be subjected. The report said: *Most of the turf has been cut from Aintree. Many hundreds of cartloads of cinders have been brought in for draining and filling. On opening day, the place will be the finest, best-equipped and most comfortable football ground in the land.*

And so we have the perfect image of Goodison Park, 1892. If only those Goodison pioneers could stand in the centre-circle now and cast their eyes around the place, I think they would be well satisfied that their labours led to something so very special.

George Mahon's Dream And The Kicking' Of King John

GOODISON Park was England's first major football stadium. Officially opened on 24 August 1892, by that giant of the game Lord Kinnaird in the esteemed presence of Mr F.J.Wall, secretary of the Football Association, and Mr J.J.Bentley, president of the Football League, it inspired gasps of admiration from all those who saw it for the very first time.

More than a hundred years on, the proud home of Everton Football Club continues to set standards of excellence to retain its place as one of Great Britain's most spectacular sporting venues. The ground is very different today to the soccer citadel that rose out of a 'howling desert' which is how the original Mere Green Field was described prior to the royal blue pioneers turning it, almost overnight, into a football arena of character and quality.

Molineux, the home of Wolverhampton Wanderers, had been opened three years earlier, but was still fairly basic. Newcastle East End had become Newcastle United in 1892 and moved from their original Chillingham Road ground in Heaton to St James' Park, but it was little more than a field. Anfield, the ground Everton left behind on the other side of Stanley Park following a row over the rent, was but a shadow of its new rival. And so the Everton members and leading lights like George Mahon and Dr James Clement Baxter had every right to view their 'new baby' with a bursting pride, mixed with a sense of relief that the gamble to break free of the shackles of 'King' John Houlding, their former president and Anfield landlord, had been such a resounding success.

Early Everton historian Thomas Keates, who chronicled the club's first 50 years, and John Roberts, author of the official *Centenary History* published in 1978, combine to give us a clear indication of the row that led to Everton turning their back on their Anfield home where they had played for nine years between 1884 and 1892.

Previously, of course, Stanley Park and Priory Road had played host to church team St Domingo and the Everton club it spawned in November 1879, at a meeting at the Queen's Head Hotel, Village Street, near the original Everton Toffee House.

Anfield had been a popular venue, but as Keates wrote: *A crisis in the club's affairs loomed in 1891, a smouldering fire that burst into flames.* He was referring to the increasing discontent amongst the members regarding the power game being played by Houlding, looked on either as the father of Association Football in the city, or a money-grabbing tyrant, depending on whose side you were on in an internal war that was accelerating to a climax early in 1892.

When the original move to Anfield took place, Houlding decided he was not only going to be the club's president, but also its representative tenant. The ground was but a short distance from the Sandon Hotel of which he was the proprietor. Club committee meetings were held there, the players changed there and Everton's various social gatherings were inevitably held within its walls. Many of the members, some of them still retaining strong connections with the St Domingo Church, objected to these powerful links with a drinking hostelry. But more than that, there was mounting resentment against Houlding.

The football field itself belonged to Mr Joseph Orrell and an adjacent field to Mr John Orrell, a brewer like Houlding. Joseph had given the club permission to use his field on the basis that 'the Everton Football Club keep the existing walls in good repair, pay the taxes, do not cause themselves to be a nuisance to Mr Orrell and other tenants adjoining, and also pay a small sum as rent, or subscribe a donation each year to the Stanley Hospital in the name of Mr Orrell'.

It was clear that he intended the club to benefit from any monetary advantage gained by the use of his field, an extremely generous gesture. But as soon as the prosperity of the new Anfield location seemed assured, Mr Houlding changed the ground rules and, instead of being the club's representative tenant, was suddenly their landlord. He intimated that as the Everton profits increased, so would the rent. It soared from £100 in 1885-86 to £240 in 1888-89 and then £250 the following year.

On 24 July 1888, the club's executive made a very sensible decision by refusing to spend funds on stands and expensive accommodation on the annual tenancy. Instead, they applied for a lease. Houlding immediately refused, but said that as long as the club paid a fair rent (or his interpretation of a fair rent) and did not interfere with the boundary walls without

George Mahon, whose vision and determination inspired the move from Anfield to Goodison Park.

his permission, he would not disturb the tenancy. At the same time, he added the rider that if any refreshments should be required on the Anfield ground, the landlord should have the sole right to supply them.

The complaints of the members flared into open anger. The men who would now prove inspirational leaders, the Mahons, Baxters and Claytons took centre stage.

They wanted to form the club into a Limited Liability Company for the express purpose of acquiring the Everton Football Ground (Anfield). This was put in the form of an official resolution at a special committee meeting held on 22 May 1889. It was going to be a long drawn out war of words and deeds. Houlding and his supporters tried to take the upper hand with the trump card of possession. A general meeting was called on 15 September 1891 at the Royal Street Hall, close to Everton Valley, where Mr W.E. Barclay, a Houlding supporter, took the chair. He gave Houlding the floor and King John, after reading some letters from Mr Orrell's solicitor, now outlined his own plans for the formation of a Limited Liability Company. A prepared printed prospectus proposed the purchase of Mr Orrell's and Mr Houlding's land, and the stands, offices, etc., at a total cost of £9,237 10s.

Mr Barclay, after taking some questions, now proposed and Mr Howarth seconded a resolution: "That the scheme as explained be adopted." Now Mahon climbed to his feet. He put a bold amendment, seconded by Mr Montgomery: That the scheme proposed be not entertained and that the committee have authority from this meeting to negotiate with Mr Houlding as to the renting of such further land as may be required, subject to Mr Houlding making the necessary arrangements with Mr Orrell." The amendment was carried.

There was now a succession of executive meetings and deputations without any progress being made. Mr Houlding sent a letter to the Committee pointing out the existing conditions of tenancy. To try and head off the growing

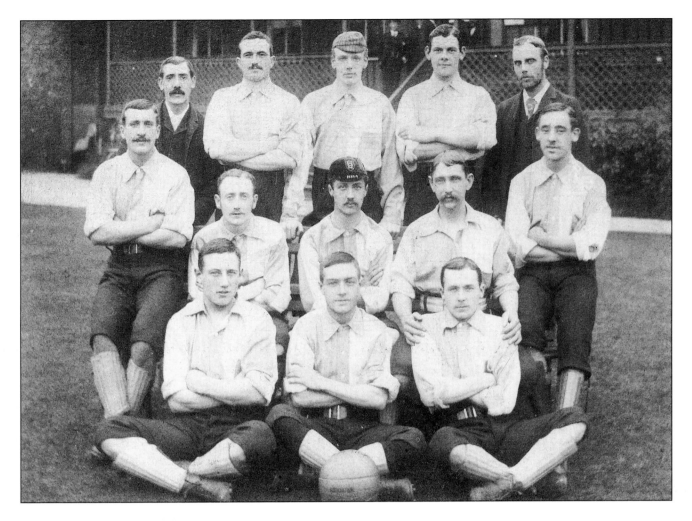

agitation for a move to a new venue, Houlding also made it clear that he would not give any undertaking whatsoever about the stands.

This new move was intended to be an effective obstacle to any change of ground, but it only served to fire up Mahon and his supporters. Keates has left us with a clear picture of Mahon's character and constitution. The man who, more than most, had a clear sight of a new beginning away from Anfield was respected as an accountant and a member of the Walton Local Board. By his own admission, he had been anti-football earlier in his life, but when he became the organist at St Domingo Church, he was gradually converted to the pastime being increasingly taken up by members of the congregation.

Bearded, extremely smart and articulate, Mahon inspired confidence in all those around him. His qualities as a fearless leader, some might call him a revolutionary, would now be put to the test. The 'split', as people now referred to it

throughout the city, was looming large on the horizon. Keates summed up the intense pressure being put on key individuals like Mahon when he said: 'It involved considerable sacrifice of time, mental anxiety, diversion from their urgent business responsibilities, monetary risks, partisan denunciation and misrepresentation. The constructive responsibility entailed was intimidating; the finding of a new ground, the drudgery and expense of levelling, draining and sodding; the formidable items of stands, offices, dressing-rooms, etc., and of incalculable (in advance) tons of bricks, woodwork, roofing, were enough to scare average men from the undertaking. But having voiced their discontent and dared the risky role of leaders, they shut their eyes to the consequences and the certain abuse that failure would ensure them.

The time had now come, in Mahon's mind, to stop talking and take action. At a special general meeting at the College, Shaw Street, on 25 January 1892, it was

Everton in 1889-90. Back row (left to right): D.Waugh (trainer), A.Hannah (captain), R.E.Smalley, D.Doyle, Mr R.Molyneux (secretary). Middle: A.Latta, J.Weir, J.Holt, G.Farmer, E.Chadwick. Front: C.Parry, F.Geary, A.Brady. While this happy group was being photographed on the bowling green of the Sandon Hotel near Anfield, trouble was brewing behind the scenes over the increase in rent.

once again made clear that a proposal to form the club into a Limited Liability Company, in accordance with Mr Houlding's prospectus, would not be entertained.

With the loss of the Anfield ground now a virtual certainty, Mahon played his ace card. He had been weighing up alternatives for some time and now spoke up about a possible new ground. A voice from the main body of the hall shouted: "Yer can't find one!" Mahon retorted: "I've got one in my pocket."

He was, of course, referring to Goodison Park, or the Mere Green Field as it was known at that moment in time. Those Everton stalwarts Dr James Clement Baxter and Mr W.R.Clayton now stood firmly by Mahon's side. They were an intriguing mix. If Mahon was the reasoned tactician, Clayton was the temperamental militant. As Keates wrote: *He added a dash of bitter to the mild.*

Dr Baxter was different again. He was said to have a sunny smile, a merry note and an optimism that improved his patients' well-being, not so much with a

medicine bottle as with a cheery glance. He would prove to be Everton's 'Good Samaritan' in terms of easing their financial worries in those worrying times before and just after the opening of Goodison Park. But more of that later.

For now, the battle was still to be won with Houlding indicating that he fully intended to carry on with an 'Everton Football Club' at the Anfield ground. This now became the subject of a major dispute after it was learned that Houlding had registered a new company in Somerset House with the title of 'The Everton Football Club and Athletic Ground Company Limited'. The signatures appended were Robert Berry, William (not John) Houlding, Alexander Nisbet, John James Ramsey, John Dermot, William Francis Evans and John McKenna. The battle lines were now firmly drawn up. Mahon knew exactly who and what he was up against.

There was much comment about the underhand way the new 'Everton' company had been registered without the full knowledge of the members and their committee. There were those who felt that Houlding had a case, but Mahon argued vehemently that his committee would fight tooth and nail to protect the interests of the majority of members who were clearly on his side. After all, there could only be ONE Everton, as laid down in the rules of both the Football Association and the Football League.

Messrs Clayton and Molyneux now attended a hearing in London at the Football Association's headquarters to settle the dispute once and for all. The FA Council adopted the following resolution: 'The Council, in accordance with its past decisions, will not accept any membership of any club bearing a name similar to one already affiliated with this Association in the name of the Everton club, and will only recognise the action of a majority of its members at a duly constituted meeting.'

This resolution effectively wiped out Houlding's dream of carrying on with an 'Everton' of his own at Anfield. The

Everton in 1890-91. This was the year Houlding increased the Anfield rent to £250, infuriating the vast majority of club members. The team, meanwhile, got on with the business in hand. Back row (left to right): D.Waugh (trainer), R.Stockton (umpire), A. Hannah (captain), J.Angus, D.Doyle, R.Molyneux (secretary). Middle: A.Latta, D.Kirkwood, J.Holt, W.Campbell, A.Milward. Front: A. Brady, F.Geary,

Everton committee now met in February 1892, with Mr Jackson in the chair. Those present were Dr Baxter and Messrs Atkinson, Griffiths, Nisbet, Ramsey, Howarth, Stockton, Clayton, Carrier, Coates and Molyneux (secretary). Resignations were on the agenda and accepted from Houlding men, Barclay and Williams. Mr Nisbet then made an application, on behalf of Mr Houlding, that the book containing the list of members be sent to that gentleman. The request was supported by Mr Ramsey. Several members commented on the adverse attitude which Mr Houlding had assumed towards the club, and it was resolved to refuse the loan of the book.

Nisbet and Ramsey now came under intense pressure. Mr Clayton proposed that the action of the pair in supporting Houlding's claim to the name of 'Everton' should now result in a severe censure, and the resolution was carried. The majority of the committee went further by declaring that they fully expected to have notice regarding the resignation of the president (Houlding) in time for the next meeting, as well as those of the people who had attached themselves to his interests.

Houlding would indeed be 'kicked out with the whole city captivated by this very public battle. The meeting at which the Everton president would finally be declared 'Offside' took place on Tuesday, 15 March 1892. I particularly like the report carried in the subsequent edition of the *Liverpool Review*, a weekly publication described as being 'Of Politics, Society, Literature and the Arts'. The Everton business obviously came under the heading 'Politics'.

It said: *There is a terrible racket going on in Liverpool just now. The city, for all that is known to the contrary, may be on the eve of a dire calamity. It is not that Mr De Bels Adam is going to resign the mayoralty and be succeeded by 'Plain Joe' or that coal is going up to 30s an ounce, or that another line of pipes is to be laid down between Liverpool and Vyrnwy. These would be simple trifles compared to the catastrophe in view. Hush! Break it gently, breath it with care, it is a football crisis, or, in other words, 'King Houlding' of Everton has been kicked. Not kicked physically, but kicked out of the presidency and from the committee of the Everton Football Club. Circumstances have been leading up to this for a long time, and on Tuesday night the 'kicking' process came off amid a great deal of enthusiasm. Oh! Football. There seems to be as much gratitude in you, in so far as 'King Houlding' is concerned, as there is for politics.*

Lord Kinnaird, the most respected figure in the game, who officially opened Goodison Park on 24 August 1892.

Dr James Clement Baxter who eased Everton's financial burden during the move to Goodison in 1892. He served the club unrelentingly until his death in 1928.

Years ago 'King Houlding' advanced the then struggling but rising Everton Football Club funds at a small rate of interest. He also assisted the organisation in other ways, for which the members were righteously thankful. As a landlord he lent the club a ground at a moderate rental to play on. He advanced money to erect grand stands, and provide all the rest of the paraphernalia of a first-class football club. Things went on swimmingly, *and the Everton players made a name second to none in the football world. Then came a change of scene. Things were not what they seemed. As the club prospered, the rental of the ground increased, and the interest asked by the landlord for money advanced went up perceptibly. There were mumblings and grumblings, and finally the storm burst. 'King Houlding' insisted that he was in the right; the great majority of members insisted that he was in the wrong. The 'King' began to assert his power; his subjects broke out in open rebellion. Very soon it became a war to the knife.*

On one side were the 'King', the sinews of war, and a small and chosen band; on the other side were a big army of malcontents. Fighting, armistices and stratagems, first on the part of the 'King' and then on the part of the rebels, followed alternately. Finally, the 'King' has been 'kicked' and the victorious host have elected to migrate to pastures new and a fresh field, where a heavy rental will cease from troubling and the footballists will be at rest.

The *Liverpool Review* now chastised both parties. It said: *This business is very sad, and, as a large number of onlookers think, very stupid. There can be no doubt that 'King Houlding' has done a very great deal for the Everton Football Club, and no doubt the club has done something for 'King Houlding'. But neither of the contending parties seem prepared to admit this. 'The more foolish of them' say the onlookers. And it really is a pity that a man like 'King Houlding' should be mixed up in such an unseemly wrangle as that which has been going on in Everton football for months past.*

The *Review* now posed an intriguing question as to the future and the possibility of rivalries reaching fever pitch. It said: *The fat is in the fire now. There is just this to be said. Perhaps 'King Houlding' will run a new football club on the present Everton ground (Anfield). If he does, the migrators to the new ground in Goodison Road will have a rival bad to beat. The two organisations may prove more beneficial or more hurtful to local football generally than the one organisation under the old order of things. That remains to be seen. Meanwhile, the football loving public may anticipate the future outcome with perfect composure. One thing is certain, however. After the 'kicking' of Tuesday night it would appear to be hopeless to expect 'King Houlding' and the old Everton Football Club to come together again. To use a football term, 'King Houlding' is palpably offside. The organisation on Tuesday night numbered some 500 members, and of these only eighteen or 20 stood by the 'King'. The king is dead; long live the king'.*

This very colourful description of one of the most important meetings Everton have ever had highlights the remarkable level of support Mahon had from the grassroots membership. It was a case of: 'Power to the people'. There were a considerable number of Press reports suggesting that the whole affair somehow had political undertones. The lively *Liverpool Review* belittled this idea in that same 1892 article, saying: *The split is purely a business one. If not, why all the talk and twaddle about 'King Houlding' reaping incalculable wealth from his hotel (The Sandon), which adjoins the old ground; and why all the talk and twaddle about some other brewer or brewers finding the funds to open the new ground -brewers with tied*

This unusual drawing depicts the sale of famous forward Jimmy Settle from Bury to Everton in 1898 for the princely sum of £400. Settle was the original goalpoacher, a skilful inside-forward who netted 97 goals for Everton between 1898 and 1908.

houses in the immediate vicinity? Judging by the statements, pro and con, there would seem to be more beer than anything else mixed up with the row, though surely the game of football is not going to be prostituted as a means of selling XXX. This would be kicking 'offside' indeed'.

There is, of course, a certain irony about this last statement. Exactly 100 years on, in their Centenary season, the club formed at Anfield after Everton departed to Goodison Park, found themselves backed officially for the first time by a world-famous brewery! I suggest that Houlding, looking down from above, is well pleased. His old rival, Mahon, still conducting a heavenly battle of words, is almost certainly saying: "I told you so!"

Laughter, Hisses, Uproar —
And A New Home

WE CAN gain a fascinating insight into the meeting in which John Houlding – the Everton president, Anfield landlord and proprietor of the Sandon Hotel – was expelled from the presidency on 15 March 1892. The 'Liverpool Review', in its 26 March edition, carried some rough notes, written by one of the Everton members who attended that historic gathering. They capture the mood of the occasion perfectly.

8.05: Business starts. Houlding asked to take the chair. Won't. Minutes. Guarantee Fund. Hartley's amount received with loud shots of 'good old jam!' Hudson's with equally loud shouts of 'good old soap!' Chairman's speech. Lasts 40 minutes. In my opinion settles the matter at once. Members liability. Satisfactorily answered by Cornett. Tom Howarth rises and is received with cries of 'How many shares are they giving you?' – laughter, hisses, uproar, 'sit down', 'company', & few feeble cheers completely drowned.

9.00: All present wildly excited. Howarth fearfully and wonderfully interrupted as he wanders away from the question.

9.30: McKenna rises and is received with terrible howls of execration and yells of 'Lie down McKenna!' 'Traitor!' etc. This is kept up all the time he is on his feet. Is cried down. Cheers. Jumps up again. Howled down ditto.

More cheers. Howarth resumes, but is again interrupted. Members say he is only spouting to waste time.

9.45: Vote taken now for Goodison road. No questions as to majority.

9.50: Mr Clayton moved that Mr Houlding, Howarth and Nisbet be removed. Nisbet says he will resign. Loud cries of 'We won't have it" 'We'll give you the sack' & Barclay says he would like to hear Mr Houlding defend himself.

10.10: Houlding's speech (the chairman hopes members will give him a silent hearing as he has been ill). This is given with but a few exceptions. General opinion of speech is that he might have treated communications as a gentleman should and have acknowledged the members.

10.25: Mr Houlding's speech lasted quarter of an hour. Wilson deeply regrets having to leave the old ground though the majority of the committee have his entire sympathy. Loud cheers and cries of, 'Good old Bob,' & Motion put to meeting. Honestly think there were not 50 voted against it (the move to Goodison). Howarth waits to speak, as regrets being removed from the committee. But meeting will not hear him. Motion as regards Ramsey. This seemed to ravel things.

Now 10.35: Members in hurry to close as there is only a few minutes to sup ale. Vote to chairman and loud cheering.

The Terms Of Settlement And On To Goodison

ON 30 April 1892, it was reported in the *Liverpool Echo* that there had finally been a settlement. The report said: *On Monday evening, a conference of representatives of the Everton Football Club and of the company recently formed with a similar title* (Houlding's Everton) *was held in the rooms of the Football Association, London, at which Mr Clayton presided. After some friendly discussion it was agreed to abide by the following terms of settlement:*

'The company to leave the name 'Everton' with the Everton Football Club, each side paying its own costs.

£250 to be paid to the Everton Football Club for all stands and hoardings as set out in the statement of claim – signed George Mahon (on behalf of the Everton Football Club), William Houlding (on behalf of the company). The new company has become affiliated to the Association under the title of Liverpool Football Club, and has now equal rights with any other affiliated body; and the long-standing dispute has thus terminated amicably.

Everton now prepared for the daunting task of turning the Mere Green Field into a major football ground in a matter of months. What is not widely known is that Mahon considered other possible venues, the main one being a plot of land a couple of hundred yards down Lower Breck Road, not too far from the present Liverpool Supporters Club.

But Mahon had set his heart on the Mere Green Field, running alongside Goodison Road, and work would now start immediately to turn it into a first-class football ground. First of all, the debris was cleared away and a basic system of drainage carried out. At the same time, the surface was levelled and re-sodded. A Mr Barton agreed to do this on 29,471 square yards at fourpence-halfpenny per square yard. This was a formidable amount of initial expenditure. The club now employed Mr J.Prescott, a prominent

local architect and surveyor. Historian Keates described him as a man who revelled in sport in his spare time and who lived in a fine old house on the border of the estate.

On 7 June 1892, a contract was made with Kelly Brothers, the Walton builders. They were instructed to erect two uncovered enclosures at the goal ends to accommodate 4,000 spectators each, and a covered stand to accommodate 3,000 fans, for £1,640 with a penalty clause in the event of non-completion by 31 July (the new League season was due to start on 3 September). On 20 June, another contract was made with Kelly Brothers to erect outside enclosing hoardings at a cost of £150. Twelve turnstiles were ordered at £7. 15s each and, on 9 August, a third contract was entered into for gates, sheds, etc., for the sum of £132 10s 0d, to be completed by 20 August.

Everton had £805 3s 0d cash in the bank, plus the £250 allotted by the FA for the properties left at Anfield. The limited company was formed with £2,500 in £1 shares and 2,212 applications for allotments represented £1,659. But Mahon still felt the worry of the financial outlay weighing heavy on his shoulders. As a leading city accountant, with offices in North John Street, he was a man of figures and everything needed to be exactly right. Fortunately, Everton were given a timely boost by one of their biggest supporters, Dr James Clement Baxter, who quietly advanced £1,000, free of interest and without asking for any security.

And so the great challenge would be met and the new ground completed in time for the official opening on 24 August 1892, preceded by a celebratory dinner at the Adelphi Hotel.

George Mahon, the Everton chairman, presided over the VIP gathering and the principal toast, proposed by Lord Kinnaird, the game's most distinguished football figure, was: 'Success to the Everton Football Club.'

The formalities over, the guests now joined Mahon in a drive to Goodison Park in open-topped carriages. On reaching the Walton area, they were cheered by crowds of spectators, the local tradesmen literally putting out the flags to give the day a real carnival atmosphere. There were 12,000 spectators inside the ground and the very first Goodison roar now echoed around the new stands as his lordship declared the new stadium open.

Ironically, there was no football, but a varied sporting programme in which the club's own players participated. Lord Kinnaird started the first event by firing a pistol and the band of the 3rd Liverpool Regiment, conducted by bandmaster T.Rimmer, cheered the gathering with a lively musical programme.

The day ended in spectacular fashion with fireworks exploding over Goodison Park.

The Mere Green Field would cost Everton £8,090. The total outlay in transforming it into a major football venue in the summer of 1892 was in the region of £3,500. The decision to actually purchase the ground was taken at a board meeting on 22 March 1895 with Mahon in the chair. It was proposed: 'That this meeting do approve of and adopt the contract entered into by the Everton Football Club Co Ltd on the 12th inst for the purchase of the Football Ground now used by the club. The resolution was carried unanimously.'

The Epitome of Contract indicated that the parties involved were Christopher John Leyland and Everton Football Club. Completion of purchase took place on 1 August 1895 and the mortgage was eventually cleared during 1904-05.

When Everton played at Anfield. The programme from a game against Glasgow Rangers in October 1886. The match was originally scheduled as an FA Cup game but became a friendly when Everton scratched because several of their best players were ineligible.

A Ground Fit
For Kings And Queens

THE NEW Goodison Park was so impressive that it was chosen as the venue for the 1894 FA Cup Final in which Notts County beat Bolton Wanderers 4-1. Improvements would now be made and, in 1895, a new Bullens Road stand was built at an outlay of £3,407. The original construction was perfectly adequate. Possibly the new work involved major spectator facilities. A further £403 was spent on roofing the Goodison Road side.

The club was amongst the richest in the land and a £3,718 profit was made following the successful 1906 FA Cup-winning campaign. They would now invest £13,000 in a double-decker stand at the Stanley Park End. Then, in 1909, a vast Main Stand emerged on the Goodison Road side of the ground. This new structure cost £28,000 and housed all the offices and dressing rooms. It survived until 1971 at which point it was completely demolished to make way for the present towering structure. Also in 1909, £12,000 was spent on concreting the terracing and replacing the cinder running-track.

The 1909 main stand was one of the wonders of the sporting world. The architect was Archibald Leitch, whose trade mark was his criss-cross front balcony walls. An example of this can still be seen on the Bullens Road side of Goodison Park. The stadium was now so highly thought of that it hosted the 1910 FA Cup Final replay between Newcastle United and Barnsley, won by the Geordies. The attendance was 69,000.

Goodison Park got the seal of royal approval on 11 July 1913, when it became the first League venue to be visited by a ruling monarch. George V and Queen Mary were the honoured guests, inspecting local schoolchildren at the stadium. During World War One, the ground was used for army drill practice and there were other unusual visitors in

The tablet installed to commemorate the visit of the King and Queen in 1913. It can still be seen in the Main Stand.

the shape of US baseball teams, the Chicago Whitesox and New York Giants. It is recalled that one player hammered a ball right over the Main Stand.

In 1926, a double-decker stand was built on the Bullens Road side of the ground for £30,000. Everton now picked up on an idea they had spotted during a trip to Aberdeen and installed dug outs at Goodison for the trainers, the first in this country.

Work was completed in 1938 on a new Gwladys Street stand, just in time for another royal visit, this time from George VI and Queen Elizabeth. This structure cost £50,000 and the stadium was now in magnificent shape, the first in the country to have four double-decker stands. The ground would subsequently suffer damage during World War Two and the club received £5,000 for repair work.

The magnificent old main stand, so futuristic in its day, would now make way for the present Main Stand in 1971. The old structure had cost £28,000. The new one would top £1 million. Eleven executive boxes would be sited along the front of the Main Stand in time for the 1981-82 season. There was standing in the Enclosure area in front of these boxes until the 1987-88 season when seats were installed to accommodate the ever-growing Family Club. The famous Gwladys Street terraces, the traditional home of the club's most vociferous supporters, became all-seater in time for the start of the 1991-92 season. Finally, the Park Stand was demolished and rebuilt in 1994 with a capacity of 6,000 seats. The £2.3m structure was officially opened in the August. Thus, Goodison Park became the all-seater venue we see today.

Minutes Leading To Golden Hours And The Naming Of Goodison Park

GOODISON Park is a very different place today to the ground that rose on the Mere Green Field site in 1892. But there is still history all around you and the club retain the original minute books that reveal so much about those pioneering seasons prior to the turn of the century, not least the famous year of 1892 when George Mahon made the bold decision to give up Anfield and find a new home on the other side of Stanley Park.

To handle those books, still in perfect condition and all handwritten by Mahon and his colleagues, is a very eerie feeling. You can almost hear Mahon's confident voice speaking to you, powerful and full of hope for the future. He had led the 'split' from Anfield with allies like Dr J.C.Baxter, W.R.Clayton, A.T.Coates, J.Griffiths, J.T. Atkinson and J.Davies, men whose names would be found on the list of provisional directors on the prospectus of the Limited Liability Company into which the club was formed at Goodison Park.

It's worth dipping into those minutes books, particularly the volume for 1892, to pick out one or two gems of day to day business. For instance, there is a casual two-line reference in the minutes of the 27 June board meeting that is truly historic. Under the hand-written heading of *Name of Ground* it simply says: *Resolved that the Football Ground be called Goodison Park.*

Prior to its development as a major football ground, the Mere Green Field had been a nursery which, it is said, had been sadly neglected and had turned into a howling desert'. It took its name from Mere Lane which ran between the old field and Stanley Park. There was another Mere Lane on the Anfield side of Stanley Park, off Robson Street and the City Engineers eventually eased the confusion by extending Walton Lane which originally

Copy of the minute from 1892 in which George Mahon, in his own hand, records a simple motion that: "The football ground be called Goodison Park."

ended at the top of Spellow Lane. Walton Lane now extended down as far as Queens Drive, as it does today, and so the old Mere Lane disappeared off the map.

Goodison Road and all the small terraced streets running off it were in existence when work was started on the new football ground in the summer of 1892. So it was a straightforward matter for Mahon & Co to call the stadium Goodison Park. There was no mystery or intrigue about it. The road itself was almost certainly named after a civil engineer by the name of George William Goodison who, in 1868 while representing the company of Reade-Goodison, gave a report on sewage to the Walton Local Board. By coincidence, Mahon would later become a member of the Walton Local Board, an enlarged parish council.

Mr Goodison was born in 1843 at Holbeck in Leeds, the son of Samuel, a milk seller, and Elizabeth. By 1881 he was resident in Hawkshead, Cumbria, and in 1886-87 in Monk Coniston, now Coniston, Cumbria. The Liverpool City Engineers street-naming department cannot confirm that Goodison Road was named after him, but research would seem to suggest that this is the case.

And so Goodison Park was officially, if not formally, named in the time it took Mahon to pen those two lines in the 1892 minute book. There were other matters of equal importance. For instance, it was resolved at the same June meeting that Mr Griffiths go to Scotland to sign on Dumbarton star Richard Boyle, a centre-half who would go on to make 243 rock-solid appearances for the Blues.

An indication of the wages paid at that time came in a reference to Fred Geary, the club's ace marksman. It was resolved that he would be offered £3 per week during season 1893-94 with the net proceeds of a midweek benefit match adding to his salary.

Under the heading *Payments in Advance* it indicated that star outside-right Alex Latta was earning £3 a week while his teammate Edgar Chadwick was on only £2 10s (£2.50).

The following week, on 2 August, the minutes included a full list of forthcoming fixtures, other than Football League, with an indication of the gate receipts and guarantees on offer. For instance: *1 September, Bolton Wanderers (h) pay guarantee of £35,. 19 September, Heart of Midlothian (a) Receive guarantee £50 plus half of everything taken over £100.*

Opponents in these various friendlies included contrasting names like Burton Swifts, Queen's Park, Newcastle East End, Grimsby Town, Middlesbrough Ironopolis, Liverpool Caledonians and Northwich Victoria.

On 4 August 1892, the directors met at Goodison Park, when it was resolved that the main club office be fixed near the gateway opposite Eaton Street on Goodison Road, elevated four feet and having an entrance from the road. The main office remained opposite Eaton Street until 1994 when the club's administration was switched to the new Park Stand.

An unusual entry made on 8 August, 1892, concerned the appointment of a 'Rubber-down' who was presumably the club's first physiotherapist. The wages on offer were ten shillings (50p) a week and the man approached was a Mr S.Orme. Publicity was clearly top priority and it was resolved that certain members of the local Press would have their expenses paid to all away League matches and Cup ties. At this meeting, the club accepted Lord Kinnaird's offer to officially open the new ground on 24 August while deciding that the ceremony would include a sports day and firework display.

On 5 September 1892, just two days after the first-ever Football League game at Goodison Park (a 2-2 draw with Nottingham Forest), an entry appeared in the directors' minutes concerning *Soldiers, Police and Postmen*. It was resolved that these gentlemen, in uniform, be admitted free to the ground through the season-

A fine view of the old grandstand on the Bullens Road side which originally housed the dressing-rooms and various offices. This picture was taken around 1905.

ticket entrance and that this fact be advertised. All one can assume is that the club felt that the presence of these 'uniformed' fans might be a good deterrent to any potential crowd trouble.

Admission prices were set at a meeting on 8 September 1892. For League and 'big' matches it would be 6d (2½p) for the ground, one shilling (5p) for the covered stand and the front of the same and two shillings (10p) for the reserved covered stand. Combination and small matches, half-price.

Everton were always quick to reward their players for outstanding work and, at the September 13th meeting, it was decided to pay each individual a bonus of ten shillings for the victory over Heart of Midlothian. At the same time it was decided that 200 children from the local industrial schools would be admitted free to the next match, the Blues clearly looking ahead with a view to capturing the fans of the future.

An interesting 'minute' concerned the purchase of a horse for ground work. No automatic lawn mowers in those days! It was also decided that the team would be requested to purchase and wear blue stockings in the matches. How would modern players react to buying their own kit?

The links with the local Press continued to be nurtured. When the *Liverpool Echo/Express* sought the use of the brand new Goodison Park for their annual Boxing Day match, the board readily agreed.

One of Everton's stars when they first moved to Goodison was Fred Geary, the Dixie Dean of his day. He would return to Anfield in 1894 and end his playing days as a Liverpool player.

On 22 August 1894, with George Mahon in the chair, the minutes reveal that the rift with Liverpool Football Club had been healed to a degree. The split and the move to Goodison had caused a lot of ill-feeling. John Houlding – Everton's old landlord and master' – had formed his new club and gained admission to the newly-formed Second Division of the Football League. It was now resolved to send complimentary tickets to the directors of Liverpool FC, who were celebrating promotion to Division One.

The Anfield club's elevation to the top flight meant that the 'Cold War' would have to be brought to an end and Everton took the first steps with this hands-across-the-park gesture. All this is revealed thanks to the meticulous way the minute books were kept. The superb organisational qualities of the club's officers are there for all to see.

The Goodison Road side as it looked in 1905. Originally, this was just a cinder bank. A vast Main Stand was built along Goodison Road in 1909 which stood for the best part of 62 years.

Training For The
High Standard Of Efficiency

WE ARE given a clear picture of the club's training methods during the early years at Goodison Park, thanks to a schedule that was drawn up by the secretary of the day, R.Molyneux. On 26 October 1896, on the orders of the directors, he issued each and every player with a printed card regarding the *Rules As to Training*.

Those rules are listed here as they appear on the card:

1. Monday - Walking exercises or Salt Water Baths.

Tuesday and Wednesday - Sprinting or Walking Exercises.

Thursday - Sprinting and Skipping Rope Exercises.

Friday - Walking Exercises.

A couple of swells — trainer Harry Cooke (right) and assistant trainer Bert Smith prepare for the 1929-30 season.

2. *Every player must be on the ground not later than 10am and must sign his name in a book kept by the Trainer for that purpose (shades of that famous disciplinarian Harry Catterick 78 years later!) At this hour, such book will be removed and any Player whose name is not entered will be required to give the directors a sufficient reason thereafter.*

3. *Each player shall bring to the ground suitable clothing, necessary for the practice of the day.*

4. *The Players shall, if required by the Trainer, indulge in the practice of Football.*

5. *The Players shall undergo any other mode of training or practice as the Trainer may, under any circumstances, deem expedient.*

6. *The Players shall, so often as the Trainer may think desirable, take such medicines which are prescribed by the Trainer.*

The Directors, in framing these rules, desire the co-operation of the Players in the observance thereof, and trust that the Players will assist them in maintaining the high reputation of the Everton Football Club by obedience to the commands of the Trainer in whom the directors have vested the necessary authority.

Tom Griffiths and Tommy White (left) enjoy a training session early in the 1929-30 season. Sadly, unhappy days were on the horizon, culminating in the club being relegated for the first time with a defeat against Sunderland in May 1930.

Local schoolchildren join in this summer training run along Queen's Drive in July 1953. Parker, Stewart (a new Canadian player), Farrell, Leyland, Lindsay, Easthope and Clinton are the Everton joggers. The footwear was very basic, a mixture of baseball boots, pumps and leather shoes. Clinton is wearing a pair of open sandals. No fancy training shoes in those days.

The Directors look to the Trainer for the maintenance of the high standard of efficiency which the Players of the Everton Football Club have attained hitherto.

On occasions, the players were given special 'treats' at the discretion of the directors. Motor cars were few and far between in those days and so they were taken for a drive out into the greenbelt for tea, the greenbelt being places like Childwall, which are now so densely populated.

It's interesting to compare training *c.*1892 with the training of 1998. Howard Kendall painted me a picture of how the modern Blues prepare for a big match.

He said: "Training starts each day at 10.30am but many of the lads are out before then, doing their own stretching exercises or some weights. Many of them join together for a keep-ball routine in a circle or in pairs to help with their touch on the ball. It's all very lighthearted before we start in earnest.

"They get their legs going with a fairly long run and then it's into a stretching routine before the ball-work starts. The coaching staff make it as interesting as possible. Then the small-sided games begin and the goalkeepers are brought into it.

"If we are working on particular patterns of play, it's a case of going into a full game. There are quite a lot of finishing routines which are worked on. Training is obviously reduced as the week goes on and a match looms. When you are playing as often as we are now, you don't need to hammer people on the training ground. The games take care of themselves.

"Different clubs obviously have different routines, but ours involves a lot of ball-work. I know in the old days, the players rarely saw a ball in training. The idea was to make them hungry for it on a Saturday. But the game is a lot quicker now and that is reflected in the amount of work we do."

Howard Kendall describes how modern training is very different to the early days. He is pictured showing off the club motto: *Only the best will do.*

Hail Goodison, Hail Everton!

Saturday, 3 September 1892
Everton 2 Nottingham Forest 2

THE first game played on Goodison Park took place on Friday, 2 September 1892, when Everton entertained their old rivals Bolton Wanderers in a friendly encounter, winning 4-2. Fittingly, George Mahon was allowed to kick-off, a tribute to the visionary chairman. But this was only a warm-up act to the star turn, Everton's very first League match on their magnificent new ground against Nottingham Forest.

This fixture also marked the start of an exciting season and the fans who had been so used to wending their way to Anfield now swarmed to the new venue with great hope and expectation. The crowd was estimated to be in the region of 14,000, a magnificent turn-out considering the weather. The wind was blowing a gale and the rain was sweeping down, but the new pitch was in good condition.

The home team emerged first in their blue and white strip and they received a most enthusiastic welcome. Forest were also applauded warmly and promptly won the toss.

The *Liverpool Football Echo* reported: *Little time was cut to waste and Fred Geary kicked off with a rush, but was well collared. Johnny Holt came in and enabled his partners to again move up, but Scott accounted for a dangerous move by the homesters.*

Holt was a powerful centre-half, virtually unbeatable in the air and nicknamed the 'Little Everton Devil' by his followers on the terraces. Thomas Keates explained why, saying that Holt was an artist in the perpetration of clever minor fouls.

When they were appealed for, his shocked look of injured innocence was side-splitting. In this opening League encounter, Holt was always to the fore.

Edgar Chadwick shot over the bar, but Forest stunned the home fans by taking

Richard Boyle played in Everton's first Goodison Park League game, a sturdy half-back who joined the club in 1890 from Dumbarton.

the lead. And so it was a Nottingham star with the unlikely name of Horace Pike, who had the honour of scoring the first League goal at Goodison Park.

Alex Latta now got stuck in and Alf Milward just failed to equalise after an outstanding cross came in from the right.

The previous year, Milward had been one of five Everton players to turn out for England against Scotland at Blackburn. He made a habit of confusing defenders with his rampaging runs down the left flank. Milward was a winner in every sense, never accepting defeat until the very

Alf Milward made 27 League appearances in Everton's first Goodison campaign, scoring 11 goals. He was a skilful outside-left with an excellent football brain.

final whistle, no matter what the score.

Geary now produced an outstanding leveller and Everton finished the half on the attack and in determined mood. On the restart, Chadwick and Milward both made some skilful runs and Latta distinguished himself with a stinging shot that dipped over the bar. Geary charged into Brown and a Forest player was cautioned after remonstrating with the referee.

Then Milward scored for Everton and Higgins for Forest to leave the score level

at 2-2, a disappointing result for the home fans who had been banking on Everton getting off to a flyer. But as they looked around their splendid new ground before wending their way home, they surely knew instinctively that great days and magical moments lay ahead. Goodison Park would prove a very happy home.

Everton: Jardine; Howarth, Dewar, Boyle, Holt, Robertson, Latta, Maxwell, Geary, E.Chadwick, Milward.
Attendance: 14,000

First League Victory At Goodison

24 September 1892
Everton 6 Newton Heath 0

EVERTON had kicked-off their very first season at Goodison Park with that 2-2 home draw against Nottingham Forest and had then lost 4-1 at Aston Villa and drawn 2-2 at Blackburn Rovers.

Now Newton Heath came to Merseyside for a clash that was causing great excitement amongst the Evertonians. They desperately wanted to see a Goodison triumph and felt the players were in the mood to see off the club that, ten years later, would take on the name of Manchester United.

The *Liverpool Echo* reported the match in some depth. It said: *Newton Heath, one of the newest acquisitions to the League, were the visitors to Goodison Park and a large crowd assembled to witness the encounter. Amongst Evertonians, jubilation was great at the return to form of their pets, for they had gone to 'Auld Reekie' during the week and taken 3 to nil out of the formidable Heart of Midlothian , the leaders of the Scottish League. Their display in the Northern City was indeed powerful and finished and this being the first time the Hearts had been defeated on their own ground since April 1891, made the Everton victory all the more praiseworthy.*

The question was asked: *Would the toffee boys maintain their form today and add a couple of points to their League credit?* The general opinion was in favour of a solid home victory as the Heathens had previously lost to Blackburn, drawn with Burnley and then succumbed to Burnley in an early return.

The weather was perfect when Fred Geary, the Dixie Dean of his day, kicked-off for Everton. Geary, a player who had scored a hat-trick on his England debut against Ireland in 1890, was renowned for his powerful running and finishing.

He was on the mark inside a minute and the fans in the new Goodison stand and enclosures erupted. The Newton Heath forwards now rushed down the field, but right winger Carson was dispossessed by Collins as he tried to thread his way through.

Geary, watching this spell of visiting pressure from the front line, now decided to do something about it and he claimed his second goal, taking a pass from the left wing and drilling in a low shot from long range. There was now a real spring in Geary's step and he made a magnificent run into the area, the move fizzling out through lack of support.

Edgar Chadwick now got on the scoresheet, a player who had signed for Everton from Blackburn Rovers in time for their inaugural season in the Football League in 1888. A mobile inside-left with a superb ability to read the game, he made a mockery of his slight frame (he was only 5ft 6ins) and was always in the thick of the action. His goal was well received and the home side were basking in a 3-0 lead.

Edgar Chadwick played for Everton for a decade between 1888-89 and 1898-99. A tricky inside-left, he netted for England after only 30 seconds against Scotland in 1892, the year of the switch from Anfield to Goodison.

One of Everton's star turns when they moved to Goodison was centre-forward Fred Geary.

Alex Latta, one of the Goodison playing pioneers who operated at outside-right and appeared in the 1893 FA Cup Final. He had been a member of the 1891 Championship winning side.

But Newton Heath were still full of running and goalkeeper Pinnell had to punch clear from Mathieson. The second half belonged to Everton in every sense and they peppered the visitors' goal. Winger Alex Latta, who had the rare distinction of being a Scot and a tee-totaller, struck the crossbar with a fierce shot. Chadwick took the rebound and made it 4-0.

The *Echo* now reported that the Evertonians *pursued their course merrily, constantly keeping their opponents on tenterhooks.* Maxwell and Milward completed the scoring as the home side leapt from 13th position to eighth. They would go on improving and finish a memorable first season at Goodison Park in third place, their home record being:
Played 15, Won 9, Drawn 3, Lost 3.

There were also three Goodison victories in the FA Cup – against West Brom, Nottingham Forest and Sheffield Wednesday – prior to a three-match semi-final marathon against Preston North End that produced a Cup Final test against Wolves.

At Fallowfield, Manchester, Everton lost 1-0 to the Midlanders, but the fans could look back on a dramatic year. Their days at Anfield were now firmly behind them. Goodison Park felt very much like home and the club would go from strength to strength.

Everton: Pinnell, Howarth, Collins, Boyle, Holt, Robertson, Latta, Maxwell, Geary, E.Chadwick, Milward.
Attendance: 10,000

Southworth's Record Six-Goal Blitz

Saturday, 30 December 1893
Everton 7 West Brom 1

JACK Southworth spent a comparatively short time at Goodison Park, somewhere in the region of 15 months. But during this time, he managed to write his name into the Everton history books with his outstanding goalscoring feats. The six goals he plundered against West Bromwich Albion in 1893 still stands as the club's individual scoring record.

Southworth was described by respected judges as the best centre-forward of his era. He first played for Blackburn Olympic and at the tender age of 16, scored six goals for them against Leigh. He moved to Blackburn Rovers and when they crushed Sheffield Wednesday 5-2 in May 1890, it was Southworth who registered all the home goals.

His scoring feats came to the attention of Everton and they paid £400 for his services in August 1893, by which time the player already had two FA Cup winners medals in his collection. The fee was a large one by the standards of the day, bearing in mind that it would be 12 years before the first ever £1,000 transfer was recorded (Alf Common from Sunderland to Middlesbrough in February 1905).

Southworth scored on his debut at the County Ground, Derby, although the Blues lost 7-3. But he would soon be making his presence felt in a big way and hit four in an 8-1 demolition job on Sheffield Wednesday.

The following week he would go two better and score his record-breaking double hat-trick against West Brom. The Throstles didn't know what hit them on a foggy Goodison Park afternoon.

Creative right winger John Bell, a player with a fascinating background in his own right, scored in the opening minute. The Scot had won a League Championship medal with Dumbarton before joining the Blues in 1892. He was chairman of the first attempt to form a players' union and is reputed to have once saved the life of a fellow First Division player by repositioning a dislocated neck with a wrench of his powerful hands. Bell, having scored against West Brom, now turned creator with an accurate centre that Southworth headed home.

Jack Southworth scored six goals against West Brom in December 1893, to set an individual club record.

The same combination produced the third goal, Reader failing to hold Bell's shot and Southworth racing in to make it 3-0. The unstoppable centre-forward then scored an outstanding individual effort to complete his hat-trick, dribbling the ball into the centre and powering home a shot.

The crowd was increasing by the minute, along with the score. In those days, because of people's working patterns it was often impossible to make the kick-off. Hence, there were 12,000 in Goodison at the start of the match, 18,000 present by half-time and up to 25,000 in the ground by the end. These, of course, are figures estimated by the reporters of the day, but they had a keen eye and were usually spot on with their guesses.

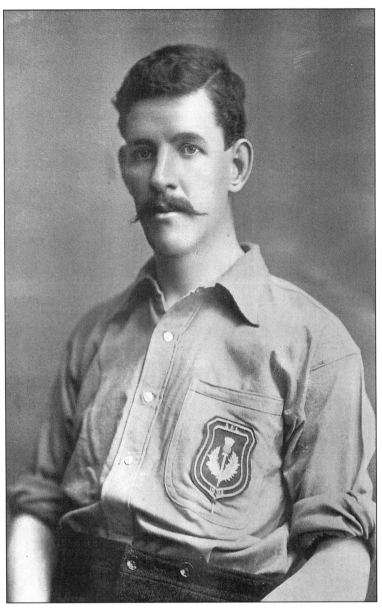

John Bell's skilful dribbling down the right flank thrilled the Goodison fans and helped Jack Southworth claim his record-breaking six-goal haul in 1893.

in the area to finish off the move and make it 5-0. Norman pulled one back for the visitors, but Southworth's strong shot made it 6-1. He was now on the brink of a double hat-trick and achieved it after meeting a Latta free-kick from the right.

In modern times there would have been pictures galore, quotes and headlines as big as your fist to salute such an achievement, but the coverage was much more modest in those early days.

The *Football Echo* headline, across a single column, simply said: *Everton v West Bromwich Albion, League Division One.*

But it did not need fancy words to explain the way the fans thought of Jack. Sadly, injury and illness brought his career to a premature end. He finished the 1893-94 season with 27 goals in 23 games and managed nine in nine matches the following year before he was forced to retire.

He would remain a great entertainer, although he would earn his applause on a very different stage. Southworth was an accomplished violinist and he became a professional musician, being good enough to join the famous Halle Orchestra. But it was the roar at Blackburn and Goodison that had been music to his ears. He will be remembered, first and foremost, as one of the deadliest strikers in the business.

Everton: Williams; Parry, Arridge, Kelso, Holt, Stewart, Latta, Bell, Southworth, Chadwick and Milward.
Attendance: 14,000

Bell continued to thrill the crowd as much as his famous teammate. He dashed clear and Southworth joined him

THE BIG BATTLE AT LAST!

EVERTON *versus* LIVERPOOL.

Houlding Kicked Again —
In The First 'Derby'

13 October 1894
Everton 3 Liverpool 0

EVERTON'S 1892 departure to Goodison Park led to the formation of another team in the city. Anfield landlord John Houlding, having been 'kicked' out of the Everton presidency during the historic 'split', now found himself guiding the fortunes of the new Liverpool Football Club.

They had seized the opportunity to play in Second Division of the Football League in 1893-94 and gained promotion at a gallop after winning 22 of their 28 games and drawing six.

And so in early October 1894, the only topic of conversation on Merseyside was the impending top-flight battle at Goodison Park between George Mahon's Everton and Houlding's Liverpool – the very first League derby. Newspapers were not in the habit of sensationalising things in those days, but here was the ultimate sporting battle. The game was given a full-page spread in the 13 October edition of the *Liverpool Review* and they made no apology for 'going over the top'.

The article said: *There are some people in this world who are foolish enough to hold in light esteem, to speak words of scorning of and to elevate their noses at, a pastime which has been known to draw together at one assemblage a vast congregation of persons numbering between forty and fifty thousand strong, amply sufficient to people a good-sized town or a fairly formidable army. None of these superior creatures will be discovered at Goodison Park on Saturday afternoon and none of these people will be missed. A man who can wax sarcastically superior to the hundred and odd thousand sport-lovers who crowd the football enclosures of the United Kingdom every Saturday is altogether too elevated for common comprehension.*

He is a chap no fellah can understand. So we will not apologise to Mr Minority for having introduced so much football fare into this issue of the 'Review'. Our end is to entertain the thirty thousand odd footballists who will throng the great Goodison enclosure on Saturday afternoon. For the hour of the big battle has arrived, and Everton and Liverpool are to meet – at last!

The second teams of the two great rivals had met in the Liverpool Cup, each claiming a victory. But there had been no clash of first teams, basically because Everton believed they were of far superior stock to the new occupants of Anfield.

The *Review* explained: *Whenever local competitions made it necessary for the clubs to meet, the Evertonians would not condescend to place more than their second string in the field against any kind of string of Liverpudlians, against which treatment the Liverpudlians naturally stood on their*

The nearest you will get to a sensational headline in 1894. How the *Liverpool Review* previewed the first-ever Football League derby, played at Goodison in 1894.

Billy Stewart was a solid half-back who joined Everton in 1893 from Preston North End. Billy was a long-throw expert, although his running and jumping routine was later outlawed.

dignity by sending only their second string, with the consequence that the clubs never representatively met – until now!

Because here was a First Division fixture that required and received the total attention of both parties. The *Review* was reluctant to predict a result, although Everton were most definitely the form favourites. They topped the table, having played seven and won seven. Liverpool had played eight, won none, drawn five and lost three. But they were fired up as they had never been before. These days we talk about the 'old enemy'. In 1892 it was simply the 'enemy'.

The *Review* provided pen pictures of the leading characters. George Mahon, now the president of Everton, was said to be a man whose tact and business ability made him an invaluable member of the Everton organisation. His presence was welcomed in all football circles and his association with the leading men of the city made him a perfect emissary for the game amongst the influential members of society.

Jack Southworth was the captain of the League leaders, described as the most famous centre-forward living. James Adams was Everton's sub-captain. Signed from Hearts, he was a solid fullback with a perfect physique.

The opposing ranks had a familiar overlord in John Houlding. Once Everton's chief mainstay, his decision to increase the Anfield rent had led to the parting of the ways. He had survived the 'split' to build a new Anfield team and he was desperately keen for Liverpool to beat the Blues, especially at Goodison Park.

Andrew Boyd Hannah was the skipper of the Anfield club. He was perhaps the most familiar soccer figure in the city, having captained Everton previously. He was a model full-back, steady, reliable and cool. He was backed up by Jimmy McBride, one of the smallest, but pluckiest half-backs in the League.

And so to the game itself. For hours on the Saturday afternoon, Scotland Road was congested with vehicles of all sizes. There was an endless supply of cabs and hansom carriages, backed up by scores of buses and trams which were besieged by the multitudes heading for Goodison Park. The approaches to the ground, said the *Liverpool Review,* seethed with struggling humanity for hours before the event.

The magnificent football arena presented a spectacle imposing in the extreme. It only needed a glance at the packed masses of spectators rising tier above tier in every quarter of the enclosure to make even the most hardened footballer utter expressions of astonishment at the drawing power of the great game.

The form book proved to be right. Everton won 3-0, although the visitors managed to carve out a considerable number of chances. Up to the last half hour, it was anybody's game. The *Review* observed: *If Liverpool were a little less unscrupulous in their tactics, they would be a popular team.*

Houlding's men were very physical and two-thirds of the fouls went against them. Liverpool's kick and rush tactics had disrupted a number of teams, but Everton had too much quality.

Blues' winger John Bell limped off after

Charlie Parry, a Welsh international defender who joined Everton as a junior in 1889. He played in the first Merseyside 'derby' game at Goodison.

some over-zealous tackling from his marker, but he soon returned to a deafening roar of approval. The lead was secured when Hannah handled and McInnes headed home Stewart's excellent free-kick.

But it was just 1-0 at half-time and Liverpool made a robust start to the second period without having any luck in front of goal. Then Alex Latta whipped in a powerful shot and it was 2-0. Bell finished off the battling visitors when he chested home a right-wing cross and the Blues had made a record start to a campaign with eight wins from eight games, scoring 30 and conceding only seven.

Sadly the run came to an end in the following game at Blackburn and the side finished the season as First Division runners-up to Sunderland.

But the most important thing as far as the fans were concerned was that Liverpool had been well beaten at Goodison. Less than a month later, the Blues returned to their old Anfield home and secured a 2-2 draw. Houlding would have to wait some considerable time for his revenge.

Everton: Cain; Adams, Parry, Boyle, Holt, Stewart, Latta, McInnes, Southworth, Hartley, Bell.
Attendance: 44,000

Shouts, Shrieks, Groans, Cheers And Then Handshakes All Round!

EVERTON'S second season at Goodison Park, 1893-94, was very much a mixed bag. The Blues, having finished third the previous year, now went backwards and dropped to sixth. They also crashed out of the FA Cup at the first time of asking to Stoke. But there had been much to admire as well. This was the year in which Jack Southworth bagged his six goals against West Brom, a feat that still stands to this day as a club record. The Blues won that match by 7-1 and twice recorded 8-1 triumphs, against Darwen and Sheffield Wednesday.

And yet there was a little bit of infighting going on. behind the scenes, a mini power battle that would reach a climax at the club's annual general meeting, held in the imposing Picton Lecture Hall. It was a gathering that started in explosive fashion and then really warmed up! Shareholders meetings are traditionally occasions that can turn mere mortals into raging bulls. Football, like religion and politics, can prove to be a dangerous subject on which to air extremist views.

Football is a passionate game, even on a bad day. At this particular shareholders' meeting, with vacancies on the board the main topic of conversation, it was not so much pistols at high noon, as a display of sabre-rattling throughout the night.

I reproduce below every dot and comma from a report of the proceedings, written by a gentleman calling himself 'The Linesman' in the *Liverpool Review*. It is a most wonderful piece of descriptive writing, significant because it reveals the debating skills of one George Mahon – the man who led Everton from Anfield to Goodison. There is also reference to a 'Mr Keates', who distinguished himself at the meeting with his sound oratory in the face of tough opposition. Could this have been the famous Goodison historian Thomas Keates, whose most superb *History of Everton Football Club* was published in 1929, leaving us with so many valuable memories about the early Blues? It is an intriguing thought.

But back to the June meeting of 1894. Present shareholders will, I am sure, enjoy the report, taken from the old *Liverpool Review*. It's a classic example to any would-be journalist of how to paint a picture with words. We thank 'The Linesman' and salute his writing prowess. This was his report:

On Monday evening, at the Picton Lecture Hall, the long expected thunderbolt was hurled, and nobody was killed. But there were great ructions all the same, and many a time during the three hours' sitting of the directors and shareholders of the 'igh and mighty Everton Football Club a 'fite' appeared imminent. But it is all over now, and, as I say, nobody is assassinated. On the contrary, the whole club is decidedly the better for an annual meeting which commenced rumblingly, continued with shouts, shrieks, groans, hisses, pale faces, and personalities, and concluded with humorous speeches, facetious commentaries, votes of thanks, congratulations, and hand-shaking all round. After which let us hope that patriotism will take the place of dissension amongst the members so the Everton FC, and that the coming season will see better management, better results, and hatchets buried by the score.

To a disinterested onlooker the proceedings in the Picton were of a most humorous description. A spectator who knew not football would probably have been amazed at the intensity of interest displayed by the five or six hundred club members who for three hours howled and gesticulated themselves blue in the face, Everton-blue in the face, over the affairs financial and governmental of their body. Personally, it was the most entertaining partisan experience which I have come across since Liverpool beat Everton at Hawthorne Road in the final for the Liverpool Cup in 1893.

It really was great fun. On the platform there sat Mr George Mahon, chairman of the meeting and president of the club. On his left was Mr Molyneux, and on his right Mr Clayton, and in the rear a number of directors. The shareholders were mostly seated in the body of the hall, but grouped on a tier of seats to the right, and facing the platform was a partisan body whose business it appeared to be to play the very holocaust with the directorate in the way of criticising its management, to push forward certain members of its party for the vacancies which had occurred amongst the directorate, and to vigorously protest against the right to vote of certain newly acquired shareholders and members of 'the trade'.

Thus we had the elements of a nice little thunderstorm, and little time was wasted in getting to words. The chairman, a thin little man with a caustic tongue and a personality powerful enough to keep the riotous spirits at his fingers' ends from first to last, confessed right away that he was in a bad temper, and then proceeded to make the best that was possible of the clubs' finances for the past season, which he admitted he expected would be warmly discussed. These he got through with fairly little interruption, but when he came to the subject of certain by-meetings which had been held by the afore-described factionists, the storm which had long been brewing burst forth in all its frenzy, and almost shook the volumes in the huge library above out of their shelves.

It was very warm indeed. Mr Mahon said that the test of the problem lay to his mind in the question: Were or were not such meetings to the advantage of the club? Whereat he was greeted with a perfect bombardment of 'Hear, hears, noe's' and 'Ayes'. And the state of things was not improved when he proceeded to name the leaders of the factionists, and expressed it as his opinion that 'Messrs. Nelson, Green and Wilson would woefully regret that they had

allowed their names to be brought forward at the meeting to receive such scant support:' and he trusted they would in future have a little more modesty, which would certainly be an advantage both to themselves and the Everton club. In fact it was a vigorous speech altogether, and at times the speaker carried the audience with him to such an extent that they cheered him again and again, expressing their approval in such cries as 'Bravo, Mahon!' 'Good old chairman!' and so on. All of which approvalisms were levelled truculently at the factionists, who sat with their faces set loweringly towards the directorate on the platform and the stormy mass in the body of the hall.

And then one of the leaders of the minority party rose to his feet, and was rewarded with a roar of mingled hoots and cheers such as that which used to greet the name of Gladstone at the pantomime, only more so. Mr Keates was the would-be

Thomas Keates, author of the invaluable *History of Everton Football Club 1878-79 to 1928-29*, who died in his 79th year while the volume was in process of publication. Keates was a former director. Was he also the man who challenged George Mahon from the floor at the 1894 annual meeting? It is a fascinating thought.

speaker, a middle-aged man with a bull-doggy countenance and a voice which would have done justice to a ship's captain. 'In a friendly way' (which was obviously a very iconoclastic way) he desired to discuss the statement of accounts which had just been approved and passed. He talked, between the whirlwinds of hooting and jeering, of the high expenditure re players; of the injurious nature of the bonus system; and of the threatened rivalry which they had to fear from a neighbouring club. He contended in opposition to the chairman that the directorate lost nothing by being subjected to such criticism as that which he and others had brought forward; and altogether Mr Keates fought so well in the teeth of the wind that several times the meeting heartily echoed his sentiments, and the three gentlemen at the table on the platform visibly appreciated the Cromwellian attack. Mr Keates subsequently distinguished himself by rushing on to the platform with a letter from a firm of lawyers, handing it triumphantly to a director in answer to a point of legal difference which had arisen, striding up to the chairman's table, seizing a glass of water and gulping the contents down, and then striding back to his place in the arena as quickly as he came. This feat simply brought down the house, and probably will have immortalised Mr Keates in the Extraordinary Annals of the Remarkable Football Club of Everton.

Mr Keates was seconded by Mr Fisher, at whose up-rising the sensation was even more tremendous, for it was evidently anticipated that this gentleman meant business, Mr Fisher had not quite the bull-doggy appearance of Mr Keates and his diction was a trifle more refined, but if anything he was even more energetic. He was a born orator, suiting the word to the action, the action to the word with a facility and effectiveness which electrified his hearers. Mr Fisher had very great difficulty in making himself heard. He evidently had something to say which the majority of the audience didn't like to assimilate, but in spite of the opposition he stood his ground, and waving his arms and shaking his first utterly defied his antagonists to shift him from his position. It was no use

trying to howl him down, for howling wasn't controverting, and they were facts, facts, facts, beastly, Gradgrindish facts, which he had to retail. In his opinion a crisis had been caused in the affairs of the club by the manipulation of paper shares and the distribution of scrip among 'the trade'. There! It was out! The trade! what trade? 'Tell us the trade,' they roared; and a rotund gentleman at the speaker's side grew absolutely purple at the insinuation, and threatened the plucky speaker with all sorts of dire mishaps. But, bless them, the imperturbable Fisher was not to be daunted, and he told them 'what trade'. He referred them to the meeting which took place at the Star and Garter at half-past seven; at which kind reference the disorder grew so awful that even Mr Fisher had to sit down.

Here the Chairman interposed, looked round at the clock, and thought it would be as well if they did a little business by way of relaxation – the election of three new directors, six being nominated on the spot. But before this was proceeded with, Mr Clayton, a dark-faced, long-faced, eloquent young man, rose from his seat at the side of the chairman, and in a big voice which made the ashphalt flooring quiver, proceeded to butter a couple of the directors, of whose merits he appeared to think the meeting was not becomingly cognisant. His speech was greeted with sympathetic applause, and at the conclusion the chairman added to the two directors mentioned the name of Dr Baxter, regretting that Mr Clayton had omitted a pat of butter for that popular gentleman, the reference to whom was received with unbounded delight. To this Mr Clayton rose to respond, whereupon a little gentleman from the rear of the writer, who had been indulging in sententious but somewhat silly asides throughout the evening, called upon the speaker to 'sit down', which so roused that gentleman that he turned his long dark face full upon his interrupter and exclaimed that he wasn't going to sit down for a new shareholder, not he; that he had worked morning, noon and night for the club before the said shareholder was dreamt of; which retort was received with a hurricane of applause, although the

The colourful 1894 annual meeting featured the superb debating skills of Goodison founder-father George Mahon, who was backed by the likes of W.R.Clayton and Dr.J.C.Baxter. Three influential Evertonians were still in high office when this photograph was taken in 1906 with the old FA Cup. Back row (left to right): A.R.Wade, W.C.Cuff, Dr Baxter, D.Kirkwood. Front: W.R.Clayton, B.Kelly, E.A.Bainbridge, George Mahon, Dr W.Whitford, R.Wilson.

sat-upon gentleman looked daggers at the dark-faced director, and eventually, I have reason to believe, called him out for a duel, to take place in the Goodison ground Press Box, with Mr Mahon as referee and Mr Wilson (who reminds me of Cattermole every time I look at him) as goal-keeper.

But this is getting a bit mixed, as Mr Mahon said at 10.30, when two hours and a half had gone and no work had been done, and he felt tired. So the voting was proceeded with (by ballot), and while the scrutineers were scrutineering the flimsies, which took them an hour to do their satisfaction, the audience congratulated itself all round upon the happy termination of the blow-up, and hoped things would go on all the smoother for it, as indeed I hope and expect they will. The man with the lion voice extracted a vote of thanks for the directorate, which request was responded to with all the jollity imaginable, for all the world as if the said directorate had been the best boys possible, and had done everything they would have done and nothing they should not.

Then it was announced that the voting

was as follows: Mr Wilson, 254; Dr Baxter, 239; Mr Leyland, 204; Mr Brooks, 170; Mr Davies, 105; and Mr Bainbridge, 100; Messrs Wilson, Baxter, and Leyland being accordingly elected.

Mr Secretary Molyneux added an interesting item to he proceedings by giving the names of the players for the coming season, these being received in silence, without sign of approval or the other thing. The names are: Goalkeeper: Cain, R. Williams, and Jardine (as an amateur); fullbacks: Adams, Kelso, Parry and Arridge; halfbacks: Boyle, Holt, Stewart, Walker and Storrier; forwards: Latta, M'Innes, South-worth, Hartley, Chadwick, Milward, Bell, Geary, Reay, Murray, W. Williams, M'Millan, and Elliott.

And that's all. I have tried to reproduce for your benefit a spice of the enjoyment which I experienced at this Annual meeting of the Everton Football Club. It was very amusing indeed, and a little thrilling at times. Seriously, though, I believe the blow-off has done the club all the good in the world.

The Goodison Turnstile Fraud of 1895

FOR some time prior to the 1895-96 season, the club's Finance Committee were concerned about the amount of gate money being handed over in relation to the number of people in the ground. Estimating crowds was a national pastime in those days and directors and reporters alike were expert at it. They could usually tell you before the end of any game what the official attendance would be, simply by casting an experienced eye around the various enclosures. They were never very far wrong.

But around this time, estimated attendances suddenly began to differ wildly from the figures being shown on the turnstile 'counters'. The money always tallied with the turnstile numbers, but there was this 'gut feeling' that many more people were in the ground than the 'official' figure suggested.

The turnstiles were fairly new and of a good make. They were checked regularly for any minor flaws. And yet there still seemed to be this anomaly. It was possible that an operator might be sixpence or a shilling short at times by giving the wrong change, but it appeared to go much deeper than that.

The club hated the idea of any of their men being dishonest. It was felt that there might be a major fault with the turnstiles and so it was decided to check things out at the next big match, against Sunderland on 12 December 1895. Mr John Davies, one of the oldest and most respected of the directors, went around as usual with the groundsman half an hour before the gates were opened and took the numbers.

But 20 minutes later, ten minutes before the gates opened, Dr Baxter made a second check with Mr Davies. With their own key, they checked the numbers already noted, which should have been the same.

The results were startling. In quite a number of the stiles, the 'clock' had been put back 200 units. Yet no one appeared to have access to them and only the groundsman had a key. One employee was questioned and taken to Westminster Road Bridewell and detained. Meanwhile, the men went as usual to their allotted stiles and the gates were opened to the public. Watching every money taker was a plain-clothed officer and when the gates were finally closed, seven men had exactly £5 more than their stile registered.

The trick was clear. Having been put back 200 units, it would take 200 sixpences – amounting to £5 – before registering against the stile operators. But each man questioned still pleaded ignorance and it was not possible at that stage to charge anybody.

The fraud was finally solved when the young employee at the Bridewell confessed, implicating over a dozen stilemen and the mechanic whose job it was to repair the stiles. The groundsman, the man whose duty it was to check the stile numbers with a director before and after each match, was also involved. That evening, and in the early hours of the following morning, 15 individuals were arrested. The famous Everton Turnstile Fraud had been solved and it led to a brand new type of machine being introduced soon after.

The Goodison Park Riot

28 December 1895
Everton 0 Small Heath 0

(abandoned after 30 minutes)

DECEMBER of 1895 will go down as one of the maddest months in the history of the Everton club. For no sooner had the 'Turnstiles Fraud' been solved, than a riot unfolded on the day of the First Division game against Small Heath, the club which later became Birmingham City.

The date was 28 December 1895, and the big game coincided with one of the wettest spells for some considerable time. It had rained non-stop for three days and the Goodison pitch was heavily water-logged in the morning.

There was much confusion as to whether it would drain in time, but when the gates were eventually opened at the normal time in a torrent of rain, the referee seemed quite satisfied that the pitch was playable. But a large number of supporters, fearing a postponement, stayed away and the attendance at kick-off time was around 6,000, only one-third of the average.

Play was farcical from the off. The players were slipping and sliding and the heavy ball was immovable at times. The players stuck at it for 30 minutes before the official signalled a halt and pointed to the dressing-room.

The crowd remained fairly patient for 15 minutes, waiting for a restart. The people in the seated areas, accepting nothing could be done, began to disperse. But a small section of fans made their way to the club office and demanded their money back. What was not clear was exactly how many of these people had paid to get in. Did they include late-comers?

The secretary tried to make himself heard from the balcony, but someone aimed a stone at him. Then the senior director, George Mahon, tried to get a hearing. He offered to give everyone present a free ticket for when the game was replayed, but the mob wanted money, not tickets. A stone shattered the glass of the large clock above Mr Mahon's head. A shower of missiles followed and the police immediately sought help from Dale Street headquarters. Sections of the palisading were ripped away and the staves used as weapons.

Every pane of glass in the pavilion was shattered. Meanwhile the 'rioters' began to march over the pitch and clamber into the stands, causing damage all the way. Others made for the dressing-rooms and there was even a shout to 'fire the stands'. Many of the police had head wounds, but they held their line to prevent the mob from reaching the main offices.

The police reinforcements suddenly arrived and, on command, drew batons. The crowd still seemed in the mood for a fight, but soon they were on the run, swept from the main gate near Spellow Lane. Goodison Road was cleared and the Everton riot was over. A small force of police were left on duty at the ground to retain the peace of the area overnight.

The game was eventually replayed on 3 February 1896 – on a Monday afternoon – and some 8,000 spectators saw the Blues win 3-0 with goals from Hartley (two) and Goldie to lift Everton to second place in the table. They eventually finished third.

Everton's Biggest Ever First Division Victory

**Monday, 3 September 1906
Everton 9 Manchester City 1**

DOWN the years Everton have had their fair share of runaway victories. In 1889 they beat Stoke 8-0 in a highly one-sided Football League encounter. They crushed Plymouth Argyle 9-1 in the Second Division in 1930 and put eight past Southampton without reply in a memorable Division One clash in 1971.

On the FA Cup front, an 11-2 success over Derby County raised more than a few eyebrows in 1890 and an 8-0 League Cup win over Wimbledon in 1978 and 5-0 UEFA Cup rout of Finn Harps the same year are also worthy of mention.

But it is the 9-1 hammering of Manchester City on 3 September 1906 that is rated as the club's greatest scoring achievement because of the game's top-flight status. And the players who produced the goods so magnificently at Goodison Park were members of one of Everton's greatest-ever teams.

In goal was Irishman Billy Scott, whose younger brother Elisha would become a legend in his own right across the park at Anfield. Billy was Everton's custodian in the 1906 and 1907 FA Cup Finals and he won three League Championship runners-up medals. Two local men filled the full-back berths, Walter Balmer and Jack Crelley. Balmer, whose younger brother Robert also played for the Blues, was famous for his powerful tackling and he represented England and the Football League. Crelley, although a Merseysider, arrived at Goodison from Millwall.

The vastly experienced half-back line consisted of Walter Abbott, Jack Taylor and Harry Makepeace, a truly outstanding trio in any company. Abbott had joined the Blues in 1899 and he flourished as a hard-shooting left-half. He was one of the original marathon men, covering every

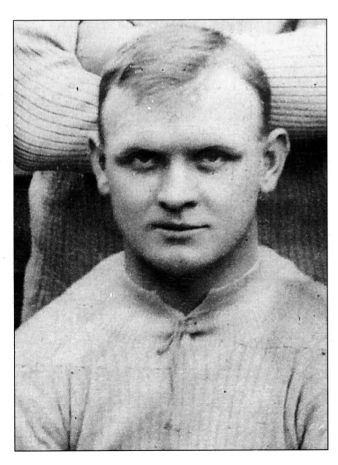

Left: Jimmy Settle, a classy inside-forward with an eye for a goal, who was on the mark when Everton beat Manchester City 9-1 in 1906.

Right: Centre-half Jack Taylor was not just a steadying influence in Everton's biggest-ever First Division victory in 1906. He also scored the first of the Blues' nine goals.

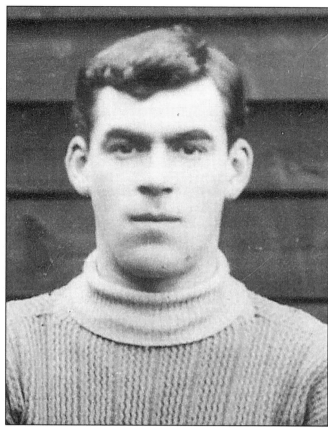

inch of the pitch. Taylor was one of the old school, a versatile character who arrived at Goodison in 1896 and played in the 1897 Cup Final on the right wing. He was still going strong when Everton reached the Final in 1906 and again in 1907.

By now, the skilful winger had developed into a solid centre-half. Alongside him, Makepeace thrilled the fans with his fierce tackling and pinpoint distribution. Makepeace was as famous a cricketer as he was a footballer, representing Lancashire and England along with his Goodison teammate Jack Sharp. Not surprisingly, the Blues were extremely proud of their talented all-rounders. Sharp was Everton's regular right winger for 11 years. He mixed speed with accuracy and strength and was once described as a 'pocket Hercules'. On the cricket field, Sharp scored 105 for England against the Australians at The Oval. But his first love was Everton and he later became a director, as did his son, while running a famous sports shop in the Liverpool city centre.

Add to these stars, men like Jimmy Settle (a clinical finisher), Harold Hardman (a great Corinthian whose skills on the wing won him an Olympic Games

soccer gold medal with Great Britain prior to him becoming one of the game's great administrators and later a Manchester United director for 50 years) and it is easy to see why Everton were amongst the great teams of the day.

And this is without mentioning the legendary Alex 'Sandy' Young. He sunk Newcastle United in the 1906 FA Cup Final and claimed crucial goals throughout his career, which brings us neatly back to 3 September 1906 and Everton's greatest First Division goalscoring feat against Manchester City.

Having mentioned that the Blues won this one-sided affair 9-1, I should now add that Young plundered four of the goals. The team were making their first appearance at Goodison following their April Cup triumph achieved in front of 75,000 people at the Crystal Palace. This, in itself, made it a special day.

The previous Saturday the side had opened the season with a 2-2 draw at Middlesbrough, a game which gave no indication of the goal blitz that was to come. The record books might suggest that City were always going to be on a hiding to nothing at Goodison against the supremely confident Cup holders. But the real reason for the goal rush could also have had something to do with the weather!

The Saturday had been the 'Glorious First' – the start of the partridge shooting season. It had coincided with the start of the football season with sportsmen shooting for goals, not game. To say there was a heatwave is an understatement. Temperatures in the mid-80s were reported throughout the country with Liverpool itself basking in 13 hours of sunshine and a high of 86 degrees.

Manchester City had entertained Woolwich Arsenal at Hyde Road (their home until 1923 when they moved to Maine Road). The heat was described in one report as being 'terrifying' and the end product was that City finished the afternoon with just six men on the pitch. Just as remarkable is the scoreline which reveals that The Arsenal won by only 4-1.

The City players seemed incapable of

Two contrasting shots of Everton's 1906 FA Cup winning team. One photograph is taken at Goodison Park, the other being a grander picture in front of a mock back-drop depicting the Crystal Palace, the Final venue. The names in the latter group are: Standing (left to right): Mr A.R.Taylor, H.Makepeace, Mr W.C.Cuff, A.Young, Mr J.Davies, Mr E.A.Bainbridge, J.D.Taylor, Mr G.Maon, W.Scott, Mr B.Kelly, Wm Balmer, Mr H.Wright, J.Elliott. Sitting: Mr W.R.Clayton, Dr J.C.Baxter, J.Sharp, H.Bolton, W.Abbott, J.Settle, J.Crelley, H.P.Hardman, Dr W.Whitford, Mr D.Kirkwood.

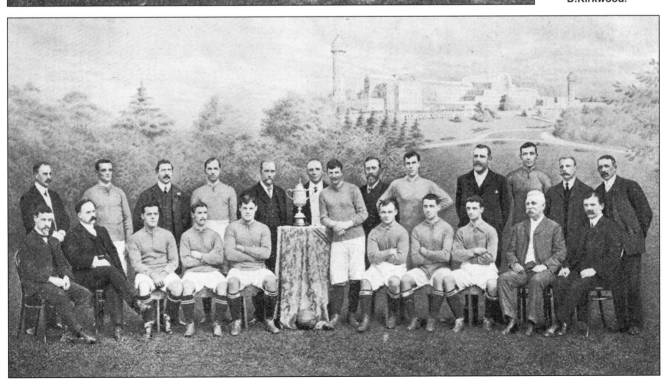

dealing with the hot-house conditions. They had eight men on the field when the second half started and the referee offered to stop the game. The Londoners, two up at the time, politely declined the official's offer of an early cold bath. But it appears they held back on their struggling opponents and settled for the 4-1 winning margin. It was described as a novel and unique incident in the history of the First Division.

City now came to Goodison to face Young, Sharp, Balmer, and the rest. Whether they were still feeling the heat or whether they simply did not fancy the challenge is open to debate. It's enough to say they turned up and were promptly played off the park. The *Liverpool Daily Post*, reporting the game the following day, said: *The inglorious display of City against Woolwich on Saturday before their own supporters did not suggest a tough job for the Toffees at Goodison. The evening was fine and 10,000 spectators were there at the start. Makepeace was absent and Tom Booth substituted. The Blues worked with determination and, keeping the leather well in, gradually forced back the Mancunian defence.*

That 'old warhorse' Taylor was not just a steadying influence in defence, but also scored the first goal, shooting beyond 'keeper Davis who would finish the game totally shell-shocked. Settle beat him easily to make it 2-0 and the cheers had only just died down when a smart pass from Young to Settle produced goal number three.

Abbott scored the fourth after a brilliant interchange between Taylor, Wilson and Young. It was surprising that Young had not found the net himself, but he soon put that right when he met a Wilson corner-kick. It gave the home side a 5-0 interval lead and it seemed that Everton could stroll through the visiting defence at will.

A clever pass by Settle enabled Young to bag number six and the centre-forward then completed his hat-trick with a 'rattling good shot'. Amazingly, City pulled one back on the break as the light began to fade. Two minutes from time, Bolton made it 8-1 and Young made it a match to remember when he headed home Sharp's centre for a record-breaking 9-1 win. The record still stands and, like Dixie Dean's League scoring feat, is never likely to be beaten.

Everton: Scott, W.Balmer, Crelly, Booth, Taylor, Abbott, Sharp, Bolton, Young, Settle, G.Wilson.

Attendance: 16,000

Everton in 1909. Notice the high waist-band and familiar snake-belt of Sandy Young, the 1906 Cup Final hero. Back row (left to right): Harris, R.Balmer, Scott, Maconnachie, Taylor, Makepeace. Front: Sharp, Coleman, White, Freeman, Young, Turner.

JACK SHARP – MILLENNIUM GIANT
1900-1910

IN the days when wingers were the skill merchants of British football, Jack Sharp was an undisputed wizard. Signed from Aston Villa in 1899, he was short and stocky, but full of power. His contemporaries called him Everton's "Pocket Hercules" and there is no doubt whatsoever that he was one of Goodison Park's original superstars.

Sharp's strength complemented his lighting fast speed and full-backs at every level had to be on their mettle to have even the slightest chance of containing him. The Everton outside-right was not just admired within the walls of Goodison. He was a national hero, not least because he was as exciting with a bat in his hand as he was with a ball at his feet.

Sharp was one of British sport's great all-rounders and when he wasn't dashing down the flanks on a soccer stage, he was lashing balls to the boundary on the country's great cricketing venues.

He won three Test caps for England and scored 105 against Australia at the Oval in 1909. A Lancashire regular between 1899 and 1925, his first class career produced a magnificent 22,715 runs which included 38 centuries. He was also a more than useful fast-medium bowler who took 440 wickets and held 223 catches.

As if this wasn't enough, he is described as being particularly brilliant at cover point.

Sharp was a sporting natural whose summer and winter activities endeared him to all who were lucky enough to see him play.

These were the days when your popularity was measured by the number of times your portrait appeared on cigarette cards. Sharp had 14 created in his image and it is said that only two Evertonians bettered this – the legendary Dixie Dean and Harold Makepeace who would follow in Sharp's illustrious footsteps as a football and cricket international.

Sharp played originally for Aston Villa, but headed for Merseyside in 1899. A Hereford lad, he made his way in the game with Hereford Thistle before breaking through with Villa in 1897. He would make only 23 appearances for the Midlanders, but Everton recognised his rich potential and he repaid them by holding down his wing position for eleven seasons, making 300 League appearances and scoring 69 goals.

Sharp also enjoyed great success in the FA Cup in

FACTFILE

Born: Hereford 1878
Everton appearances: 342
Everton goals: 81
Everton honours:
FA Cup winner: 1906
FA Cup runner-up: 1907
First Division runner-up: 1901-02, 1904-05, 1908-09.
England caps: 2.
Football League appearances: 3.

which he played 42 times for the Blues, scoring 12 goals. This gave him an Everton career total of 342 games and 81 goals. His consistency was quite remarkable, considering the effort he also put into his cricket career.

Sharp's three England cricket caps were supplemented by two for soccer, against Northern Ireland in 1903 and Scotland in 1905. He was renowned for his pinpoint centres and J. T. Howcroft, a referee for 30 years, said Sharp was the best outside-right he had ever seen, more effective even than a Billy Meredith or a Stanley Matthews. This was praise indeed.

Jack's brother Bert, a strong full-back, added to the family pride by also turning out for Villa and Everton.

However, even Bert would admit that the real star was Jack, from the day he made his debut against Sheffield United on the opening day of the 1899-1900 season. The Blues lost 2-1. Indeed, they lost all three of their opening games as defeats followed against Newcastle and Aston Villa. But Sharp tasted victory in memorable fashion in a 2-1 away win against the old enemy Liverpool at Anfield. Three games later he would score his first goal in a Blue shirt as Everton beat Nottingham Forest 2-1 and another wonderful moment came on December 2 that year when the Sharp brothers lined up together in an Everton team for the first time, helping to overshadow Derby County 3-0. Jack was amongst the scorers along with Jimmy Settle and Jack Taylor.

Jack's early career saw him going so near yet so far on the trophy front. Everton finished runners-up in the Championship in 1902, third in 1904 and second again in 1905. Sharp also suffered the agony of failing to reach the Cup Final in 1905, despite scoring in a 1-1 semi-final draw against his old club Villa at Stoke's Victoria Ground and also netting in the replay at Trent Bridge, Nottingham in the 2-1 defeat.

However, the glory game was Jack's game and the following year his outstanding wing play was one of the key factors as Everton set off on another tremendous FA Cup run which would this time end with a sensational 1-0 win over Newcastle at the Crystal Palace in front of 75,609 spectators. Alex 'Sandy' Young was the match winner, scoring from a Sharp centre 15 minutes from time as the Cup came back to Merseyside for the first time. A newspaper report described the moment of magic . . .

"Sharp resisted the attentions of McWilliam and, dashing along, centred like a flash, clean into the goalmouth, where Young, smartly following up after the leather, finished the job in style. Needless to say, the pent-up feelings of the Everton multitude broke forth in such a volume of sound that it was a wonder the threatening rain clouds overhead did not discharge their deluge."

Sheer poetry! This was the age of the train in the shape of the unstoppable Sharp. His day of triumph was fittingly shared with team mate Harold Makepeace, two of only 12 men who have played both football and cricket at full international level for England. It is worth noting that Makepeace remains the only man to have won a Cup winners medal, a League Championship medal (1915), a County Cricket Championship and played for England at soccer and cricket.

No wonder Everton were looked on like sporting royalty in this famous era. The Goodison travelling army had no doubt who was their man-of-the-match in the 1906 Cup Final – the indefatigable Sharp.

The following year, the Blues would return to the Crystal Palace in the FA Cup Final and Jack, having been a provider the previous year, would actually score in front of 84,584 fans. However, the Merseysiders finished up on the wrong end of a 2-1 defeat against Sheffield Wednesday.

Sharp would never achieve his dream of winning the League Championship. A third runners-up experience would follow in 1908-09 and the great winger finally hung up his famous boots on the final day of the 1909-1910 season. However, the impact he had made on the Goodison faithful had been quite remarkable. A club historian declared: "No player's brilliance on the field was more vividly impressed on the minds of the Everton faithful than Jack Sharp's."

He was invited to join the board of directors, now serving Everton with distinction behind the scenes. He died in January 1938, but his son, also Jack, maintained the great family tradition by also serving on the board. The great name also lived on for decades in a famous Liverpool city centre sports outfitters in Whitechapel.

The selection panel unanimously confirmed Jack Sharp as Everton's Millennium Giant (1900-1910).

Last Gasp Champions On A Day Of High Drama

Monday, 26 April 1915
Everton 2 Chelsea 2

FEW teams have won the League Championship with as much character and grit as Everton's school of 1915. The Blues suffered a major set-back in the run-in when they lost successive home games to Burnley and Sheffield Wednesday.

The men from Goodison now had to go on their travels, facing four away games on the trot. They won every single one of them – against Sunderland, West Brom, Bradford and Manchester City – to power from fifth place to first with just one game left.

Everything would now be decided on the last day with Everton and Oldham Athletic side by side on 45 points. As fate would have it, the Latics were up against Liverpool at Boundary Park. The Evertonians could not decide if this was a good thing or a bad thing as they prepared for their final game against Chelsea.

As it turned out, the Reds from across Stanley Park turned out to be the most reliable of neighbours. Their battling victory over Oldham and Everton's 2-2 home draw with Chelsea meant that the title trophy would reside in the board room at Goodison Park for only the second time since the inception of the League in 1888. Remarkably, the Blues were given a very low-key write-up in the local Press based on the fact that Chelsea were down amongst the First Division dead men and should have been crushed rather than held.

Certainly, the Blues were penned in for long periods in the early stages, possibly feeling the pressure after their long spell on 'tour' which had produced eight vital points out of eight. Strangely, they had been given a somewhat muted reception from the fans when they took to the field, Chelsea possibly getting a louder cheer.

Joe Clennell, a free-scoring inside-forward, figured in 36 League games during the 1915 title run, scoring 14 goals.

It was only when the Blues became fiery on the field that the supporters responded to their cause. It was Tom Fleetwood, an attacking wing-half, who stirred things up with a zig-zag run and a low cross shot that found the net to make it 1-0. Now Everton's leading scorer Bobby Parker took centre-stage with an outstanding strike to make it 2-0.

Parker had been signed from Glasgow Rangers in November 1913 and finished off that season with 17 goals in 24 League games. This latest offering took his 1914-15 tally to 36 in 35 games which made him the First Division's leading scorer.

It was a classic effort, a goal worthy of winning any Championship. Harrison powered in a corner and Parker drew back his boot, flashing a hook shot high into the roof of the net to inspire a standing ovation from all corners of the ground.

Incredibly, the Blues lived on their nerves in a tense finale and Brittain pulled one back before Logan equalised with a penalty. Thanks to Liverpool's triumph at Oldham, the point was good enough to secure the Championship. Everton finished on 46 with the Latics on 45. It had been a long and tense campaign, but no one at Goodison was complaining.

Everton: Fern; Thompson, Weller, Fleetwood, Galt, Grenyer, Chedgzoy, Kirsopp, Parker, Clennell, Harrison.
Attendance: 30,000

(Far left) Everton's team which won 5-1 at Villa Park during the Blues' 1914-15 League Championship season. Back row (left to right): Fleetwood, Grenyer, Thompson, Gait, Fern, Maconnachie, Makepeace. Front: Chedgzoy, Kirsopp, Parker, Clennell, Roberts. Centre-forward Bobby Parker scored four goals that day. For outside-left Roberts, though, it was his only appearance for Everton, standing in for the injured George Harrison.

Tom Fern's goalkeeping was an important feature in the title success of 1914-15. He made 231 appearances for the Blues.

Tom Fleetwood, an attacking wing-half, scored a crucial opening goal against Chelsea as Everton claimed the Championship in 1915.

Ten Thousand Holes In Blackburn Lancashire's Defence!

Saturday, 4 January 1919
Everton 9 Blackburn Rovers 0

FOOTBALL was played on a regional basis during World War One. Everton played in the Lancashire Section Principal Tournament which they won in season 1918-19, suffering only one defeat (at Manchester City) in 30 matches. The Blues subsequently lost to Midland Section winners Nottingham Forest in a two-legged Championship decider before finishing the campaign in the Lancashire Subsidiary Tournament.

The highlight of the year was undoubt-

Alan Grenyer was a left-half who played his best football for the Blues during World War One.

edly a 9-0 thrashing of Blackburn Rovers at Goodison Park. It does not stand as a record of any sort because of its county status, but it is still worth recording, if only for the five-goal blast from centre-forward Billy Gault.

It was reported that the ground was sticky and that there were 'pranks and miskicks aplenty', although it would appear that most of the action occurred in the Rovers penalty area. Early in the match, the Blues were criticised for producing very little at the end of graceful combined movements. Someone even commented that the shooting was not what you might call deadly.

It was as if the team picked up on these jibes because they opened the scoring after 15 minutes and then proceeded to swamp their opponents with an avalanche of attacks and goals.

Gault was the first on the mark, driving the ball low and wide of Gaskell's left hand and Everton soon increased their lead with an effort that was poetically described as a 'Miller thriller, a goal in a thousand'. The skilful right winger took the ball along the flank, beating the half-back and then the full-back before veering infield and hammering home a terrific low shot.

Rovers were being outclassed in all departments and Gault snatched the third after the 'keeper mishandled. On the half-hour a Joe Clennell header crashed into the back of the net to make it 4-0. The inside-left was all smiles, having joined the Blues from Blackburn in 1914. Clennell had been a virtual ever-present in the 1914-15 Championship-winning side. In wartime football he managed to amass 114 goals in only 104 games and this effort against his old club was a typical opportunist effort.

Clennell would make it 5-0 early in the

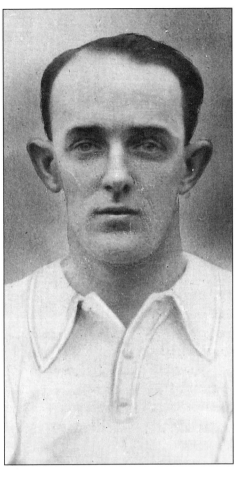

second half, netting from close range after a solo run. Then Gault took a centre from left winger Joe Donnachie to bring the total to 6-0 with the light fading fast over Goodison Park. Donnachie's far-post centre was his speciality. He was a real crowd favourite with his jinking runs and is one of that elite band of individuals who enjoyed two spells at Goodison Park.

The Blues now dropped down a gear,' one report suggesting they were 'fiddling around a lot, plainly refusing to rub salt into Blackburn's wounds'. In truth, the players were just catching their breath before producing a storming finish with Gault unstoppable. He made it 7-0 with a low shot and 8-0 with a cheeky backheel which meant he had claimed a traditional hat-trick and five goals in all. Wareing scored the ninth and the crowd were still shouting for more. Clearly, there had been a fresh delivery of salt!

Everton: Mitchell; Thompson, Maconnachie, Fleetwood, Wareing, Grenyer, Miller, Jefferis, Gault, Clennell, Donnachie.

Attendance: 8,000

Above, Left: Frank Jefferis helped to demolish Blackburn Rovers 9-0 in a Lancashire Section clash in 1919. Jefferis was a scheming inside-forward and a top-class tactician.
Centre: John Maconnachie was a highly polished left-back from Scotland, showing skill at a time when most defenders opted for the long punt downfield. He starred against Blackburn in that 1919 massacre at Goodison.
Right: Billy Gault scored 38 goals in only 29 appearances in 1918-19, including five in the 9-0 hammering of Blackburn Rovers. The following season, the first proper post-war campaign, he netted 12 goals in 21 League games but in May 1920 was transferred to Cardiff City.

Left: Billy Wareing, who scored the ninth goal against Blackburn. Southport-born, he joined Everton from Preston in 1912 and moved to Swindon Town in 1919 after scoring six goals in 64 appearances with the Blues.

SAM CHEDGZOY – MILLENNIUM GIANT
1910-1920

WINGERS and centre-forwards have always been very special to Evertonians. It has probably got something to do with the fact that the two go together like peaches and cream, Jack Sharp and Sandy Young, Dean and Critchley, Eglington and Hickson, Scott and Alex Young, Morrissey and Royle, Thomas and Latchford, Steven and Graeme Sharp – to name just a few of the great providers and strikers of the 20th century.

It is therefore no surprise that Everton's first Millennium Giant was a number seven, Jack Sharp, and that their second official legend also wore the same shirt.

Sam Chedgzoy filled the great Sharp's boots with a dash and a verve that won him eight England caps. He was first spotted as a 20 year

Born in Ellesmere Port , Chedgzoy spent his first three seasons at Goodison learning the ropes from great professionals around him after making the big step up from non-League football, but when he got into his stride in the 1914-15 campaign it was the start of a remarkably consistent run that saw him retain his place in the side for the next eight years.

It is not insignificant that Chedgzoy's first full season coincided with Everton winning their second League Championship. The winger, now very much part of the scene, played in 30 of the 38 games and scored two goals. Sammy's unselfish play would help centre-forward Parker grab 36 goals in 35 games.

Chedgzoy would help the Blues reach the semi-final of the FA Cup, scoring in the quarters in the 2-0 win over Bradford. Chelsea would prevent the Merseysiders reaching a Final that was played at Old Trafford, an emergency venue because the Crystal Palace had become a war depot. But that League title medal was more than enough compensation for Chedgzoy.

FACTFILE

Born: Ellesmere Port, 1890.
Everton appearances: 300
Everton goals: 36
Everton honours:
First Division Championship winner: 1914-15.
England caps 8.
Football League appearances 5.

The winger has another claim to fame that made him the talk of British football as his Everton career began to draw to a close. In June 1924, the Football Association reworded the corner kick rule and in doing so left a loophole that was spotted by famous *Liverpool Echo* sports editor Ernest Edwards. This is the same Edwards who is credited with the naming of Anfield's Spion Kop, picking up on a phrase used by local soldiers returning from the Boer War in South Africa when talking about a steep hill.

old, operating down the right flank for the Burnell Iron Works in the West Cheshire League. Fittingly it was a centre-forward who spotted him, but then you would expect a marauding number nine to appreciate the potential of a flying winger for laying on pinpoint crosses.

Fred Geary had been a record-breaking Everton striker of the Victorian era, amassing 86 goals in just 98 games. The first time he saw Chedgzoy he knew that the player would go to the very top of his profession and become a major wing ally for Goodison centre-forwards of the future.

Bobby Parker was the man who benefited most from Chedgzoy's intelligent play down the right. The winger had this knack of hanging balls in the air, inviting big centre-forwards to leap for glory.

The astute journalist had long discussions with Everton officials about the wording of the new offside law and it was decided that Chedgzoy, the club's regular corner taker, would seek to exploit it to see if he could gain an advantage.

Edwards declared. "There is nothing in the book

as it stands to prevent you dribbling the ball right into the middle, instead of taking the kick from the corner flag. Why not try it out and see what happens.?"

Chedgzoy was up for the challenge and in a match early that season he stunned the crowd, officials and opposing players by calmly placing the ball down and then dribbling it towards the goal. The referee whistled and began to lecture the Everton winger, but with the words of Ernest Edwards ringing in his ears, Sammy argued: "What's in the rules to stop me ref?"

Later, the official had to admit that there was nothing whatsoever. An emergency meeting of the football authorities had to be called and the law was clarified. It remains unchanged to this day.

Chedgzoy would have just one more season in English football's top flight, but once again it was a significant one. He would play 38 games in 1925-26 as a young man by the name of William Ralph Dean began to get into his free flowing stride.

Sammy would be a more than useful provider for young Dixie who plundered 32 goals in just 38 League games that year. It was the vastly experienced winger getting a supremely confident young striker up and running in a big way. Sammy managed seven goals himself, but by now he had been on Everton's books for 15 years. He had figured in 300 games, but this figure would have been over 400 if the First World War had not brought a halt to mainstream soccer between 1915 and 1919.

Nevertheless, Chedgzoy had much to look back on as he considered retirement plans that would take him to the United States.

There was that 1915 Championship medal to treasure, those eight England caps, secured against Wales (3), Scotland (2) and Northern Ireland (3) and that amazing episode when he played a part in the rewriting of one of the laws of the game.

Sammy Chedgzoy bridged two Everton decades, but the selection panel saluted him for the period 1910-1920 during which he was a Championship hero and one of the game's great characters.

The famous Sammy Chedgzoy, who was an established wing star when Dixie Dean made his home debut against Villa. Chedgzoy had won a League Championship medal in 1915 and was responsible for a change to the law concerning corners. At White Hart Lane in 1924, after it was decreed that a goal could be scored direct from a corner, Chedgzoy took a corner by dribbling along the by-line before hammering the ball into the Spurs' net. Afterwards the rule change was amended so that the player taking the corner could not play the ball twice.

Dixie Signs In For A Goal-Den Future

Saturday, 28 March 1925
Everton 2 Aston Villa 0

TRANSFER speculation was rife around Goodison Park as the 1924-25 season, a disappointing one for Everton, entered the home straight. In mid-March the *Liverpool Echo* reported that the Blues were on the verge of making some bold moves with a view to rebuilding the team. Many people were asking why they did not move locally for talent with the main topic of conversation surrounding Tranmere's talented teenage striker Dixie Dean.

The *Echo's* respected columnist, one 'Bee' (Ernest Edwards), was quick to point out that many clubs had been testing the water at Prenton Park and that *the time is ripe for the transfer of the boy.*

Edwards added: *Price is everything and Tranmere won't part with such a money-producer for a mere song. He ought not to go far from our doors, seeing that to all extents and purposes he is a local. He is, to my mind, the most promising centre-forward I have seen for years.*

The following morning, Tuesday, 17 March 1925, the *Liverpool Daily Post* was able to report that the Blues had scooped the likes of Manchester United, Aston Villa, Albion, Birmingham, Huddersfield, Liverpool, Middlesbrough, Chelsea and a host of other clubs to sign Dean.

The 18-year-old centre-forward had plundered 27 goals in 27 games for Rovers, who were reported to have put a £2,500 price tag on his head as well as seeking a gift of other players from the club securing his signature. The *Post* said: *It is probably the heaviest transfer fee that has ever been paid for a mere boy. It is impossible to state the figure with any degree of accuracy, but we can state definitely that £2,500 was Tranmere's original claim for their treasure.*

The paper then made a personal plea to the Evertonians, saying: *Everton once had another boy on their books who started well, but eventually fell through the frailty of human nature and the sickly adulation of the crowd. It is to be hoped the crowd will not make a 'god' of Dean. He is very human and*

Opposite page: Dixie Dean shows his legendary heading power to plunder another Goodison goal.

Everton in 1923-24, the season before Dixie Dean signed from Tranmere amidst tremendous local exitement. Note the square wooden goalposts.

has many boy-like touches. It is not so much what he has done but the way he has done it. He is a natural footballer with a stout heart, a willing pair of feet and a constitution that will stand him in good stead.

'Bee' picked up on the debate in the *Echo* in typically humorous fashion, writing an imaginary postcard from the 'Echo Hive, 17 March 1925'. It said: *Dear spectator. Pardon my intrusion, but you may have heard that Dixie Dean has been transferred by Tranmere Rovers to Everton. It is not a world-making move; it is just the movement of a local boy from Prenton Park to Goodison Park. At Tranmere there has been too much talk of Dixie-this and Dixie-that. If it continues, the boy – he is but eighteen years old – may easily lose his balance and his football form. Do not imagine that I am intruding or that I am not not going to take a firm hold on my own writings about the boy. Do be normal – and let him be likewise.*

The message was a simple one. Give Dean a chance to develop without undue pressure. As it turned out, there was no need for concern. The player remained the most level-headed individual in the game, even when he was at the very height of his success and scoring goals hand over fist for Everton and England.

Young Dixie made his Everton debut at Arsenal on 21 March 1925, a 3-1 losing experience. Seven days later he was selected for the home game against Aston Villa. The *Echo* reported: *It is as plain as daylight that Everton are going to sweep away the tradition of a year ago and aim at young men with a push and go that has been missing from some of the ranks of the side. Everton have been very pretty; they have been tantalisingly so. Now the club directors have shown a firm hand, and are in effect stating that the side has not nearly been good enough and must be amended. The new Everton shall be forceful and enterprising.*

And so Villa came to Goodison Park, the bridesmaids at Dean's wedding. The young man with a glorious future ahead of him was soon into his stride, getting in a snap shot after Smart had miskicked. The ball struck the goalkeeper's body and spun across goal with Talbot dashing in to clear. But Dixie's dream of making it a Goodison scoring debut was realised when his partner Kennedy bamboozled the Villa defence into thinking he was going to allow a forward ball to run out for a corner. Instead, he hooked a centre-back to Dean, who hammered it into the back of the net. The crowd gave their new hero a standing ovation.

In the second half, Dean began to direct headers wide to both flanks, giving the wingers the kind of service that would be his hallmark in years to come. He was always looking for openings around the box and directed an Alec Troup centre just over the top. Late on, another Troup cross, this time from a corner, was drilled home by left-half Reid to make it 2-0. It was very much the start of a new Goodison era.

Everton: Harland; McDonald, O'Donnell, Brown, McBain, Reid, Chedgzoy, Irvine, Dean, Kennedy, Troup.
Attendance: 25,000

Dean's First Goodison Treble

Saturday, 24 October 1925
Everton 4 Leeds United 2

IN A memorable Everton career, Dixie Dean would score many hat-tricks for the Blues. His first came at Burnley on 17 October 1924. His first Goodison treble arrived the following Saturday when Leeds United came to town.

It took Dean just three minutes to find the mark, a fine shot cannoning into the back of the net off an upright. Dean's anticipation of the early forward ball served him well and the 28,000 crowd showed their appreciation. There was an amazing scramble on the Leeds goal line soon afterwards with the ball trapped under several players until goalkeeper Johnson somehow managed to clear, but it was not long before Dean increased the lead with an unusual goal.

Sam Chedgzoy got away down the flank and hoisted the ball into the centre. Dean came charging forward and although he was hampered by the close attentions of a defender, he somehow managed to head the ball into the corner of the net.

Chedgzoy was possibly Everton's best forward at this stage with his spurting runs and effective centres. The Blues, though, failed to cash in until the 37th minute when Kennedy netted with a first-time drive following more outstanding work by the winger.

The 3-0 interval lead was well deserved, but Leeds were not going to give in without a fight. Centre-forward Jennings rattled the woodwork with Menham well beaten, but Dean responded by making it 4-0 after 55 minutes, thus completing his first home treble for the Blues. It wasn't a hat-trick in the old-fashioned sense (three successive goals) but it was still an achievement the young man from Birkenhead could be extremely proud of and the crowd gave him a

Tiny Scottish winger Alec Troup, who had previously played for Forfar Athletic and Dundee, was the man who helped Dean to many of his 377 goals for the Blues. Troup wasn't on the scoresheet against Leeds, but he had another good game, causing opposing defenders all sorts of trouble.

rousing cheer. Once again, Chedgzoy was the provider. Dean got a foot to the centre and the ball dropped just under the bar with the 'keeper nowhere.

Wainscott pulled one back for Leeds after 63 minutes, but a minute later he was badly injured and taken to hospital with a dislocated elbow.

The ten men now battled gamely and Jennings reduced the lead still further with a fine drive a minute from time. But the day belonged to Dean as so many others would in the future. In the space of two weeks he had bagged six goals to suggest that glorious days were ahead in a blue shirt.

Everton: Menham; McDonald, Livingstone, Brown, Bain, Hart, Chedgzoy, Peacock, Dean, Kennedy, Troup.
Attendance: 28,660

A Goodison Christmas Cracker

25 December 1926
Everton 5 Sunderland 4

EVERTON had not won for six weeks when they entertained Sunderland on Christmas Day 1926. They were desperate for a holiday victory and secured it in the most dramatic of circumstances, winning at Goodison Park by the odd goal in nine.

Dixie Dean, playing his tenth game after recovering from a nightmare motor-cycle accident, was the undisputed hero of the day with an outstanding four-goal haul. But elsewhere another famous centre-forward, Middlesbrough's George Camsell, was bettering Dean's achievement by scoring five against Manchester City at Maine Road.

Head and shoulders above the rest, as usual, Dixie Dean rises above another frustrated 'keeper to power a header on target. This time it is Aston Villa who are on the receiving end.

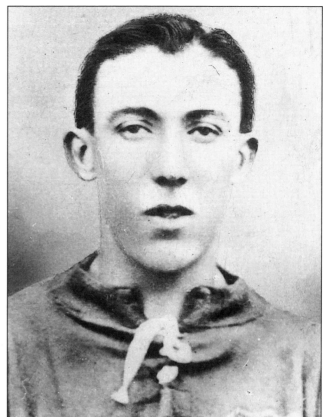

Camsell would go on to claim 59 League goals and set a new Football League scoring record. Dean would take note and do something about it 12 months on, but for now it was all about a crucial win over the men from Roker which finally brought to an end a worrying barren spell.

The Blues had lost 5-1 to Burnley, 1-0 to Cardiff, 5-3 to Aston Villa, drawn 1-1 with Bolton, thanks to an own-goal, and lost 2-1 at Manchester United. There were those who said relegation was not so much a possibility as a certainty. The Everton players now gave the fans the perfect Christmas present.

Over 37,000 turned up for the clash, the biggest Christmas attendance at Goodison for years. A young man by the name of Ted Critchley, signed from Stockport for a nominal fee, was handed his debut. It was hoped he would eventually prove an admirable replacement for famous right-winger Sammy Chedgzoy, the man who had been responsible for a major change to the offside law.

Chedgzoy had recognised a glaring loophole in the laws and exploited it in a game against Tottenham, dribbling the ball in along the by-line and then hammering it into the net without any other player touching it. Twelve months later, the football authorities were forced to introduce a new rule whereby the taker of a corner could play the ball only once before a second player had touched it.

Chedgzoy had retired at the end of the 1925-26 season, crossing the Atlantic to live in America. It meant the number seven shirt he had worn over a period of some 15 years was up for grabs and men like Irvine, Parker, Moffatt, Millington and Woodhouse had all worn it that season before Critchley stepped into the frame on Christmas Day. The *Liverpool Echo* reported: *The Stockport boy did well. His one run the full length of the field was something to memorise, but allowing for his over-anxiety, which made him run the ball out, his old mannerisms and passes and centres augers well for future days.*

Those words proved prophetic. Critchley, with his tight control and speed, would provide teammate Dean with countless goals and serve the club well for eight years. Dixie rattled in four against Sunderland, but the best goal of the day was scored by inside-forward Bobby

Dixie Dean the family man, taking a golfing break in the Isle of Man.

Irvine, who was a magnificent dribbler. He lashed home an outstanding first-time drive in an end-to-end affair that finished 5-4 in Everton's favour with Sunderland more than playing their part.

Everton: Davies; Raitt, O'Donnell, Brown, Bain, Hart, Critchley, Irvine, Dean, Dominy, Troup.
Attendance: 37,500

One Down, Fifty-Nine To Go

Saturday, 27 August 1927
Everton 4 Sheffield Wednesday 0

THE dawning of the 1927-28 season was a significant one for Everton. The previous year, star striker Dixie Dean had been badly injured in a summer motor accident in which he fractured his skull. His durability was such that he was pulling on his famous number nine shirt just four and a half months later and scoring in an October fixture at Leeds.

Dean went on to claim 21 League goals in 27 games with three in the Cup for good measure. It was as if the accident had sharpened his appetite for big-match action rather than dulled it and so when the new campaign kicked-off with a home clash against Sheffield Wednesday, there was tremendous anticipation amongst the Evertonians that the season would hold something very special indeed.

It turned out to be a record-breaking year in every sense, a goal-packed Championship charge in which Dixie would find the back of the net 60 times on League duty to claim a VIP place in the Goodison Park Hall of Fame.

The first of those goals came against Wednesday on a day when new captain Warney Cresswell led the team out for the very first time. The pitch was in perfect condition and while Cresswell lost the toss, it mattered little because there was no bright sunshine or wind to give an advantage.

The Blues almost scored in the opening 60 seconds when Alec Troup lobbed the ball into the area. It seemed too high to kick and too low to head, but Dixie made the most of it with a magnificent dive that very nearly produced a headed goal.

Dean now went from the sublime to the ridiculous. The referee stunned everyone by ignoring Wednesday's bold

Dean was virtually unstoppable in the air as the Huddersfield Town defence found to their cost at Goodison. The challenge is decisive and the ball just a blur as it flashes over the goalkeeper's head.

Albert Virr, a no-nonsense half-back who was prominent against Sheffield Wednesday the day Dixie Dean scored against the Owls to begin his push for the legendary '60'.

offside appeals and Cresswell was allowed to break forward and slide an inch-perfect pass into the box. It seemed as if Dean could not miss in front of the posts, but he pulled his shot wide and the visitors couldn't believe their luck. Stirred by this miss, the centre-forward then bulleted a header against the bar.

Everton's first-time football was a treat to watch. The ball flashed from one man to the other to leave Wednesday gasping. It was no surprise when the lead was claimed after 26 minutes. Winger Troup was the scorer, squeezing home a shot from what had seemed an impossible angle to startle goalkeeper Brown. The lead was increased within a minute when inside-left Weldon hammered home from long range. At the other end, Everton's solid Scottish centre-back Hunter Hart ensured that opposing centre-forward Jimmy Trotter didn't get in a single shot.

At the start of the second half, the Blues began to pepper the Wednesday goal as Dean, Forshaw and Virr all went close. Forshaw made it 3-0 after 62 minutes, Dean heading into his path after O'Donnell had launched the ball in. The victory was completed when Dean took Irvine's well-timed pass on the run and slipped his shot wide of the helpless Brown.

For the Goodison number nine it was a case of one down, 59 to go. George Camsell's League scoring record was clearly in his sights.

Everton: Taylor, Cresswell, O'Donnell, Kelly, Hart, Virr, Irvine, Forshaw, Dean, Weldon, Troup.
Attendance: 39,485

DIXIE DEAN – MILLENNIUM GIANT
1920-1930

WHEN it came to naming Everton's Millennium Giant of the 1920s, there was no argument, no debate, no question whatsoever that the panel and the fans would be anything other than unanimous in their verdict.

Back in what was a golden age for Everton FC, the cry was always: "Give it to Dixie."

In the famous Goodison board room, 62 years after the record-breaking centre-forward left his beloved Blues, the shout was still the same as the Millennium Panel considered some great candidates: "Give it to Dixie!"

And we did, with an admiration and affection that is reserved for true greats. The famous exploits of William Ralph Dean, including his remarkable 60 goal haul in 1927-28, are well documented in a variety of chapters in this official history of Everton's famous stadium.

Therefore, in paying tribute to him in this "Giants" section, I will take you on a whistlestop journey through his life, letting his own words give you some indication of how much he loved the great game and how fans all over Britain were dazzled by his sheer brilliance.

At 13, Dean was playing three games each Saturday for school and junior teams in Birkenhead. He recalls: "I remember one day in particular because I scored 18 goals. Yes, 18 in three games that followed almost one after the other, so I wasn't too surprised when I got 60 in one season for Everton."

Knowing Dean and having had the honour to meet him many times, I know that those words were said tongue-in-cheek. You see, this particular immortal was one of the most modest men you could ever wish to meet.

He would tell you: "I was no use whatsoever as a scholar at school. I could just about write a bit, but I couldn't put two and two together, and I spent all my time playing football."

One day, he was presented with a medal for football. "It turned out to be one of my best days at school," he recalls. "I asked the teacher if I could slip home and show the medal to my mother. He let me go and I stayed away for three days just to celebrate. They were great times."

Modern superstars have everything at their feet. Dean left school on a Friday and started work the following Monday. He said: "It was shift work and the other apprentices with me didn't like the night work. I revelled in it, because it gave me more time in the day to play football."

Although he lived on the other side of the river

FACTFILE
Born: Birkenhead 1907.
Everton appearances: 431.
Everton goals: 377.
Record 60 League goals in one season, 1927-28.
Everton honours:
First Division Championship winner: 1927-28 and 1931-32.
Second Division Championship winner: 1930-31.
FA Cup winner: 1933.
Charity Shield winner: 1928 and 1932.
England caps: 16.
Football League appearances: 6.

to the city of Liverpool, he was an Everton fan all his life. "I didn't care if Liverpool were licked 3-0," he said. "That wouldn't affect me at all. If Everton lost? Well, let's just say I couldn't get over it."

Mention "Dixie" to Evertonians and they immediately see him in their mind's eye, standing there like a giant at Wembley in 1933, clutching the FA Cup. "I'll never forget going up to the Royal Box at Wembley to collect the FA Cup," he would say. " I received it off the Duchess of York, the mother of our present Queen. She congratulated me and said it was a very good game (Everton beat Manchester City 3-0). She really smiled and said she had enjoyed it. That made me feel so proud. I was walking ten feet tall because it meant I had won every honour in the game. That cup medal completed the collection."

Incredibly, the powerhouse Dean was never spoken to or cautioned by a referee, even though it was a rough and tumble world that he played in. One ref called him over and Dixie thought his proud record was going to be broken. "Do you want a mint to suck, Billy" the official declared. Dean said: "Thanks very much," and sprinted back into the action!

Naturally, defenders did their level best to kick Dean off the park. He had 15 major operations during his career and recalled that trainer Harry Cooke seemed to spend half his life in hospital with him at that time. Dean had broken bones, bones taken out of his ankles, broken ribs, broken toes and cartilage operations. Cooke took great delight in keeping the bits of bone and cartilage in a pickle jar. When new players joined the club, the first thing Harry did was thrust it in their faces and say: "That's what it takes to be a real player!"

Later in his life, Dean paid the ultimate price for his bravery. He had to have a leg amputated, a direct result of the catalogue of injuries he picked up during his no-holds-barred football career.

Nothing phased Dean, certainly not intimidation from big defenders. But there were a lot of very hard men around. Dean remembers one particular game in Yorkshire. He said: "I scored two goals and this Rochdale fella says to me... 'Thy'll get no more bloody goals today.' I said . . . 'You're too fat and too old, what are you talking about?' But he was right. The next time I tried to dribble past him, he kicked me up in the air. I finished up in hospital for an operation. He was a good tipster, that fella!"

Dean was the undisputed King of the Air and he would say: "The secret of heading is to catch in on your forehead. If you get it on the top of the head it will knock you daft in no time. I was not as tall as many of the centre-halves I played against, but I never had any difficulty beating them in the air. It wasn't a case of leaping higher than they could. It was just a matter of going up at the right time."

Dean was idolised by soccer fans all of

his life. He said: "I never stopped signing autographs, day in, day out. I'll never forget the Everton fans for the way they treated me, not only when I was playing, but long after I left the club. I felt that these fans belonged to me and I belonged to them. I was born and bred an Evertonian and I knew that would never change.

William Ralph "Dixie" Dean, the club's undisputed Millennium Giant for the 1920s will always hold his place at the head of the Goodison immortals. He was simply the best.

Dixie Dean's Finest Hour

Saturday, 5 May 1928
Everton 3 Arsenal 3

IF there was such a thing as a soccer time machine and Evertonians were offered just one magical trip into the past, I suggest that they would opt, to a man, to be whisked back to Goodison Park on Saturday, 5 May 1928 to witness William Ralph 'Dixie' Dean's finest hour.

The League Championship had already been won. Now the greatest number nine the game has ever seen was standing on the brink of immortality with George Camsell's Football League scoring record of 59 goals locked in his sights.

Could Dean rewrite the record books by equalling and possibly beating the Middlesbrough striker's formidable tally? The challenge against the mighty Arsenal was all too clear. Dean needed three goals to become a record-breaker. For most strikers, the task would be a mountainous one. But Dixie was no ordinary player. Here was the complete footballer, fast and powerful, possessing a lethal shot in both feet and the undisputed king of the air.

There was a genuine sense of history in the making as thousands of fans converged on Goodison Park in bright sunshine. It was as if the gods themselves wanted to be part of football's greatest day.

Incidentally, most reports give a crowd figure of 60,000 for this match, but the official figure returned to the Football League was just over 48,000. Years later, half of Merseyside would claim to have been present on this historic day.

Arsenal were never going to be pushovers. One of their most successful players, Charlie Buchan, was playing in his final match before bowing out. The Gunners were not interested in Dean. They wanted to win it for Charlie. The game had so many aspects, not least the fact that the League Championship trophy was going to be presented on the final whistle.

Copying Wembley's lead, amplifiers had been spread around Goodison so that every fan in the ground would be able to hear League president John McKenna during the post-match celebrations. The fans had been encouraged in the local

A proud Championship group pose in May 1928 with the Gwladys Street terraces behind them. Notice there is no stand. The houses are clearly visible. From the left: Harry Cooke, Critchley, Martin, Kelly, Cresswell (captain), O'Donnell, Mr W.C.Cuff (chairman), Hart, Dean, Davies, Weldon, Virr and Troup.

Press to keep off the pitch at all times. All they had to do was cheer Everton and Dean in particular every inch of the way.

Reflecting on the big match, the *Liverpool Echo* reported: *In many clubs, success such as one man (Dean) has won would have been fatal. There would have been petty jealousies, but at Everton that is not the case. They all recognise Dean's worth and his great help, and naturally they are as keen as Dean to see Camsell's record go by.*

A new entrance from Bullens Road had been created for the first time, from which the mounted police could be brought into the ground at any given moment, if required. The trophy was already on display and a supporter shouted to the Goodison officials: "Where are the colours?" The hint was taken and secretary Tom McIntosh immediately tied royal blue ribbons to the trophy. This was a day for single-minded bias.

Chairman Will Cuff opened the proceedings by urging the crowd to remain in the places on the final whistle. Then there was a sensational Goodison welcome for skipper Warney Cresswell as he led out the team. The warmth of the supporters also touched Buchan as he emerged from the tunnel, wearing an Arsenal shirt for the last time.

Referee Mr W.P.Harper of Stourbridge took the unusual step of giving Dean a hearty handshake. And all eyes were on the centre-circle as the official finally got the proceedings underway. Carried forward on the crest of an almighty roar, Dean had an early chance, but did not score.

The Arsenal now attacked themselves and snatched the lead dramatically with just two minutes on the clock. Shaw appeared to handle as he moved through, but he got away with it and his shot went straight through the 'keeper's hands into the back of the net. The match was clearly not going to script and the fans were temporarily stunned, but the man of the moment now responded with a quite sensational double with the game only three minutes old!

The crowd went absolutely wild when a Ted Critchley corner was turned on by George Martin to Dean. The centre-forward sent a header into the extreme left-hand corner of the net and it was 1-1. The ground now rocked as tens of thousands of voices picked up on the moment with Dean closing in on goal for a second time. Long-legged centre-half Butler ran across him and the Everton ace crashed to the ground. The cry of 'Penalty'! was so loud, it rattled the slates on a thousand and one houses in the surrounding streets.

The referee immediately pointed to the spot and Dean got up, placed the ball himself and drilled it wide of Bill Paterson to equal Camsell's 59 goal record (the Middlesbrough player had achieved his feat in the Second Division).

The prince of goalscorers now needed just one more to be king. At the same time, Everton were nearing the 104 goals record total achieved by West Brom shortly after World War One. The Blues total was 101 and the statisticians in the crowd were beginning to think about a possible team record as well as an individual achievement. After all, the game still had 87 minutes to run.

At the same time, the play was enthralling. Paterson claimed a hot-shot from Dean who was now pumped up to fever pitch. The big attacker followed in with a shoulder charge that nearly sent the 'keeper sprawling into the back of the net. The crowd would have been happy to see Dixie pick up the Arsenal custodian and throw him over the line, ball and all.

The Gunners had already beaten Everton twice at Highbury, 3-2 on Christmas Eve and 4-3 in the fourth round of the FA Cup. The Blues were now intent on a very special revenge, but Buchan and Shaw demonstrated their artistry to indicate that the match would be fiercely contested to the finish.

In his anxiety to get the record, Dean began to fall into Arsenal's offside trap. Everton's frustration reached new heights when the Londoners equalised ten minutes before the interval. Goalkeeper Davies was about to pick the

If Dean was blasting home goals, he was pitching for glory in other areas. He enjoyed a game of baseball and won honours playing for local club Caledonians. Everton secured his baseball medal at a Glasgow auction in October 1991, along with his 1931-32 Championship medal and other key items of memorabilia.

ball up when left-back O'Donnell contrived to turn it over his own line to make it 2-2. It had been a pulsating opening 45 minutes and the players and the fans were grateful for the half-time whistle and an opportunity to catch their breath.

On the resumption, the tension was unbearable. Paterson made an outstanding save as Dean got full power on a wickedly spinning ball. He now showed the other side of his game, slipping a neat pass to Critchley, who hammered a shot against the angle of the post. Everton had the sun in their eyes and were almost certainly trying too hard, but such frantic play was inevitable with so much at stake. Dean now found himself crowded out for a spell, but he broke through with power on the hour to swing a shot narrowly wide.

The minutes were now ticking away. Dean headed inches over and then overran the ball on the break. He sent a left-foot shot wide and as the game went into the final ten minutes, hope was turning to despair. But Dixie was the man for all occasions and he seemed to grow visibly when the Blues gained a corner-kick after Paterson had punched Martin's shot over the bar.

Tiny Scottish winger Alec Troup, the man who had provided most of the ammunition for Dean throughout that famous year, now hoisted the ball high into the box. Dean rose out of a ruck of players to head home with all the power and accuracy that was his trademark.

The 60-goal haul that many felt was impossible had been achieved and the centre-forward was congratulated by all of his teammates. Two spectators broke through the police barrier and one was bundled off by the referee. The other managed to reach his hero and give him a kiss! Goalkeeper Paterson took off his cap and scratched his head, accepting that he had been beaten three times by the master.

There were still eight minutes left and during this closing spell the crowd never stopped cheering for a single second, even when Arsenal centre-forward Shaw levelled matters on the rebound after Davies had turned a Peel effort against the upright. As Everton shaped to take a corner at the other end, the Gunners' goalkeeper Paterson took the opportunity to shake hands with Dean. And even while the kick was being taken, centre-half Butler was seen to shake hands with the man who had given him such a torrid afternoon.

Suddenly it was all over. Cresswell stepped up to receive the Championship trophy from Mr McKenna. Everton's famous chairman Cuff tried to make himself heard over the loudspeakers, congratulating the team on their title success, adding that it had been the most wonderful season the game of football had ever known.

The toast was Everton Football Club and Dixie Dean …the greatest centre-forward of all time.
Everton: Davies; Cresswell, O'Donnell, Kelly, Hart, Virr, Critchley, Martin, Dean, Weldon, Troup.
Attendance: 48,715

Famous *Liverpool Echo* cartoonist George Green saluted Dean's 60-goal League haul with an extra-special drawing. The fans loved it.

Another historic George Green cartoon hails the 1928 Champions. It was hats off to Everton.

Sagar Begins His Goodison Marathon

18 January 1930
Everton 4 Derby County 0

TED Sagar was the Goodison Park marathon man. He spent an astonishing 24 years and one month with the Blues between 1929 and 1953 to set up what was then a club record of 463 League appearances (some record books give the incorrect figure of 465). The goalkeeper who became an Everton legend first appeared on the scene on 18 January 1930, named in place of the experienced Davies. As a boy, he had played for Thorne Colliery in the Doncaster Senior League and was on the verge of signing for Hull City when Everton nipped in smartly to secure his services.

The fans turned up for the clash against the Rams, fascinated by the debut appearance of the young 'keeper who had been earning himself good reports with the Reserves. He soon demonstrated a safe pair of hands, claiming a shot-cum-centre from Bobby Barclay. This apart, there was very little for the young Sagar to do. Ted Critchley secured the lead after 22 minutes with a well-placed side-foot shot. Derby now made what was only their second attack of note and once again Sagar was equal to a high forward ball.

The initiative remained with the Blues although their new 'keeper earned applause when he dashed out to collect a ball that Harry Bedford had headed in. Dean made it 2-0 after 51 minutes after Derby 'keeper Harry Wilkes had failed to hold a fiery shot from Jimmy Stein.

Sagar now showed the bravery that would become one of his hallmarks, plunging down at the feet of Bedford. His other strength was his confidence going for crosses and he leapt to make a good catch after George Mee had centred across the goalmouth.

Soon after, he punched away in similar circumstances and the *Football Echo* reported: *Sagar had undoubtedly justified his inclusion, although it was Everton's teamwork which had gained the day.*

The Blues went three up after 75 minutes, Dean having the simple task of guiding the ball in with his body after Wilkes had failed to claim a Stein centre. Three minutes from time, Stein's hot drive made it 4-0. It had been a successful debut for Sagar, but he now stepped down for three games to allow Davies to return.

Sadly, things were now deteriorating for the Blues in terms of all-round results. Sagar was able to get a seven-match run, but relegation-haunted Everton lost five of these matches and conceded 19 goals in the bargain.

The young 'keeper's confidence might have been destroyed when Billy Coggins, signed from Bristol City, now claimed the first-team jersey for the remainder of a frustrating relegation season. More than that, Coggins was an ever-present the following year as the Blues swept back to the top flight at the first time of asking.

But Sagar's quality was such that he was the man in the driving seat when a bright new First Division challenge loomed on 29 August 1931. The supremely talented goalkeeper never looked back.

He won two League Championship medals and an FA Cup winners medal with the Blues and finished up with a marvellous total of 495 League and Cup games under his slim belt. He had many memorable moments, but that debut clean sheet against Derby County always gave him particular pleasure.

Everton: Sagar; Williams, O'Donnell, Robson, Hart, McPherson, Critchley, Martin, Dean, Rigby, Stein.
Attendance: 35,436

TED SAGAR – MILLENNIUM GIANT
1930-1940

TED Sagar's claim to fame as Everton's Millennium Giant for 1930-40 is not just that he was a remarkable goalkeeper whose career spanned an astonishing 24 years and one month at Goodison Park, although that in itself would have been good enough to secure him a place in any Football League Hall of Fame.

No, it was the fact that Sagar claimed the final vote in an era when Everton FC was packed full of legends that makes his achievement so special. With the legendary Dixie Dean already assured of his place on the pedestal as the 1920s Giant, Sagar still had to contend with such outstanding candidates as magnificent centre-forward Tommy Lawton and fans super hero Joe Mercer.

That he came out on top suggests that we are talking here about a very special individual, a modest man whose career bridged three decades and who won Championship and FA Cup honours as well as playing for England and the Football League. Not surprisingly for such a relentless marathon man, he also held the club's appearance record until another famous custodian, Neville Southall, finally surpassed his 463 game League total.

Some people might say that it was easy playing behind such players as Dean and Lawton. Certainly, the opposing goalkeepers in this era inevitably had a tougher time of it and a typical Dixie double on Sagar's debut ensured that most of the headlines that day were dominated by the great striker.

Nevertheless, Sagar was so respected that a newspaper report in 1934, discussing an impending appearance for the Football League, declared: "There is no finer goalkeeper in football today."

Evertonians literally grew up with Sagar. The penalty areas at Goodison Park became his domain and he dominated them with tremendous athleticism and bravery.

Ted came to Everton from Thorne Colliery FC who played in the Doncaster Senior League in Yorkshire. He quickly impressed in the reserves and kept a clean sheet on his debut against Derby County. He was fairly thin for a keeper in an age when it was perfectly legitimate for marauding centre-forwards to shoulder charge the man between the posts. The young goalkeeper began to rely on his positional play and sound judgment and his big strength was judging and claiming high crosses.

This was the age of the winger and goalkeepers who could not deal with the ammunition fired in from the flanks would be exposed in every game. He would later say: "I tried to make collecting crosses my life's work. I would practice for hours on end, week in, week out, with a couple of lads pushing high balls into the box while another came in to challenge me. I very seldom got it knocked out of my hands."

Sagar would make just nine appearances in that first 1929-30 season with Davies and Coggins also competing for the jersey. But the fact that the Blues used three keepers in one campaign suggests that they were going through a time of change. Indeed, at the end of Sagar's first campaign, Everton were relegated.

The young arrival was devastated, but he continued to learn his trade with the reserves as

FACTFILE
Born: Moorends, Yorkshire, 1910.
Everton appearances: 495.
Everton honours:
Football League Championship: 1931-32 and 1938-39.
FA Cup winner: 1933.
FA Charity Shield winner: 1932.
England caps: 4.
Football League appearances: 5.

rival Coggins helped Everton bounce back at the first attempt as Second Division Champions.

Indeed, Billy Coggins played in all 42 League games as well as being an ever-present as the Blues reached the semi-final of the FA Cup. Many outsiders might have believed that young Sagar's chances of forcing his way back into the reckoning were slim, but his form in the reserves never dipped below excellent and it was Coggins who was the odd man out when the 1931-32 season kicked off with the Blues back in the top flight.

Sagar didn't just step out of the shadows, he leapt into the limelight and literally never looked back for a quarter of a century.

Everton won the title during the goalkeeper's first full season between the posts and the following year he was a Wembley winner as the Blues beat off the challenge from Manchester City to claim soccer's most famous trophy.

Sagar's second Championship medal followed in the last big season before the outbreak of the Second World War, 1938-39. He has the distinction of playing both for and against Northern Ireland on an international stage.

The Everton star made his international debut for England against the Irish in October 1935.

Later, Sagar would actually pull on a Northern Ireland jersey in a war-time international against Southern Ireland. He was proud of this remarkable achievement of having played at the highest level for two separate countries. His other England caps came against Scotland, Austria and Belgium.

Sagar's final Everton appearance was fittingly at Goodison Park against Tranmere Rovers in the Final of the Liverpool Senior Cup in May, 1953, making him the club's longest serving player by a mile at that time.

In his retirement, Ted was Mine Host at the well known Blue Anchor Pub in Aintree, close to the racecourse. He died in 1986 at the age of 76. The final tribute came from another great, Joe Mercer who described him as a spectacular player who was truly out on his own. "I can't compare him with any of the modern players," said Mercer. "I can only describe Ted Sagar as a total one-off."

What better tribute could any player receive.

Relegated After A Storming Victory!

Saturday, 3 May 1930
Everton 4 Sunderland 1

A DISASTROUS six-game losing spell between 5 March and 12 April had left Everton in a precarious position as the 1929-30 season reached a nail-biting climax. Aston Villa, Newcastle United, West Ham, Birmingham, Leicester and Grimsby Town had all overshadowed the Blues in a disappointing spell and now Dixie Dean, scorer of 109 League goals in a richly productive three-year spell, was suddenly unavailable for selection.

It was doom and gloom at Goodison Park, but the side had shown its fighting qualities, embarking on a four-match unbeaten run (three victories and a draw) that had brought the Blues to the final game with a mathematical chance of staying up. Sadly, Everton's fate would depend on results other than their own.

All they could do was produce the goods against Sunderland at Goodison and keep their fingers crossed. Not surprisingly, the game attracted the club's biggest gate of the season with over 51,000 people in attendance. It was a sultry, humid afternoon and the Everton players were looking distinctly nervous as play got under way.

Warney Cresswell made a couple of uncharacteristic mistakes for such an old warrior and it served to unsettle the crowd. But the tension eased after 23 minutes when inside-left Tommy Johnson cashed in following a free-kick. Goalkeeper Robinson had punched away off Tommy White's head. There was something of a scramble until Johnson claimed the loose ball with the fans screaming for a shot. It was a long time in coming, but when it did, it flew home with the scorer mobbed by his delighted teammates.

Everton's elation lasted just six minutes. After some loose play in front of goal, Clunas arrived with a first-time drive to equalise. The supporters groaned in disappointment, but their frustration was shortlived because the Blues regained the lead almost immediately with a magnificent goal from White. He met a lobbed centre and headed the ball downwards. Robinson managed to parry

This 1929-30 squad of players had the misfortune of taking the club down for the first time, although they bounced back at the first time of asking. Back row (left to right): Thompson, Bryan, Sagar, O'Donnell, White, Martin, Coggins, Cresswell, Hart. Centre: Cooke (trainer), G Cook, Webster, Britton, Gee, Dean, Common, Stein, Tucker, Robson. Below Centre: Wilkinson, McClure, Critchley, Williams, Griffiths, McCambridge, Johnson. Front: Low, Rigby, Chedgzoy, junior, Towers, McPherson, Dunn.

the effort, but White had followed in and he netted with a deft touch of his boot.

Everton went in with a 2-1 interval lead and all eyes immediately focussed on the scoreboard, an ABC guide to the goings on elsewhere. There was a huge sigh when the Burnley score went up because it showed them winning 1-0. But Grimsby and Newcastle had failed to score and so there was still some hope.

The home players responded by making it 3-1 after 65 minutes. White was the scorer after Ted Critchley, George Martin and Johnson had all tried their luck in a packed area. Sunderland now lost Lawley through injury and it helped Everton's cause.

White did well shrugging off the powerful Shaw before firing home a great goal for his hat-trick. The giant crowd were now waiting on news from elsewhere. Would Everton be relegated after three successive victories? There was a strange hush around the famous ground and then total despair when it was revealed the Blues would be going down.

The *Football Echo* summed up the agony in a page one leader. It said: *Everton relegated! There is a sad ring about the words. Everton stood for the real football. Throughout forty-two years of League football, they have carried millions of people to heights of admiration uncommon for all but a few fortunate clubs. Of those millions, a tolerable minority will accept that even a classic club like Everton must go the way of the world and be relegated to Division Two. Their regret is ours. A noteworthy record has been broken.*

Since 1906-07 it has been the boast of three clubs – Everton, Aston Villa and Blackburn Rovers – that they alone of the original twelve clubs in the League had not been relegated to Division Two. It was Everton's particular boast that, of those three, they alone had not been helped out of relegation by voting in or extension of the League. Derby County were the previous club of the original 12 to break their connection

in Division One in 1907. Everton have withstood the strain for an additional 19 seasons, but now leave Villa and Rovers to share the record that was theirs. Sunderland's unbroken run dates only from 1891.

Everton had flirted dangerously with the big drop in 1922 and 1927 when they finished third from bottom. Now the unthinkable had finally happened. The *Echo* then listed the order in which the ten 'originals', were relegated: Stoke 1890, Accrington and Notts County 1893, Burnley 1897, Bolton 1899, Preston and West Brom 1901, Wolves 1906, Derby 1907 and now Everton 1930.

The report concluded: *Those League derby days at Goodison Park and at Anfield leave fond memories. It depends upon Everton how soon they are resumed.*
Everton: Coggins; Cresswell, O'Donnell, McPherson, Griffiths, Thomson, Critchley, Martin, White, Johnson, Rigby. *Attendance: 51,132*

A Whole New Second Division Experience

3 September 1930
Everton 2 Preston North End 1

EVERTON, founder members of the Football League, were not relishing their very first home game in the Second Division on 3 September 1930. But at least they were in good company. Their Goodison Park opponents were Preston North End, who had won the very first Football League Championship back in 1888.

The difference was that North End had been down since 1925, having also experienced the drop in 1901, 1912 and 1914. For the Blues it was a whole new experience and they were intent on getting back to the top flight at the earliest opportunity.

They had won on the opening day of the season at Plymouth Argyle and now the opportunity was there to take another step up the ladder on home soil. But while they secured a 2-1 success over the men from Deepdale, there were those in the crowd who were suggesting that, on this

performance at least, the Blues would not go far in Division Two.

There was even criticism of Dixie Dean who failed to score for the second week running, but *Liverpool Echo* correspondent Ernest Edwards took a very different tack. The forward line was ill-balanced, but he acquitted Dean of any blame, claiming it was the service and the support-play that was at fault.

Edwards wrote: *He went for every ball that was within hailing distance and his work with his head made him quite a force. Others may disagree with this view, but it is a considered opinion about a player who only had the ball passed to him on the turf but twice during the game. His heading is so deadly that I suppose I should not be critical of the perpetual height at which he had to take a 'pass', but I do say that his method is to present goals to those who should be at his side when they see him rise to the ball with his face towards his own goal. He can do no more than enlarge the position and create openings by his leap and header.*

In other words, Dean needed more

Stepping out at the start of the 1930-31 season, Everton's first-ever in Division Two, are George Martin, Tommy White, Dixie Dean, Billy Coggins and Tom Griffiths. The purposeful stride in a street near Goodison told its own story. Within eight months, the Blues would be back at the top.

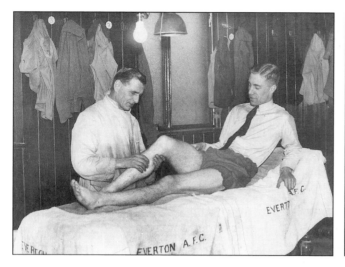

Left: Everton were determined to make their stay in the Second Division a short one. They opened up with five straight wins, getting off the mark at Goodison with a 2-1 win over Preston. A young Cliff Britton would soon make his bow an go on to become one of the most cultured wing-halves Everton have ever had. He is pictured receiving treatment from Harry Cooke.

Right: Trainer Harry Cooke packs Everton's kit before another away game.

support alongside him and a greater sense of anticipation from his attacking teammates. This was a day when the Blues relied on the class of defender Warney Cresswell and the control and speed of Ted Critchley on the right wing.

Centre-half Tommy Griffiths was also influential, although this would be his last season in an Everton shirt. He would be injured halfway through the promotion campaign, lose his place to Charlie Gee and then be transferred to Bolton Wanderers. The Blues seemed to give Preston too much respect in the main. Tommy White failed to cash-in on a series of gift offerings from Dean's head. The message from the fans was a simple one. Everton were being too easily brushed aside and hustled off the ball. The Second

Division, it was said, would teach them a great lesson in this respect.

But while they were outpaced and outmanoeuvred, the home side still snatched the points. Griffiths opened the scoring from a lobbed centre by Cresswell. Harrison equalised with a scorching shot and White edged the Blues back in front.

The critics soon faded into the background as the Goodison outfit got their act together, opening with five straight wins. An intriguing campaign was gaining momentum with every passing week.

Everton: Coggins; Williams, Cresswell, McPherson, Griffiths, Thomson, Critchley, White, Dean, Martin, Rigby.
Attendance: 29,908

Seven Goals Before Half-Time

Saturday, 28 February 1931
Everton 9 Southport 1

EVERTON'S total frustration at being relegated to the Second Division for the first time in their history proved to be a powerful motivating force in season 1930-31. The Blues produced a string of outstanding performances to link a memorable promotion campaign with a powerful FA Cup run.

Local rivals Southport, members of the Third Division North, provided the opposite in the quarter-finals and it turned out to be a record-breaking afternoon at Goodison with seven goals scored by the home side before half-time! The Seasiders were out-powered and out-classed on a mud-bath of a pitch. But it was snow that was the biggest worry to the fans on the morning of the game.

There was a severe fall, the likes of which had not been experienced all winter. Most people presumed the game would have to be postponed and yet, as if by a freak of nature, only the corners of the pitch were snow-capped with the middle area completely clear. Rumours were rife in the city that the tie might have to be abandoned because the snowflakes were so large, they might 'blind' the players and the referee. Yet by 2pm, a large crowd had already gathered inside the ground, each and every one of them banking on a thrilling cup clash.

Plymouth, beaten earlier in the competition by the Blues, were generous enough to send a telegram to Goodison, wishing the home side well. Someone recalled that on the morning of the match in Plymouth, Everton had been greeted by a military band playing the 'Funeral March'. But their Cup dreams were still very much alive, even though Southport were promising them a rough ride with a lucrative semi-final place up for grabs.

The Evertonians shrugged aside all of this bold talk from their opponents. It was the Mayor of Southport's birthday and they were intent on making it an unhappy

Everton scored a magnificent seven goals before halftime when beating local rivals Southport 9-1 in 1931 on a mudbath of a Goodison pitch. Dean scored four, including this spectacular header.

one, but the visitors arrived in considerable numbers, clearly identifiable Southport schoolboys with their maroon and black-striped caps and two young mascots, each wearing top hats. Everton wanted to win it for the skilful Ted Critchley, whose wife presented him with a daughter on the morning of the game.

Among those present was Mr John McKenna, the League president and Anfield stalwart who, in spite of the cold, climbed the giddy heights of the main grandstand to sit alongside Everton chairman Will Cuff. The pitch was in a dreadful state. The *Football Echo* declared: *The Everton mud was in prime condition. At about 3.15 pm it was high tide!*

Southport, anticipating being up to their ankles in it, had trained secretly on a ploughed field. The wags in the crowd suggested they could have borrowed Goodison. Four times, Everton captain Williams tossed the coin before the kick-off, only to see it stuck upright in the mud.

The visitors won the toss at the fifth attempt and attacked the Stanley Park End. Southport advanced immediately down the left, but the ball appeared to turn into an oversized snowball as it rolled along the surface. The Blues claimed it and launched it forward, the opposing 'keeper completely misjudging the flight of the ball. Dean darted in behind him and ignored the presence of a full-back on the line, blasting home to make it 1-0.

The lead was increased after 12 minutes. It was Dunn who powered home after Dean had seen a shot kicked away. The Blues were in full flight and Dunn made it 3-0, once again inspired by Dean. Rather foolishly, the visitors now tried to use the offside trap against one of the

liveliest forward lines in the business. Dean cashed in on a gift, set up by Johnson, and he completed his treble at the 35th-minute mark with a crack shot into the bottom right-hand corner. It was 5-0 and there was no sign of a let-up.

Critchley then gave his new baby a present by moving into the centre-forward position to claim goal number six after 37 minutes. Smiling broadly, the same player now celebrated in style with a pacy run that took him clear for what can only be described as 'The Magnificent Seven'.

The half-time whistle provided Southport with some much-needed respite and they staggered back to the

Factfile: Everton lost 1-0 to West Brom at Old Trafford to miss out on Wembley. But as the next report reveals, promotion was now to be achieved at the first time of asking.

dressing-room feeling distinctly shell-shocked. They actually managed to pull one back after the break, but the rampant Dean and his partner Johnson increased the lead to 9-1.

The visitors consoled themselves with a financial bonanza. Everton's ambitions stretched much further than the nearest bank. Wembley was now just one game away and it was a tantalising thought, even though promotion was priority number one. But for the time being, the mud-kings were happy with their emphatic quarter-final triumph.

Everton: Coggins; Williams, Cresswell, McClure, Gee, Thomson, Critchley, Dunn, Dean, Johnson, Stein.
Attendance: 45,647

An unusual angle of Everton's ninth and final goal against Southport in 1931. The scorer is tricky inside-forward Tommy Johnson. Note the snow and mud which put the game in some considerable doubt. The fans are also standing under the Stanley Park Stand, an area which was later blocked off.

Promoted At The First Attempt

Saturday, 18 April 1931
Everton 3 Burnley 2

REVENGE and celebration were in the air as Everton prepared for their final home game of the 1930-31 season with League president John McKenna in the main stand, ready and willing to present the Second Division Championship shield.

Burnley had crushed the Blues 5-2 at Turf Moor in mid-December, Everton's heaviest defeat of the season. Now there was a wonderful opportunity to put that right while revelling in a title success. The crowd was not that big as the kick-off approached. It was estimated that around 18,000 were in the ground, but the inevitable late-comers would swell that number. There was a biting wind and a threat of rain, but a goal inside three minutes warmed the home fans. Johnson, a tricky inside-left who was the perfect foil for the powerful Dean, lashed home a powerful free-kick to make it 1-0.

The applause had hardly died away when Critchley conjured up one of the best goals seen on the ground for some time to increase the lead. Stein laid the foundations with a great centre when the ball had seemed certain to run out for a goal-kick. Dean tried to make contact with his head, but the ball sailed over him and Critchley reacted superbly, hooking home on the volley.

It would soon be three goals in nine minutes, but this time the opposition were celebrating. Shots cannoned away in a packed box until Beel found a way past Coggins from close range. Everton's two-goal advantage was restored when the unfortunate Wood conceded an own goal when trying to prevent Critchley's centre reaching Dean who was lying in wait.

Referee Kingscott had been selected to officiate at the FA Cup Final, but he struck a note of discord with the Evertonians.

Dean showed his annoyance at a particularly bad offside decision and the crowd reacted by booing the referee from all corners of the ground. The din continued for some time, but Dean helped to concentrate their thoughts with a superb pass to centre-half Gee, who had moved forward and only had the 'keeper to beat. Unfortunately, he shot like a defender, over the bar! It left the interval score at 3-1.

Mid-table Burnley had been outclassed, but Everton had not made the most of their chances. Priest reduced the arrears with a long-range shot that squeezed inside the post with Coggins at full stretch. But Everton retained a firm grip on the proceedings to finish winners on their special day.

Mr McKenna, presenting the shield to the Blues, said there was no reason why they should not go on and emulate Liverpool's feat of winning the Second and First Division titles in successive season. They were very prophetic words indeed.

Everton: Coggins; Williams, Cresswell, McClure, Gee, Thomson, Critchley, Martin, Dean, Johnson, Stein.
Attendance: 19,144

Twelve Goals At Goodison In One Day

Saturday, 17 October 1931
Everton 9 Sheffield Wednesday 3

EVEN in the goal-mad 1930s, 12 goals in a single game was an attacking feast to be applauded by all and sundry. The irony of this sensational Goodison Park affair was that many fans were unable to fully appreciate the goal blitz because of the swirling fog that had threatened the match right up to kick-off time. There were many people outside the ground 15 minutes before the start, reluctant to venture through the gates for fear of a postponement.

It was not quite as bad as all that, but there was certainly enough fog about to make things difficult for the spectators. Visibility for the players was not too bad, but those fans at the back of the various stands were constantly straining when the ball was at its maximum distance away.

International calls robbed Wednesday of two key players, but their reserve strength was such that they still promised to be worthy opponents. But Everton were in rampant mood, having scored 15 goals in their five previous games. In the final reckoning, the Blues would be unstoppable with Dixie Dean in particular an irresistible force.

As Wednesday goalkeeper Brown picked the ball out of the back of the net for the ninth time, no doubt his mind went back to his non-League days when he had a similar experience against Spurs in the Cup while playing for Worksop Town.

Everton went ahead after 22 minutes when a neat back-header from Dean played Stein in. He thumped the ball wide of the 'keeper and the goal spree was on in earnest. The *Football Echo* correspondent reflected on Dean's scoring prowess up to that stage of the season, suggesting that it had 'not been prolific'. The big centre-forward had managed 'only' two hat-tricks in the ten opening games! Dixie, always striving for that little bit extra in front of goal, would now respond with a magnificent five-goal haul.

He took a ball from defence, played a quick one-two with White and then hammered his shot home before Brown could move.

Wednesday pulled one back when Rimmer met a Burgess cross, heading wide of Sagar to make it 2-1. The half-time whistle came with the crowd unaware that the second period would be one long catalogue of outstanding goals.

Shell-shocked Wednesday would concede three in the space of ten minutes. White headed in after 46 minutes from a Critchley centre. Almost immediately, Stein took a bad knock as he moved past Beeson, but it did not prevent him from playing a sharp pass to Dean, who wheeled round and rifled a shot wide of the startled Brown to make it 4-1. The Sheffield outfit, weakened in defence, had no answer to the threat from Dean and a perfect header from Critchley's outstanding centre made it five with Dixie celebrating his third treble of the season.

Everton were dancing through the fog and Brown didn't know what hit him when he got in the way of a fierce shot from Dean. The superb Critchley now waltzed past two defenders before claiming goal number six on the hour. Wednesday refused to give up the ghost

and they pulled two back through Hooper and Ball to make it 6-3.

Dean responded at the double with goals in the 73rd and 75th minutes to complete his nap hand and Johnson, the man with the roving commission, finished off the visitors two minutes from time.

It was pointed out that Dean had scored five without getting a hat-trick which in those days was three on the run. We accept a hat-trick as a treble of any sort in the modern game, but they were more discerning in the past!

Dean would finish this Championship season with 45 goals in 38 League games, 15 short of his League record, but still a magnificent tally and one that emphasised his standing as the most dangerous striker in the land.

Everton: Sagar; Williams, Cresswell, Clark, Gee, Thomson, Critchley, White, Dean, Johnson, Stein.

Attendance: 38,186

Hail To Sunshine Dixie!

Saturday, 28 November 1931
Everton 9 Leicester City 2

EVERTON players were scoring hat-tricks as if they were going out of fashion as the 1931-32 season progressed towards what would be a Championship finale. Dunn had opened the campaign with a treble against Birmingham. White had followed up with three against Portsmouth.

Dean's personal satisfaction reached new heights when he rocked the old enemy at Anfield with an unforgettable hat-trick. The great man went on to plunder three at Sheffield United, five against Sheffield Wednesday, five against Chelsea and four in a 9-2 win over Leicester, the game featured here.

The weather had been unkind to the Blues, but the sun shone for the first time in weeks for the visit of the men from Filbert Street. The game opened with Everton employing their famous criss-cross passing movements, Johnson spraying the ball first to Critchley and then to Stein. Four men had a hand in Dean's opener after six minutes, the ball inevitably finding the net off the number nine's head.

Four minutes later the crowd roared once again when White increased the lead. Dean unselfishly played his teammate in and while the shot lacked power, it was still good enough to beat goalkeeper McLaren. It was not all one way and Sagar made saves from four different Leicester players before Everton went three up after 17 minutes.

It was again the result of the brilliant heading of Dean. When Critchley centred,

Dixie Dean was the undisputed king of Goodison in 1931, scoring four in a crushing 9-2 win over Leicester City. His big dream, however, was to hoist aloft the FA Cup which he did in 1933. This historic picture shows Dean with the trophy on his shoulder, flanked by his delighted teammates. Albert Geldard holds the match-ball.

most people expected the centre-forward to go for goal, but Dixie's eye for a better opening saw him calmly nodding the ball back to Johnson who struck the ball so hard, McLaren didn't even see it, let alone save it.

Dean now decided to increase his own tally although he was aided by the 'keeper. He met Stein's centre with a firm header and while McLaren got to the ball, he succeeded only in patting it back into the forward's path and this time Dean steered the ball into the corner of the net.

So the Blues were four goals to the good and looking as if they had twice as many players on the field as their opponents. Leicester finally responded on the break, Hind driving home to pull a goal back shortly before half-time. But Everton would add three more goals in the space of 11 minutes at the start of the second half with the kind of attacking football that had the fans purring.

Johnson sent a header beyond McLaren after 46 minutes following an accurate Stein corner. White made it 6-1 without knowing too much about it. Gee thumped the ball forward and the 'keeper moved wide of his goal expecting to collect. But the driven forward ball glanced off White and sped into the far corner. Dean secured his hat-trick with a soaring header from a Critchley corner, but Everton were not satisfied with seven.

They even scored an own-goal, Sagar turning a corner-kick under his own bar after 62 minutes. But the rout continued when Dean claimed his fourth and Everton's eighth following a skilful run and centre by Stein. The Blues were simply unstoppable and Clark scored his first top-flight goal with a brilliant long-range effort to make it nine. It was attacking football of the highest quality. Everton were not so much a team as a goal machine.

Everton: Sagar; Williams, Cresswell, Clark, Gee, Thomson, Critchley, White, Dean, Johnson, Stein.

Attendance: 33,513

Tommy White was a first-class partner for the powerful Dixie Dean. Here, White plunders a goal in a 4-2 League victory over Sunderland in January 1932.

The Old One-Two Champs At The Double

Saturday, 30 April 1932
Everton 1 Bolton Wanderers 0

THE lowest point in Everton's long and distinguished history was undoubtedly season 1929-30 when the Blues finished rock-bottom in the First Division and found themselves relegated for the first time ever, a humbling experience for one of the League's founder members.

Wounded pride proved to be an inspirational weapon and not only did the Blues bounce back at the first time of asking with a convincing Second Division Championship success in 1930-31, they followed it up with a storming top-flight title triumph just 12 months later.

There were rousing scenes at Goodison Park as Everton claimed the game's greatest honour for the fourth time in their history with a 1-0 victory over Bolton Wanderers.

Ernest Edwards – writing in the *Football Echo* under his famous pseudonym 'Bee' – struck a little blow for all Blues' fans in his colourful report when he said: *Everton have often been chided that there was one record they could never claim compared with Liverpool, their neighbours. They had never won the Second Division Championship and the First Division Championship in successive years. Evertonians replied: 'We could, but we have never been in the Second Division'!*

Last season Everton duly felt the bump of relegation. They won that League and have now gone on to win Division One with team work, all-round ability and the study of wise play.

'Bee' also quoted captain Dixie Dean, scorer of the only goal against Bolton, in the somewhat flowery manner that was the style of the day. William Ralph was reported to have said: "The lads are splendid. This is a triumph for players who at one time found everything going against them. Today we have touched the peak and Arsenal have again been put to second place. I want to thank all our players for their brilliant work."

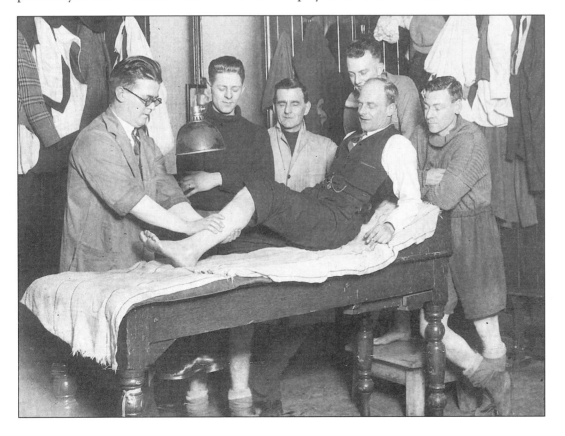

Dean never claimed to be a one-man band. Warney Cresswell, one of the classiest full-backs Everton have ever had, is pictured receiving treatment for a key game in 1932. The attire and the receding hairline gives Warney the look of a businessman rather than a top-class footballer, but he was at the peak of his playing powers and eventually completed 306 appearances for the Blues. Looking on are Sagar, White and Rigby with trainer Harry Cooke (centre).

Everton, League Champions 1931-32. Back row (left to right): Harry Cooke (trainer), Clark, Williams, Sagar, Gee, Cresswell, Britton. Front: Critchley, White, Dean, Johnson, Stein, Thomson.

The kind of 'brilliant work' Dean referred to was there for all to see in the Championship clincher against Bolton. The game had an extra edge because the Wanderers side featured centre-half Tom Griffiths, a rangy defender who had played for Everton for four years between 1926 and 1930. Indeed, he had made 26 appearances during that fateful relegation season. Now he was back, ironically trying to prevent his old club from clinching the League Championship.

As skipper of Wanderers, he exchanged a few amusing words with his former captain Dean and as they tossed up the heavens opened and there was a loud clap of thunder. Was someone up there trying to tell Tom something. Dean opted to attack the Gwladys Street End in the first half, taking advantage of a strong northerly wind. The Blues suffered an early blow when Gee had to go off for treatment on a knee injury. He hobbled back into play, bandaged and unlikely to do himself any justice in a strongly contested affair.

Everton had an anxious moment when Sagar raced out without much chance of intercepting the ball. Butler was able to get in a shot with the goalkeeper out of position, but fortunately the ball flew high and wide. Gee went off again, but reappeared with a new bandage and a real determination to play a part. In the meantime, Everton recovered their composure to build up some excellent attacking moves, one ending with the lively Dunn trying to head the ball out of the hands of 'keeper Jones.

But Dean was being well-marshalled by Griffiths and the Blues' play deteriorated as quickly as it had improved. The game had gone dead and so had the crowd until a voice boomed out from the paddock: 'Play Up Everton!'

Johnson responded with a clever overhead kick that rebounded back off the bar. Gee had battled on bravely, but he had to leave the field shortly before half-time, reducing the Champions-elect to ten men.

Thomson went to centre-half and Johnson to left-half. As often happens in adversity, the weakened team now raised their game to cover for their loss. Dean claimed possession and seemed in no hurry to move the ball on, but it had the

Bolton defenders scurrying round to try and cover. The centre-forward finally brought Critchley into play and he cleverly hooked the ball over his head before going for a strong shot which produced a corner.

The kick was punched back out towards the touchline by Jones, but the irrepressible Dunn hoisted it straight back in. Dean, seeing his moment, stretched his neck muscles and sent a solid header towards the furthest post. The tall Jones was unable to keep it out, but then he would not be the first or last to be beaten by Dean's aerial power. It gave Everton an all-important interval lead and the ten men would defend it with tremendous character after the break.

The brave Gee attempted one more return, at inside-left, but the first time he touched the ball he grimaced with pain and he headed back to the touchline.

A rainstorm now came over the ground as well as a storm of Bolton attacks. Sagar was at his best in this spell and Everton did not stand on ceremony in the closing stages, hammering the ball out at the first sign of danger. By now skipper Dean was drifting deeper and deeper to help out his defence. He desperately wanted to get his hands on that Champ-

ionship and the referee's whistle finally ensured he would.

The title had been won by clever football, all-round superior team work, leadership and unselfishness, said one report. And Anfield's historic 'double' had been equalled with Everton's very own version of the old one-two.

Everton: Sagar; Williams, Cresswell, Clark, Gee, Thomson, Critchley, Dunn, Dean, Johnson, Stein.
Attendance: 28,546

Left: There was plenty to shout about at Goodison in the 1930s and they were able to do it from the roof tops, courtesy of this searchlight. type loudspeaker which was installed above the Main Stand. The church is visible beyond the roof. This piece of '30s high-tech gadgetry was said to be able to carry sound a distance of two miles and was used for musical broadcasts and general announcements.

Bottom left: Trainer Harry Cooke shows off the FA Cup, after they beat Manchester City 3-0 at Wembley in 1933.

Right: Everton's Tommy White in action at Goodison in October 1933, when they lost 3-0 to Champions Arsenal in the FA Charity Shield game. Gunners' players are Lancashire-born goalkeeper Frank Moss and Norman Sidey.

Everton were entertained by the Lord Mayor of Liverpool at a special Town Hall function in May 1934, prior to the team's departure for a trip to Tenerife. Pictured are (left to right): Alderman Strong, W.C.Cuff, W.Cook, W.R.Dean, N.Higham, A.Geldard, J.Coulter, J.Stein, Mr Evans (director), B.Williams, A.Stevenson.

Goodison's Greatest Ever Cup Tie?

Wednesday, 30 January 1935
Everton 6 Sunderland 4

ASK Evertonians to name the greatest ever FA Cup tie seen on Goodison Park and modern enthusiasts will inevitably go for the sensational 4-4 draw in 1991, a clash of titanic proportions between Everton and Liverpool.

But senior fans will immediately recall a replay battle that unfolded in 1935 and which took the breath away of the 59,213 supporters who were fortunate enough to be present on a memorable Wednesday afternoon. One fan suggested that everybody should have been charged on the way out, as well as the way in, so entertaining was this fifth-round affair.

The crowd revelled in ten goals, six of them hitting the back of the Sunderland net. The Blues were never in arrears, twice Sunderland drew level and every goal was scored with a shot. It left the *Echo's* Ernest Edwards posing this question: *Has there ever been a greater game of skill in the mud*

in any League or Cup match? We all keep our memory cells filled with noteworthy sporting occasions, but this latest 6-4 game will top the lot by reason of its two goals in the two closing minutes, by the ordering off of a manger of the visiting side, and by the multitudinous moments of dramatic skill and art.

The referee, Mr Pinckston of Aston Villa, was saluted for the way he made the players get on with the game. Sunderland swept up the field with adroit passes and combination, only to be mediocre near the goalmouth – they scored only four!

Everton won because they had that extra bit of finishing power. Jackie Coulter's three, Albert Geldard's two and Alex Stevenson's solo effort stood out boldly. Jimmy Cunliffe, that outstanding inside-forward, played for much of the later stages in a state of semi-consciousness, having been badly concussed.

The ground was so packed that the crowd broke on to the line in the early

stages without serious consequences. But many people had to be lifted out by the police and the ambulancemen, particularly in the Goodison Road enclosure. The fans were finally able to concentrate on the action and Coulter cheered everybody with an opener after 14 minutes. It was not a great strike, but rather a tribute to Stevenson's early work. The fact that the Blues were in front was reason enough to celebrate.

Coulter made it 2-0 after 31 minutes, the Irishman moving in to crash a Geldard centre into the net. But Sunderland were far from beaten and David reduced the arrears four minutes before the interval. There were still many people outside the ground and there was a report that a considerable number had tried to rush the gates.

When the second half got underway, Roker star goalkeeper Thorpe was warned by the referee for swinging on the bar like a trapeze artiste.

Factfile: Everton, having won this Cup classic, now beat Derby County 3-1 at Goodison with Coulter the goal hero again. He scored two and Dean grabbed the other. But in the sixth round, also at home, Bolton Wanderers shocked the Mersey-siders 2-1, even though Coulter was on the mark again.

The diminutive Stevenson now thrilled the crowd. The smallest man on the field tried to charge Thorpe over the goal-line, much to the amusement of the fans. Stevenson appeared to have settled it 15 minutes from time with a close-range effort after Dean had headed in.

But Connor had the home fans edgy with a fine effort to make it 3-2 and Gurney equalised with possibly the last kick of the 90 minutes. He was probably

An action-shot from the game many senior Evertonians claim was the greatest Goodison match of all time, the 1935 FA Cup replay with Sunderland. Gee gets in a solid tackle on Bob Gurney in an eventful 6-4 triumph.

99

the only man in the ground not to see his overhead kick go in. It was now 3-3 and extra-time was called into play.

Before the match resumed, Sunderland manager Johnny Cockrane was ordered off the field as he tried to coach his players. Coulter claimed his treble two minutes into the extra spell, but the yo-yo nature of the game continued when Connor made it 4-4.

With a second replay now looking a certainty, Geldard took matters into his own hands and he put the Blues in front with an outstretched boot from a Dean header. In the closing stages, he finished off the visitors when he hoisted the ball high into the area and it sailed in over the heads of Dean and defender Thorpe.

Everton: Sagar; Cook, Jones, Britton, Gee, Thomson, Geldard, Cunliffe, Dean, Stevenson and Coulter.

Attendance: 59,213

The Master And The Pupil

Wednesday, 3 March 1937
Everton 7 Leeds United 1

THIS was a significant day for Evertonians. It was the game in which they saw the master and the pupil in action together for the very first time on home soil. The Blues had paid Burnley £6,500 for the services of teenage sensation Tommy Lawton, a Bolton lad who had scored a remarkable 570 goals in three seasons of schoolboy football.

Lawton had netted on his Everton debut at Wolves, but had very little to celebrate. The Merseysiders lost 7-2, lacking the experience and attacking know-how of Dixie Dean. The great man returned to partner Lawton in the subsequent away game at Birmingham, but once again Everton tasted defeat, going down 2-0.

Now they entertained Leeds United at Goodison Park, a game that captured the interest of fans on both sides of Stanley Park. Obviously the chance to see Dean and Lawton in tandem was of particular interest to the Goodison faithful. At the same time, here was a match that could help ease Liverpool's relegation worries. For once, Reds' fans desperately wanted the old enemy to win.

But there was a strange twist. Making his debut up front for Leeds was former Anfield favourite, South African-born Gordon Hodgson. It meant the day had genuine possibilities.

The previous weekend, Merseyside had suffered blizzard conditions. The Goodison pitch was heavy to say the least. At the toss-up, Dean flipped the coin on to the back of his hand, rather than let it drop to the floor in customary fashion because the pitch was so muddy. But it was a bright afternoon and the stands were

On 3 March 1937, Dean and Lawton played at home together for the first time. The match was a seven-goal sensation. Here three of Goodison most loved centre-forwards meet at a dinner in the 1960s. From left to right: Lawton, Alex Young and Dean.

packed with a large gathering of scouts and managers from rival clubs. Everton attacked the Stanley Park End in the first half. Hodgson was determined to impress on a Merseyside stage and he went close with one of his famous headers from a dangerous corner.

Dean showed his strength by charging Holley to the ground and he powered on through the mud to go extremely close. Lawton now came to prominence with a pacy run and a first-class shot which McInroy took with both hands. The conditions did not seem to suit the visiting defenders. The mud was six inches deep around their goal, but the home forwards seemed to revel in it, showing excellent control.

Geldard's body swerve was the starting point for many Everton attacks. Dean was inevitably the man on the end of these moves and he rifled home a shot from a central position 25 yards out that flew into the corner of the net to make it 1-0.

Lawton was not to be outdone by his famous partner. He seized control from a corner, hesitated momentarily while he selected his spot and unleashed a solid effort into the bottom left-hand corner. It was looking good for Everton – and Liverpool!

The fans were fascinated by the new attacking partnership, although it was noted that no one outshone Dean for endeavour in the heavy conditions. His heading was also of the highest class, but then this aspect of his game rarely dropped below outstanding.

Lawton had been making a name for himself with his speed of thought. He would collect the ball and deliver a shot so quickly that opponents were constantly caught out.

But this was a day for shared honours. All five Everton forwards managed to get on the scoresheet, Dean adding to his tally in the second half, aided and abetted by Stevenson (two), Geldard and Gillick.

Leeds scored a single consolation goal, swamped in the Goodison mud.

Lawton had made himself an instant favourite. He would go on to claim Dean's famous number nine jersey and score 70 goals in 95 games for the Blues before the war interrupted his Goodison career. He was transferred to Chelsea for £11,500, Everton making a 100 per cent profit on what they had paid for him. Notts County later paid a record £20,000 for the centre-forward's services and after spells with Brentford and Arsenal, his career record was 231 goals in 390 League games.

The Goodison crowd never forgot Tommy. Everton staged a testimonial game for him in 1972, a full 27 years after his last wartime appearance for the Blues. Fittingly, a Great Britain XI provided the opposition and the occasion raised £6,500. As he walked on to the pitch to take a special bow, his mind no doubt drifted back to that Goodison debut game of 1937 and the seven goals that flew into the Leeds United net. Happy days indeed.

Everton: Sagar; Jackson, Cook, Britton, Gee, Mercer, Geldard, Lawton, Dean, Stevenson, Gillick.

Attendance: 17,064

Dixie's Heading Out!

Saturday, 11 December 1937
Everton 1 Birmingham 1

THE incomparable William Ralph 'Dixie' Dean scored an astonishing 377 goals for Everton in 431 appearances. He was a legend in his own lifetime -a man whose 60 League goals in the 1927-28 season will never be beaten.

His greatest moments in the game have been well documented - his scoring feats for England, his record-breaking triumph against Arsenal and his inspirational role in the 1933 FA Cup Final against Manchester City.

But what was it like at Goodison Park the day the greatest centre-forward the world has ever seen played his last game for the Blues? What we tend to forget is that it was just another game for the fans. They didn't know the great man was wearing his famous number nine jersey for the last time.

If they had, there is every good chance it would have been a gala occasion with the famous stadium bursting at the seams, just as it was on 7 May 1928 when Dean brought the house down with the hat-trick against Arsenal that would make him immortal.

Hundreds of games and hundreds of goals on, he was selected for only his fifth League outing of the season on a bitterly cold December day in 1937 with Tommy Lawton out injured. Incredibly, the match was in doubt until 2pm with the surface covered in a skin of ice. The referee inspected the pitch at 12.30pm and, according to the *Football Echo*, found it was hard as flint.

A second check an hour later suggested that the ground was softening and the official declared he would give it another half-hour, at which point the gates were thrown open. The heavily sanded surface still seemed fairly treacherous but the *Echo* would later report: *All 22 men gave an excellent display considering the icy conditions.*

Before the kick-off Dean got a fine reception from the small crowd of just over 17,000. Once a hero, always a hero. He responded in the first minute with a neat header to Cunliffe, who should have done better from an excellent position.

Then Birmingham – they did not add 'City' to their title until 1945 – moved forward almost immediately to claim a shock lead. Richards made a pass along the touchline which Morris collected and he wasted no time in hammering in a shot. Goalkeeper Morton pulled the ball from under his crossbar but he fumbled it. He tried to recover, but the ball had crossed the line and Everton were down.

Football remained a tricky business on the rock-hard pitch and it was possible to hear the ice cracking under the players' feet. Dean, Stevenson and Cunliffe conjured up an outstanding passing move that was described as favouring a cricket pitch rather than an ice-bound football ground.

Dixie was playing in a slightly withdrawn role behind his fellow forwards. Every time the Everton 'keeper launched the ball forward, he was winning it with his head and directing headers to Stevenson and Cunliffe. Dean might have been in the twilight of his career but he was still the undisputed king of the air.

The pitch now caught out 'keeper Morton, enjoying a run in the continued absence of another Goodison legend, Ted Sagar. Morton tried to race across his own goalmouth as Beattie threatened, but he fell headlong and the crowd gasped as the shot flew narrowly wide.

As usual, though, the fans looked to Dean to find a way through. He produced a fiery drive which brought a roar from the crowd as it flew wide and it proved an inspirational moment because Everton levelled matters with their next attack. Geldard was the scorer with a long-range effort that was reported to have left his foot *like a stone from a catapult*.

It was his first League goal for nine

Dixie Dean welcomes new winger Torry Gillick to Goodison in December 1935. An £8,000 buy from Glasgow Rangers, Gillick would be a provider for Dean and score many goals himself. He figured in Dean's final match at Goodison, against Birmingham in 1937.

months and Dean's broad smile as he patted his teammate on the back summed up the mood.

The final whistle now loomed. As Dean trudged off he would not have realised that he had pulled on a royal blue shirt at Goodison for the last time. It was the end of a goalscoring era, the like of which we will never see again.

Everton: Morton; Cook, J.Jones, Britton, T.G.Jones, Mercer, Geldard, Cunliffe, Dean, Stevenson, Gillick.

Attendance: 17,108

Factfile: Dean subsequently played in a friendly at Halifax on 12 February 1938. His last game was the Liverpool Senior Cup semi-final at South Liverpool on 9 March 1938. He scored the last of Everton's four winning goals and two days later joined Notts County.

Dixie Has His 60 Goals Gordon His 60 Years!

DIXIE Dean scored his 60 goals to become a legendary figure. One of his contemporaries can now claim a very special '60' all of his own, but in Gordon Watson's case, it was 60 years plus of service to the club he joined from Blyth Spartans in January 1933.

If you wanted to know about the old days, Goodison Park as it was in that famous pre-war era when Dean, Lawton, Mercer, Sagar and the rest were the men of the people, you talked to Gordon. He could be found conducting one of the many 'tours' around Goodison or even working on the door of one of the executive lounges until he retired in 1997. He was a truly wonderful servant to the Blues, first as a player who mixed tight control with fierce tackling, and later as trainer, promotions man and finally official guide. The North-East accent was always in evidence, but here was a man steeped in Merseyside tradition.

He paints a wonderful picture of the players of the 1930s, the men who wore tough leather boots up to their ankles with solid toe-caps, kicked a 'casey' that seemed to weigh a ton when wet, lived alongside the fans and mixed freely with them, both before and after matches, and earned next to nothing for their labours on the field, even though they were often playing to crowds that dwarf the modern average attendance.

Gordon said: "Most of the players lived near to the ground, many of them in Goodison Avenue behind the Stanley Park End. It meant that the likes of Dean, Dunn, Stein and even old trainer Harry Cooke would walk to the game with the fans.

"I lived in Harewood Street, just off Breck Road and then in Ince Avenue. Me and Torry Gillick used to walk through Anfield Cemetery to get to Goodison on match days. There would be hundreds of fans walking with us. If you got beat, you stayed in the dressing-room for two hours after the match, frightened to go out and face the walk home.

Harry Cooke, Everton's dedicated trainer and the original magic sponge man. Dean once said: "Without him, I would never have broken that record."

"If Liverpool beat us, we would go home and then refuse to go out for three days!

"Goodison Park was very different to the stadium we see today. For instance, there was no stand at the Gwladys Street End when I first arrived in 1933. It was all concrete steps with an old scoreboard at the back to display the half-time scores. If the weather was bad, it was possible to do sprints under the steps behind the Gwladys Street End.

"There was a little gymnasium where the main car-park is now. We would get old balls, take the bladder out and stuff them with paper like medicine balls. We used to practise throwing them against the wall on the Bullens Road side. Dixie used to see how far and how high he could throw them. We would play wall tennis and we also did a lot of roadwork.

"When we first reported back to training, the first four days involved long road runs from Goodison. We would run down as far as the Jolly Miller pub on Queen's Drive, turn down towards West Derby Village, reach the Crown Pub at the top of Walton Hall Avenue via Long Lane

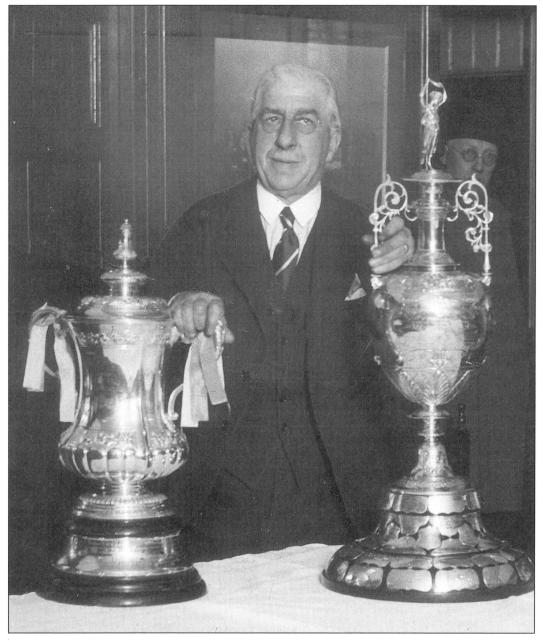

and then make our way back down to the ground.

"The old club car-park was originally grassed. The 'A' and 'B' teams used to play there. It was also a centre for the training. In those days, there was no collective work as such. You would just come in, get stripped and go out on the field. The trainer would tell you what to do and you just got on with it. No one would shirk the work, even though we never trained as a group and never really got the ball out."

Gordon revealed that the only time the players saw a ball during the week was on Tuesday mornings when there was shooting practice. Those Tuesday sessions involved the full-backs going behind the goals to field and return the balls. They

had big playing staffs in those days and 30 to 40 pros would be out there. If you came in early, you got more shots with three or four goals set up. Now and again, a few crosses would be played in, but mainly it was shooting.

There were never any complicated team discussions concerning moves and tactics. Gordon said: "You simply learned by the experience of the older players. If you played in an away match, you would arrange to 'room' with a partner who could pass on bits of help and information. I would go with Billy Cook or Jock Thompson. These were players who worked little things out themselves for corner-kicks and the like.

"But there was never any organised

coaching. You simply learned by your mistakes. The other players would make sure you didn't make the same mistake twice. There were no tactical meetings before matches. Before the season, they would call us all together and say: 'Look, this is Everton Football Club. Whether you are travelling home or away, we want you properly dressed with a collar and tie.' This was probably the only time we were addressed collectively. But we still had a tremendous side with some wonderful players."

Gordon often found himself 12th man. The sheer size of the squad and the quality of the team meant that competition was intense. The lad from the North-East was an excellent all-rounder and he would play in every outfield position except centre-forward. Gordon would play a part in the 1938-39 Championship success before the war interrupted his career.

In his early days, Dixie Dean was the undisputed star turn and yet there was never any petty jealousy amongst his contemporaries, helped by the fact that players were paid exactly the same, regardless of their pedigree. Dean was very level-headed and never sought any special privileges.

Gordon recalls: "When the club got to the Cup Final in 1933, I had only just come down from the North-East. There was a 50 shilling tailor on Walton Road. They came up to the ground and asked Dixie to advertise one of their suits. There was an ice-cream parlour next door called Fusco's and they wanted to get in on the act, picturing Dixie licking one of their ice creams.

"He refused to do it unless the whole team was involved. There is a famous photograph knocking round of the lads in a line, all wearing long raincoats down to their ankles and trilby hats. Dixie could have taken it on himself and made a few bob, but he wanted the squad to benefit from the Cup success.

"It was a big gesture because the players were only earning £8 a week and even this used to go down to £6 in the close season. When I finished as a player in

1949, I was on £20 a week with £2 for a win bonus. That was the most I ever earned as a player.

"I can remember when we won the Championship in 1939, secretary Theo Kelly took us all out for the day to Blackpool. He gave me and the wife 2s 6d (12 ½p) and said, 'Go out and enjoy yourself.' We thought it was great."

Gordon never used to drink, but it was a favourite pastime for many of the big stars. There was nothing unusual about a player having a drink on a Friday night in those days, regardless of the game the next day. The legendary Dixie was quite a lad.

Gordon recalls a famous story about the greatest striker that has ever lived. He said: "Chelsea had signed a centre-half called Peter O'Dowd. I think they paid £7,000 for him. He wrote in the *Echo* and the *Evening Express* that Dixie wouldn't get a kick in the game at Goodison on the Saturday.

"The night before the game, Dixie went out and got a little bit worse for wear. The trainer kept him at Goodison all night. They slept in the trainer's room by the old dressing-rooms, lying on the skips and the St John's Ambulance rugs. The trainer went home and brought back a flask of hot coffee, no doubt thinking that O'Dowd would be able to live by his word and play Dean off the park. Dixie went out the next day and scored five! Everton won the match 7-2."

The players were always up to different tricks. Little Alex Stevenson, one of the finest ball-players of his era, and his right-wing partner Wally Boyes, were both known as 'Mickey Mouse' because of the pranks they used to get up to.

Gordon said: "You would get back to your room on an away trip and find your bedclothes gone. Even the directors were not immune from the tricksters. Dean was another who was always game for a laugh. I remember an occasion on a bridge above Chesterfield Station. He kept shouting down to a policeman just for fun: 'Aye, Aye Copper!'

"The next minute the constable was up on the platform asking who had been

This is Goodison Park ...Gordon Watson kept these fans enthralled in one of his many guided tours of the famous stadium before retiring in 1997.

doing all the shouting. He took Dixie into this room and we all thought he was going to arrest him because it was all so serious. Suddenly they came out, side by side and smoking cigars. That was typical Dixie."

Dean was a giant figure, on and off the field. When he was playing, he never used to like to have his shirt tucked right down inside his shorts, but at the same time, the players were not allowed to have them hanging out, George Best fashion. Gordon recalls that Dixie used to get the trainer to cut his shirt level with his shorts so when he jumped you could often see his back. Whether it was because he felt freer that way or felt it helped to keep him cool is open to debate. He was just a character and a half.

The players didn't just have to cope with poor pitches and ankle-deep mud in Watson's day, they also had to play with a ball that became very heavy when it was wet.

Gordon said: "I think the regulation weight was 28 ounces, but it soaked up the water and would often split your forehead if you headed the lace. Of course, they used to say that Cliff Britton was so talented, he would centre the ball so the lace faced away from Dixie.

"And when the goals went in, which was often, there were no mass celebrations or players jumping up on to hoardings to punch the air. The scorer would just turn and jog back into position. There would be the odd shout of 'well done' but that was it. Finding the net was all part and parcel of the day to day business."

So was looking after each other. Gordon remembers a game at Brentford. He said: "I was only reserve, but Warney Cresswell took ill. They told me two hours before the match that I was playing and I was a bag of nerves in the dressing-room. As we were going out, Dixie said, 'Get next to me,' and so I followed him up the tunnel.

"They had a player called Davis and I remember he hit me early in the game, knocking me down and winding me. Jock Thomson just ran past and said, 'Leave it to me'. A few minutes later, Davis was lying down and holding his mouth. Jock was there, helping to pick him up. The lad didn't know what, or who, hit him. That's the way it was. There was an incredible spirit and we looked out for each other."

The rewards were not high considering the attendances, but Gordon always revelled in the stories and never missed a chance to pass on the many legendary tales as he reflected on a marvellous Goodison background, the definitive Everton expert.

Members of Everton's 1938-39 Championship squad are pictured at Lime Street Station. Left to right: Boyes, T.G.Jones, Cook, Caskie, Stevenson, Lawton, Gillick, Sagar, Watson, Mercer, Greenhalgh.

Champions And Then It's War

Saturday, 29 April 1939
Everton 3 Aston Villa 0

EVERTON finished the 1930s as they had begun it, their name on everybody's lips.

Herbert Chapman's legendary Arsenal held sway in the middle of the decade, but the Blues finished the 1938-39 season back on top of the pack.

They would effectively be 'Champions' for seven years with regional football the name of the game during the war years.

It was the season that Everton clinched the title on the day they lost! They went down 2-1 at Charlton, their first defeat in seven games, but Wolverhampton Wanderers failure to win at Bolton meant the Merseysiders could not be caught in the remaining two games.

The final home League game was against Aston Villa and the newly-installed Champs desperately wanted to turn it on for the fans. Manager-secretary Theo Kelly had built a new team around exciting young players like Joe Mercer, a wing-half with a superb tactical brain and Tommy

Lawton, who filled Dixie Dean's striking boots so superbly that many claimed he was an even better centre-forward than the maestro.

This in itself is a subject that could be debated around the clock. Lawton was generous to say that there was no one better than Dixie. Perhaps the argument should end there.

But there is no disputing the fact that Lawton was a very special player, possessing two outstanding feet and being virtually unbeatable in the air. He led the line. in that final home game against Villa, having already plundered 34 League goals in 36 games.

The crowd was not as big as many thought it would be but the new Champions were still showered with confetti and given a great ovation when they emerged from the tunnel.

The football was not as good as it might have been in the opening exchanges but the ball was lively and a strong wind did not help the players.

Everton soon settled down. Defender

Allen showed his fear of Lawton when he hurriedly kicked into touch rather than taking any risks but this safety clearance led to the opening goal after 11 minutes. The scorer was Bentham, a man whose strikes were few and far between. Nevertheless, it was an excellent effort, a powerhouse shot that goalkeeper Rutherford never even saw.

Gillick provided the knockout punch when he made it 2-0 after 23 minutes, but in doing so he took one on the chin and was carried off unconscious. The stockily-built winger, having made a goalwards header from Caskie's free-kick, was instantaneously caught full in the face as Rutherford tried to punch clear. He did not see the ball hit the back of the net and was lifted to the touchline where he received lengthy treatment before he was able to continue, holding a handkerchief to a bloody nose.

The Blues now had the opportunity to further increase their lead when Villa conceded a penalty after a Bentham header was handled by Iverson on the line. Cook was Everton's spot-kick expert and he scored with his usual confidence to make it 3-0 with just 29 minutes gone.

Surprisingly, Lawton had not figured in the scoring. It was not to be his day - three cannonball drives rebounding clear off defenders. The Blues strolled through the second half and while there were no

Scottish winger Torry Gillick was never far from the action during the 1938-39 Championship success. He is pictured here going close in a 2-0 home win over Brentford. Tommy Lawton (left) scored both goals.

Everton met Manchester United in November 1940 in a wartime League North game. This programme shows some famous names. Tommy Lawton scored four and Alex Stevenson also netted in a 5-2 victory. Johnny Carey, the United number ten, later became Everton's manager.

Off to war in 1939 and the *Echo's* George Green warns the enemy about some Merseyside sporting heroes including Everton's Tommy Lawton.

Goodison Park was hit by German bombs in September 1940. The club received £5,000 from the War Damage Commission to carry out essential repairs.

further goals, the crowd saluted the Champions warmly on the final whistle.

No one enjoying the carnival atmosphere at Goodison that day realised what was just around the corner. It would soon be war games only for the likes of Mercer, Gillick, Bentham and Lawton as Adolf

Hitler drew the world into a bitter conflict
that would last six long years.
Everton: Sagar; Cook, Greenhalgh, Mercer,
T.G.Jones, Watson, Gillick, Bentham,
Lawton, Stevenson, Caskie.
Attendance: 23,667

The Blues 1938-39 Football League
Championship side. Back row (left to right):
Lawton, T.G.Jones, Sagar, H.Cooke (trainer),
Mercer, Greenhalgh. Front: W.Cook,
Gillick, Bentham, Thomson, Stevenson, Boyes.
The young mascot is one J.Shannon.

T. G. JONES – MILLENNIUM GIANT
1940-1950

GOODISON Park was first dubbed the 'School Of Soccer Science' in the 1930s, a tribute not just to the ball-playing skills of the stars who graced the royal blue jersey, but also to the supporters who have always been connoisseurs of quality football.

Everton's Millennium Giant for 1940-50 was not so much a graduate of that scientific soccer academy as one of the professors.

Tommy George Jones – T. G. to avoid confusion with the

FACTFILE

Born: Connahs Quay, 1917.
Everton appearances: 175.
Everton goals: 5.
Everton honours:
Football League Championship winner: 1938-39.
Wales caps: 17.
War-time internationals: 11.

Tommy E. Jones who followed him in 1950 – was a defender with a difference. Centre-halves in this era were big and strong, built to bludgeon opposing centre-forwards as well as compete with them every inch of the way in the air.

T. G. was a different breed. He was a thinking centre-half rather than a stopper. He had the supreme confidence to glance back-headers into the arms of goalkeeper Ted Sagar, a tactic that was unheard of in an age when defenders attacked the ball and went for distance upfield rather than accuracy and skill. It was said that Sagar would scream blue murder if anyone else tried to find him with a testing backpass, but he had total confidence in T. G.

Everton paid £3,000 for Jones in March 1936. It was a substantial sum at that time for a player who had only played six League matches for Wrexham. It was money well spent, one contemporary declaring that "T. G. Jones was the best signing Everton ever made."

He would figure in just one game that first season before settling down and establishing himself in the side as the definitive class act at the back. T. G. was a key member of the 1938-39 Championship winning side which looked as if it could dominate English football for years to come.

Sadly, the Second World War would wipe out five full seasons from his first class record although Jones was clearly as influential as ever when hostilities finally ended and he returned to Goodison Park to continue his career in earnest.

Famous Echo correspondent Bee (Ernest Edwards), writing in 1947, said: "Jones is the finest centre-half playing football

today. He is in a class by himself, Everything he does has the hallmark of the consummate artist. He is the essence of style, neatness and precision and a gentleman on and off the field. I have never once seen him guilty of a shady action. He is a credit as well as an ornament to the game."

However, this colourful portrait of a football giant came on a day most Evertonians would choose to forget because in March 1947, T. G. shocked the Merseyside soccer scene by asking for a transfer. Later that year, after a further four requests for a move had been turned down, Jones would reveal that he had been unhappy with certain members of the Goodison hierarchy for the best part of three years. Clearly, a volcano had been rumbling inside him and now it exploded.

He believed that Everton's reluctance to sell him was linked directly with the sale of two other Goodison favourites, Tommy Lawton and Joe Mercer, observing: "Could it be that, having lost Tommy and Joe when both might have been kept had different methods been adopted, they are frightened of public opinion if they let me go?"

In stating his affection for the fans who still idolised him, T. G. got to the heart of his dissatisfaction with the revelation that it stemmed from a derby game at Anfield three years earlier on April 22, 1944. It was the third time the great rivals had met in ten days to try and settle a Lancashire Cup-tie.

Early on, Jones suffered an ankle injury and had to be carried from the field. He said: "While I was in the dressing room and doubled up with pain, an Everton director came down, looked at my black and swollen ankle, and poo-poohed my remark that I would not be able to return to the field. 'That's nothing,' he said. 'I've seen plenty of fellows play with worse than that.'

The director showed his annoyance when the star centre-half refused to go back on. Jones caution was linked with the experience of a young Everton colleague who suffered a similar injury a few months earlier, but who played on through the pain barrier, only to find out later that the ankle was broken. It finished his first class career.

Jones, in severe pain and vastly more experienced, was not going to take that same chance. What really annoyed him was that he was given no assistance to get away from Anfield and back to his RAF Unit (the country was still at war). As it turned out, he finished up in hospital for four months and couldn't touch a ball for six months.

He never forgot that incident. This was an era in which directors dictated team matters. T. G. might have been at odds with one or two in the corridors of power, but he remained on exactly the same wavelength as the fans who continued to support him.

His insistence that he wanted a transfer dominated the headlines throughout 1947. Jack Humphreys, another Welsh international, began to hold down the number five shirt that was once T. G.s by right. Ten games into the 1947-48 campaign, Jones regained his place and played against Liverpool and Wolves, but he was dropped when the team went to Middlesbrough. Rightly or wrongly, he was beginning to feel there was a conspiracy against him, telling respected Echo correspondent Ernest Edwards: "I am convinced that if Jack Humphreys wasn't taking my place, it would be somebody else. It is my conviction – which the trend of events behind the scenes have done nothing to dispel – that I shall never get back into the Everton first team, except in case of dire emergency."

This was an age when it was unheard of for players to speak out so strongly against a top club, but Jones was an intelligent man who felt he was being treated unjustly. He was so shaken by events that he threatened to quit football altogether when his contract expired.

Thankfully, T. G. did return to the heart of the Everton defence, thrilling the fans once more with his quality defensive play. However, the club's rivals knew of his on-going frustrations and Notts County were amongst those ready to offer a king's ransom for him.

Everton were steadfast in their refusal to sell, but there was a sensational new twist at the start of the 1948-49 season when it was revealed that Italian giants Roma were intent on capturing Jones. They were even prepared to give him a player-coach role and it finally appeared that Everton would release their unhappy star for a fee in the region of £15,500 which was five times what they paid for him. Negotiations on behalf of the Italians were carried out by Dr Claudio Ferrari, a former Roma outside-right who was now a barrister, resident in Liverpool.

The offer to Jones was sensational at the time. He would be given a lump sum in advance, a contract from two to four years, depending on his wishes, a job as a full time coach when his playing days were over, a wage of approximately £25 a week (double his Everton salary), plus bonuses, a house in the best part of Rome and other advantages. Roma declared that they would soon be moving into a new 100,000 capacity super stadium.

All seemed well, but once again Jones would have to face weeks of total frustration. A month and a half later, the deal was still on hold and T. G. himself was describing his chances of moving to Italy as 100-1 against. The player had gone as far as completing discussions, getting clearance from the FA and verbally agreeing the deal. A barrister was specially engaged to complete the final contract, but a problem arose over over the currency details.

The dream move never happened and T. G. concentrated his attentions throughout the remainder of the season on keeping Everton in the top flight. It was a worrying campaign for the Blues and they finally finished 18th. The one consolation for the fans was the great form of their favourite centre-half . It seemed all was well again when he was reinstated as captain in August 1949, in place of Peter Farrell.

But the tempestuous final years took one final twist when on 26 January 1950, the skilful defender once again asked for his release. Despite having started that campaign in the side, he lost out after ten games to his old Welsh adversary Jack Humphreys who in turn made way for Dick Falder. The unthinkable happened with T. G. Jones unable to make the reserve side at times. When he arrived at Goodison and saw his name wasn't on the teamsheet, Jones would nip away and play secretly for Hawarden Grammar School Old Boys. He joked: "They had pretty good gates when the word got round!"

On 1 February 1950, Everton agreed to the player's request for release. It was the end of an era as well as the end of a saga. Incredibly, one of the classiest defenders of his day, a man who seemed on the verge of an Italian adventure just months before, now chose a career away from mainstream football. He became proprietor of a hotel in Pwllheli and became player-coach of the town's football team.

His thoughts almost certainly drifted back to the great days at Everton. I'm sure he must have thought about the famous 1939 Championship triumph as well as the Roma dream that was snatched away from him. But T. G. Jones was an intelligent and single-minded individual who knew his own mind. At 32, he was back in Wales and ready to move forward in his own way as positively as he could. He would retain his love for football, writing an authorative column for the North Wales edition of the Liverpool Daily Post as well as enjoying a successful ten year spell with Bangor City.

Ironically this would link him again with an Italian challenge. Bangor never finished out of the top four in the Cheshire League during his stewardship and they also won the Welsh Cup. This gave them a crack at Italian giants Napoli in the European Cup. Incredibly, Bangor won 2-0 at home on a night when they could have scored eight. But the little Welsh side lost the return in Naples by the same margin and eventually went out after a play-off at Highbury.

Later still T. G. would manage Rhyl and act as team adviser to Bethesda Athletic.

His football story is truly remarkable. He had a frustrating end to his Everton career, but in the minds of the fans he remained the undisputed "Prince of Wales." The Millennium Giants panel, considering his claims half a century after he left the club, were unanimous in confirming him in his rightful place in the Goodison Hall of Fame.

The Everton squad in 1948-49. Back row (left to right): Juliussen, Falder, Catterick, Hedley, Lewis, Fielding, Eglington, Saunders, Farrell, Humphreys, Greenhalgh. Middle: T.G.Jones, Corr, Dugdale, Pinchbeck, Powell, Burnett, Sagar, Cameron, Higgins, Cookson, Clinton, Lindley, H.Cooke (trainer). Front: Boyes, Watson, Stevenson, Bentham, McCormick, Lello, Wainwright, Grant.

Everton fans ready to cheer on their favourites during a Cup tie in 1948.

Bring In The Crowds — 78,299 of Them!

Saturday, 18 September 1948
Everton 1 Liverpool 1

IN the soccer-mad post-war years, crowds of 50,000 plus were not so much unusual as the order of the day. When Liverpool crossed the park in season 1947-48 to stage an FA Cup tie against Manchester United, a staggering 74,721 people passed through the Goodison turnstiles to set a new attendance record for the ground. United had to make the venue switch because of war damage to Old Trafford.

Few people thought the attendance would be surpassed. Yet when Liverpool returned early in the following campaign to face the old enemy in a League game, it was clear that an historic day was on the cards.

The famous old stadium was bursting at the seams and the gates were finally locked with 78,299 fans inside the ground. It remains the record attendance and will never be beaten, successive ground safety rules reducing the Goodison capacity almost by half.

The *Football Echo* reported that there were many casualties, not least because of the swaying in the paddock. The teams came out side by side and the roar of anticipation inside was matched only by the roar of frustration outside where thousands were locked out!

Stevenson was Everton's captain and he won the toss, opting to attack the Gwladys Street goal in the first half. Modern tradition dictates that the Blues defend that end before the break, but this was

clearly not the case on this memorable afternoon.

Liverpool's best chance in the opening exchanges fell to Liddell, but Sagar claimed his splendid teasing centre under the bar. Liddell then tried one of those pile-driver shots for which he was famous. The ball rebounded out to Balmer who lifted his shot over the top. The Reds were on top, but Sidlow had to concede a corner after Stevenson cracked in a shot from the left. The visitors were soon encouraging their vast army of fans with a series of determined attacks but T.G.Jones was immaculate in the heart of the home defence. Cool and controlled, he extricated himself from any difficult situation with a classical touch to a better-placed teammate.

At the same time, Stevenson was delivering some outstanding passes, linking well with Boyes to cause the Liverpool defence a certain amount of anxiety. Boyes beat his man and centred

across goal for Fielding to head back into the middle.

Boyes, the instigator of the move, had followed up and Sidlow was forced to make a useful save. At this stage, Everton were playing some outstanding football.

Liddell was not having the best of games against Bentham and Saunders. But the Anfield star could never be ignored and a powerful run and shot forced Sagar to concede a corner on the stroke of half-time.

The Reds came out fighting after the interval, determined to make the all-important breakthrough and Sagar had to be on his guard to deny both Fagan and Shannon.

Stevenson, a player who could turn on a sixpence, raised the home spirits with a feint that bamboozled two defenders, but the Blues were unable to cash in on his skill.

Sagar made an absolutely stunning save after Fagan had volleyed goalwards in

A record Goodison Park day. Blues' skipper Alex Stevenson and Liverpool's Jackie Balmer step out in front of a bumper 78,299 crowd which will stand forever as the club's biggest home attendance.

spectacular fashion. The ball was powering towards the corner of the net when the 'keeper plunged down to turn it away. Late in the half, Jones had to leave the field for treatment to a leg injury. He was off for only a matter of minutes, but Liverpool cashed in to score.

Payne made a good run and flicked the ball wide to Shannon in the outside-right berth. His outstanding cross invited Liddell to crash a shot goalwards. It failed to reach the target, but Fagan was on the spot to cash in with a solid and accurate shot into the far corner.

Liverpool's delight was shortlived. A Boyes corner caused panic in the visitors defence. The ball was finally returned to Boyes, whose rocket shot beat Sidlow all ends up, only to be tipped over the bar by defender Shepherd.

Dodds took the resulting penalty and whilst Sidlow got his hands to the ball, he could not keep it out of the net. There were only six minutes left in which neither side managed to conjure up a winner. But it had been an historic day on the terraces. Like Dean's 60 goals, here was an attendance that would stand the test of time.

Far left: A fine action picture of centre-forward Jock Dodds in 1948. Real name Ephraim Dodds, 'Jock' was a giant no-nonsense striker who had previously been with Huddersfield, Sheffield United and Blackpool. He scored 37 goals in 58 Everton appearances.

Left: A portrait of outstanding inside-forward Alex Stevenson, who scored 90 goals in 271 appearances between 1933-34 and 1948-49.

Below: While the players put opponents through the mangle out on the pitch, Miss Buchanan put the kit through the electric mangle in the Goodison laundry, watched here by 'A' team trainer George Thompson. This picture was taken in 1949.

Everton: Sagar; Saunders, Hedley, Bentham, T.G.Jones, Watson, Powell, Fielding, Dodds, Stevenson, Boyes.
Attendance: 78,299 (some reports initially gave the figure as 78,599)

Factfile: On the Monday immediately following this record-breaking game it was reported that former Goodison star Cliff Britton would be taking over as manager of the Blues. Britton had been one of the greatest Goodison wing-halves of all time, figuring in the 1933 FA Cup-winning team. Described as a 'student of football', he managed Burnley and enjoyed many triumphs at Turf Moor, inspiring promotion from the Second Division as well as taking the Clarets to Wembley in the FA Cup. He would lead Everton between 1948 and 1956, but major honours eluded him. The Blues went down and were promoted during this spell and had some great runs in the Cup. He finally handed over the reins to Ian Buchan.

Aston Villa's Con Martin scores from the penalty spot and England are on the way to a Goodison nightmare.

England's First Home Defeat Against Foreign Rivals

Wednesday, 21 September 1949
England 0 Republic of Ireland 2

GOODISON Park has the dubious distinction of being the venue when England lost on home soil for the first time to a 'foreign' country – that is to say other than Home International rivals.

The Republic of Ireland was the opposition on a night when the likes of Wilf Mannion, Tom Finney, Billy Wright and the rest found themselves with red faces at the royal blue stadium.

But there was nevertheless an Everton silver lining. The Goodison club's skipper Peter Farrell scored the Republic's second goal five minutes from time, after Con Martin had given them the lead from the penalty spot in the 35th minute.

Another Everton player to enjoy the night was winger Pat Corr, who would be released to non-League Bangor a few weeks later. The Blues would have had a third representative in the Irish side, had Tommy Eglington not been injured.

The *Liverpool Echo's* report indicates the nation's frustration with England's performance. It said: *To think that Eire, who had extreme difficulty in raising eleven men of sufficient calibre for such a match, should be the first 'outside' country to beat us on home ground. It shows plainly how far we have fallen from the all-conquering England of a few seasons ago. They have fairly put the cat amongst the England selectors' pigeons.*

Finney was the star of the English front line, although his marker, Johnny Carey, later to manage Everton, was described as having a 'brilliant game'. But overall, the home attack was said to have fiddled and finessed to the point of extreme exasperation in the penalty area.

It was a proud night for the Irish, though, particularly the Shamrock Rovers goalkeeper, 22-year-old Tommy Godwin, who was snapped up by Leicester City two weeks later and went on to make over 400 appearances in the Football League.

England: Williams; Mozley, Aston, Wright, Franklin, Dickinson, Harris, Morris, Pye, Mannion, Finney.
Republic of Ireland: Godwin; Carey, A. Herne, W. Walsh, Martin, Moroney, Corr, Farrell, D. Walsh, Desmond, O'Connor.
Attendance: 52,000

Not quite today's cheerleaders! "Practical skipping to music to promote good carriage as well as a healthy physique" — that was the description of this entertainment at Goodison in the early 1950s.

The 1950-51 season began brightly enough with a 3-2 home win over Huddersfield Town. The man emerging from the Goodison players' tunnel in the centre of this picture is none other than Harry Catterick, later to become a League and Cup-winning Everton manager.

Heavy snow and plunging temperatures caused problems going into 1951. Everton were 16th in the table and hoping to move away from the danger zone, but they crashed 3-0 at home to Stoke. Moore heads away in this picture, watched by Sagar and Jones, but it proved to be a disappointing afternoon.

That Sinking Feeling

Saturday, 21 April 1951
Everton 1 Aston Villa 2

EVERTON'S final home League game of the season in 1950-51 had disaster written all over it. Only three points had been gained from the previous eight matches and the Blues were staring relegation in the face for only the second time in their long and distinguished history.

The Midlanders were themselves in the danger zone along with Chelsea and

A 2-1 home defeat against Aston Villa in April 1951, proved disastrous for the Blues. It was their last Goodison game before relegation. Peter Farrell was Everton's best player on the day and he sprints in here to try and dispossess Villa forward Thompson.

Sheffield Wednesday. But their plight was of no consequence to the 45,000 Evertonians who turned up at Goodison Park, hoping to play their part in a footballing 'Houdini act'. Could the Blues pull themselves together and snatch crucial points with a view to going into their final two away games with a fighting chance?

Hope springs eternal on the football field, but Everton gave themselves a mountain to climb when they conceded a goal in the very first minute. Villa won the toss and defended the Park End goal which meant their opponents were forced to kick into the sun in the opening period. The start was absolutely sensational.

Villa won a throw-in on the left at the end of their very first attack. Goffin took it and the ball floated over the Everton heads and landed at the feet of Walsh, who quickly invited Dixon to close in on goal from an acute angle. It seemed as if it was too tight a situation to get in a shot with the vastly experienced Sagar covering the near post, but the forward somehow drilled the ball across the 'keeper and into the far corner of the net.

The Blues were not just playing into the sun, but also into the face of a strong wind. Jones blocked a goal-bound shot from Dorsett. But the home side recovered from these faltering early moments to equalise after just five minutes. Hold picked up a half clearance and whipped the ball across the face of goal. A Villa defender lashed the ball against centre-forward McIntosh and he seized the rebound to make a goal of it.

It was a dire game, reflecting the tension felt by both sides. The crowd groaned to a man when Buckle volleyed an Eglington corner well wide. The game was balanced on a knife-edge at the interval. And so was Everton's First Division status.

As the second half unfolded, Buckle and Aldis clashed heads in a painful collision. Trainer Cooke advised Buckle to leave the field, but with a sponge held to

his damaged cheek, the Everton player sprinted around the goal at the Stanley Park End, determined to carry on. It summed up just how important the result was to the home side.

Ironically, Buckle had only just returned to the field when Villa went in front. It was a disastrous moment for the Blues. Dorsett's centre was flicked on by Dixon and Smith netted from the outside-right position. The crowd's obvious frustration bubbled to the surface.

The Second Division beckoned and respected *Liverpool Echo* scribe 'Ranger' (Bob Prole) pulled no punches in his Monday column.

He said: *Whether it was just plain jitters or something worse I wouldn't know, but certainly there wasn't enough tenacity or courage on Saturday to send the spectators away with even the slight consolation that the Blues had gone down fighting. Farrell set a great example and Potts ran himself almost to a standstill, but most of the rest seemed as infirm of purpose and lacking in determination as though it made no difference whether they won or lost.*

Goodison had certainly seen better days. The Merseysiders were going down.

Everton: Sagar; Moore, Rankin, Grant, T.E.Jones, Farrell, Buckle, Hold, McIntosh, Potts, Eglington.
Attendance: 45,254

Peter Farrell makes a flying clearance ahead of Villa's Thompson on 21 April 1951, but Everton are heading into the Second Division.

Eddie Wainwright, Peter Farrell and Tommy Eglington take to the air in training in February 1952.

Opposite page, top: Harry Potts playing head tennis under the Gwladys Street Stand in 1951. This was common practice when the weather was bad. Potts later earned fame as manager of Burnley.

Bottom: Former Everton players, on the staff in the early 1950s, are pictured here 'putting the boot in' — but only for repairs. Messrs Watson, Bentham, Leyfield and Borthwick at work in the Goodison 'cobbler's shop'.

PLAY UP THE
BLUES

EVERTON 3 IPSWICH T 2
EVERTON 1 NOTTS.F. 1
EVERTON 2 MAN.UTD. 1
EVERTON ASTON.V

Can you recognise yourself in this fans' group, taken en-route to Villa Park in the Cup in February 1953?

Blood And Thunder Cup Triumph

Saturday, 14 February 1953
Everton 2 Manchester United 1

THOSE who were lucky enough to be at Goodison Park for this FA Cup fifth-round clash between Second Division Everton and top-flight opponents Manchester United will remember it as Dave Hickson's greatest hour.

Everton's swashbuckling centre-forward scored the winning goal with blood streaming down his face from a deep cut above his eyebrow. He had sustained the injury just before half-time and at that stage it looked as if he would be struggling to continue.

But spilling blood for his beloved Everton was all in a day's work for Hickson. Twice the referee asked him to go off. Twice the Blues' number nine shook his head and launched himself back into the fray. His courage would eventually be rewarded in a quite remarkable game.

The Goodison pitch looked in fine condition for this clash, although the surface was just a little bit greasy, suggesting the turf might cut up as the game progressed.

At first sight, the crowd looked to be approaching the 70,000 mark. There were frustrating scenes on the Bullens Road side of the ground where many unlucky ticket holders did not get in until at least 25 minutes after the start although they were outside the ground in good time.

The trouble was caused by a terrific crush of people hoping to get into the paddock which was pay-at-the-gate. A mass of supporters jammed the north end of Bullens Road and the police, operating on foot, were powerless to do anything about it.

Even when the paddock turnstiles were closed, people with tickets still could not force their way through. Eventually mounted police managed to sort things out, but by now the tie was well underway.

Peter Farrell won the toss and elected

Harry Walker, the Forest goalkeeper, just manages to elude Dave Hickson during the FA Cup fourth-round tie at Goodison Park in January 1953. Everton won 4-1 to set up a famous clash with Manchester United.

to defend the Gwladys Street End. United were the reigning Champions and clear favourites to win the game. The Manchester side featured stars like Ray Wood, Roger Byrne and David Pegg, but there was experience amongst them as well in the shape of Arthur Rowley and Johnny Carey, a man who would later change sides and manage the Blues.

United attacked with confidence early on and it was no surprise when they secured the lead after 27 minutes. Berry, with plenty of space on the right, out-foxed Lindsay with a feint to centre. Instead, he turned inside and beat his man before trying a shot which O'Neill parried. The rebound went straight to Rowley, who lashed it home from close range.

The Blues refused to lie down and two fine efforts from Buckle raised the home morale. The home side's fighting qualities came to the fore when Eglington equalised in the 34th minute. Cummins had made a clever pass to Hickson in the outside-right position. He quickly moved it on to Eglington, who rounded defender Aston and scored with a solid right-foot shot from ten yards out. It was his fifth goal in as many games.

Everton's elation was tempered by an injury to Hickson sustained just before half-time. The Goodison number nine took a nasty knock in the face and was led from the field with blood pouring from a badly cut eyebrow. It looked as if he might struggle to continue, let alone play a leading part in the second-half action.

But this was Dave Hickson, a real-life 'Roy of the Rovers'. He returned to the fray with a vengeance, shrugging the referee aside when he suggested a possible early retirement. United refused to give the Everton hero an inch, but then Dave never sought any favours.

Dave Hickson was the hero of Goodison on 14 February 1953 when Second Division Everton knocked Champions Manchester United out of the FA Cup with a 2-1 victory. Hickson finished the tie covered in blood after sustaining a deep cut above his eyebrow, but he continued to head the ball bravely and scored a crucial goal. He is pictured challenging United's Ray Wood for a high ball.

Physical jerks (top) began training at Bellefield as Everton began to prepare for their 1953 FA Cup quarter-final against Aston Villa. Manager Cliff Britton (below) discusses tactics with the players. Left to right are Grant, Lello, Buckle, Farrell, Parker, Hickson, Jones, Potts, Eglington, Lindsay, Cummins and O'Neill.

The *Football Echo* reported: *When Hickson was harassed by two defenders as he tried to bore his way through, he was brought down by Carey and adopted a rather truculent attitude on getting up!*.

Truculent? The Cannonball Kid was spitting blood and breathing fire at the same time.

Ignoring his injured eye, he met a corner with his head and the ball thudded against an upright. Hickson was like a boxer who had taken a left hook, his eyebrow bursting open once more with the impact of the ball. The referee stopped the game, indicating that the player should now heed his advice and call it a day. Hickson, with the crowd roaring his name, simply trotted back into position.

Everton were now well on top. Farrell set up Eglington and the fans gasped as his superb lob sailed narrowly over the bar. United's Rowley and home fullback Clinton clashed and tempers were now getting a bit frayed to say the least.

Parker missed a golden opportunity to put the Blues in front when he screwed a left-foot shot well wide from an outstanding position, but it didn't matter.

Everton grabbed the lead after 63 minutes with a goal as dramatic as anything that had been scored on this famous ground, apart from Dixie's

legendary 60th. Inevitably, Hickson was the name on the lips of every single member of the blue and white army.

Factfile: Everton met Aston Villa in the sixth round at Villa Park. Once again, Hickson was the man of the moment, scoring the only goal of the game to earn the Blues a semi-final challenge against Bolton Wanderers. It proved to be a sensational match, Parker (two) and Farrell scoring in a heartbreaking 4-3 defeat.

Bolton went on to lose at Wembley to Blackpool in what will forever be known as the Stanley Matthews Final. If the Blues had gone all the way, would the Cannonball Kid have stolen the Wizard of the Wing's thunder? Such dreams are what the Cup is all about. It's enough to say that Hickson had a season Evertonians will never forget.

He had played the half with blood pouring from that gash above his eye. The worse it got, the more determined Dave seemed to become. His golden moment

began with a long ball from Clinton near the halfway line. Eglington claimed it and wasted no time at all in squaring it to Hickson.

Two defenders were tracking the Blond Bomber and he seemed to have little chance of making anything of the situation. But chasing the ball, he beat one man, side-stepped the other and then screwed back an angled shot that the despairing Wood failed to reach.

The crowd went wild. Hickson's grit and determination had won the day.

One side of his face was a mass of red. The top half of his blue shirt had turned scarlet. But the man was still a tower of strength. He left the field to a stand-

ing ovation. Was such a salute ever more deserved?

Everton: O'Neill; Clinton, Lindsay, Farrell, T.E.Jones, Lello, Buckle, Cummins, Hickson, Parker, Eglington.
Attendance: 77,902

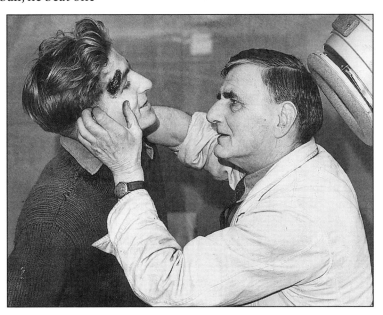

Three famous FA Cup goals en-route to the 1953 semi-final. Top: John Willie Parker scores in the 4-1 win over Nottingham Forest. Middle: Dave Hickson's memorable strike against Manchester United. Bottom: Hickson's quarter-final winner against Aston Villa.

The face of a battered hero. Dave Hickson has his badly gashed right eyebrow examined by trainer Harry Cooke after the sensational 1953 FA Cup victory over Manchester United.

The power and determination of Dave Hickson is captured perfectly in this photograph, a flying header at Goodison which produced an outstanding goal during the 1953-54 campaign.

A soccer giant at Goodison. The great John Charles of Leeds United gets in a solid header, challenged by Don Donovan in November 1953. The Blues won 2-1.

A fine action shot of Wally Fielding — a key figure in the 1954 promotion side. Fielding was a superb ball-playing inside-forward.

Sprinting back to the top ...Dave Hickson, Eglington, Farrell and Parker prepare for a return to the First Division in the summer of 1954.

Heading Back To The Big Time

The players who took Everton back to the top flight in 1954: Back row (left to right): Moore, Farrell, T.E.Jones, O'Neill, Donovan, Lello, C.Leyfield (trainer). Front: Wainwright, Fielding, Hickson, Parker, Eglington.

Saturday, 24 April 1954
Everton 1 Birmingham City 0

EVERTONIANS approached the end of the 1953-54 season with just one thought in mind. The Second Division was no place for one of the greatest clubs in the land. After close on three years in the wilderness, enough was enough.

When Birmingham City visited Goodison Park for the final home League game of the season, victory was not so much important as absolutely crucial. A crowd of over 62,000 converged on the ground, each and every one of them hoping that the Blues would overcome their promotion jitters. They had drawn the previous two games, both away from home, allowing Fulham (0-0) and Lincoln City (1-1) to share the spoils.

Birmingham were a more than useful side and there was an air of tense excitement about the crowd as they greeted their heroes with a deafening roar. The pitch had been well watered by the groundstaff and there was little doubt that the ball would zip up off the surface.

The visitors mounted two early attacks, clearly more relaxed than their opponents. The only thing the Birmingham players were playing for was their £2 win bonus. There was so much more at stake for Everton. Wally Fielding took a knock in the back although he did not require attention and then Goodison's very own Cannonball Kid, Dave Hickson, was grounded when Newman charged him as they disputed possession for a high lob.

The powerhouse centre-forward would eventually have the last word. Defenders found to their cost that Hickson was not a man to trifle with.

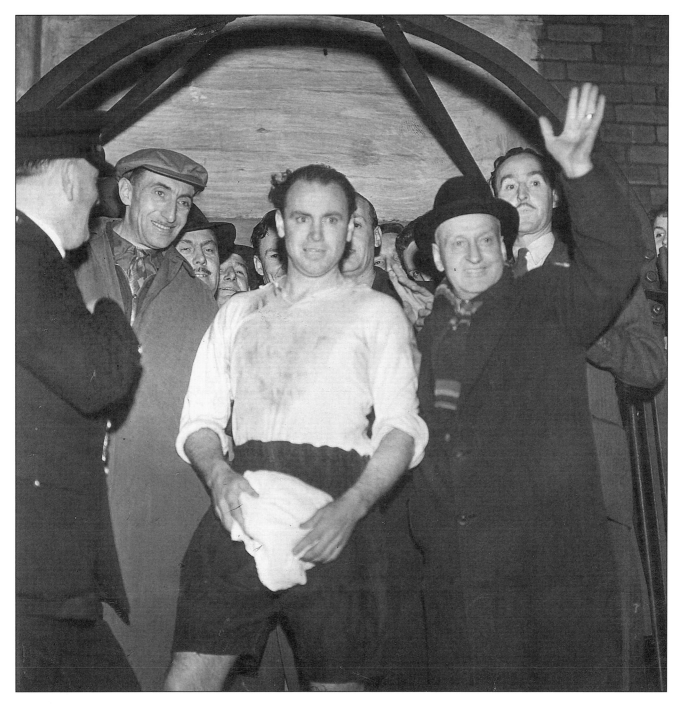

The blond number nine was spoken to by the referee for a foul on Newman just inside the Everton half. The official took the battling Blues' star to one side, waving away two Birmingham players before reading the riot act. Dave was unmoved by the ref's outstretched finger and he was patted on the shoulder by his skipper Peter Farrell.

The skirmish between striker and defender would turn into something of a war, but this was par for the course for Goodison idol Hickson.

A couple of minutes later Everton got a free-kick for a foul on Hickson by New-man. Then came a spell of incessant attacking by the home side with no end product. John Willie Parker was just too slow to take advantage of a short pass by Hickson in the vicinity of the six-yard box.

At this stage, the home side were not producing the dominance and combin-ation in attack their fans had hoped for. Fielding and Parker were not making their usual good use of the ball and the crowd were getting a little bit restless until Hickson finally made the all-important breakthrough after 38 minutes.

Cyril Lello and Farrell linked to provide Tommy Eglington with a chance

Elation for Everton's sturdy wing-half and captain Peter Farrell at the end of the promotion winning 1953-54 campaign. Farrell made 453 appearances for the Blues and played 28 times for the Republic of Ireland. He also won seven caps for Northern Ireland at a time when they could select Eire-born players for the Home International Championships.

A tip from the master, Ted Sagar passes on a few hints to his young successor, Jimmy O'Neill, who established himself as Everton fought their way back to the top flight.

Opposite page: The Goodison fans idolised Dave Hickson, seen here rising in typical fashion to head powerfully towards goal. He had two spells with the Blues in the 1950s, playing for Aston Villa and Huddersfield in between. There was uproar when Everton sold the forceful centre-forward to Liverpool in November 1959.

to get in a telling centre, but the resulting cross was too near the goalkeeper. Merrick double-fisted the ball away, but Hickson was hovering in a dangerous position and he rammed the ball back towards the net with a header that was almost as powerful as any shot.

The crowd erupted to salute their goal hero, who modestly waved back, his 24th League goal of the season in the bag.

There was an unusual incident in the second half when Hickson and Lello both went down after being charged by defenders. While the referee went to assess these painful knocks on the edge of one area, play continued just outside the area at the other end of the field. The fans screamed at the startled official who wheeled around and finally stopped play.

Factfile: Everton went on to win in style at Oldham, scoring four times without reply. Parker (two), Hickson and Jones were the scorers. It was the perfect way to complete a memorable promotion campaign.

It helped to ease the tension and the Blues were soon celebrating a crucial victory that would take them into their final game at Oldham with the First Division beckoning them.

Everton: O'Neill; Moore, Donovan, Farrell, T.E.Jones, Lello, Wainwright, Fielding, Hickson, Parker, Eglington.
Attendance: 62,965

Toffee Lady in the mid 1950s… Mary Gorry.

Lighting Up Goodison Park

Saturday, 9 October 1957
Everton 2 Liverpool 0

OVER 58,000 fans turned up at Goodison Park on 9 October 1957, for an historic occasion, Everton's first ever floodlit match.

The Blues were by no means pioneers in this field. Sheffield Wednesday, for instance, had installed a highly effective system at Hillsborough. And even non-League South Liverpool, very much Mersey minnows, had stolen a march on their famous neighbours. As early as

September 1949, South had staged a floodlit game at their Holly Park ground against a Nigerian touring XI, attracting crowd of 13,000 people.

But there was no disputing the fact that the Goodison venture was both ambitious and highly effective. There was much hype about the new technology prior to the game. It was said that enough electricity to last an ordinary house for six months would be used in just one game.

Four giant pylons, each 185 feet high and operating initially with 36 lamps each, towered over the pitch, one in each corner

FA Cup fever gripped Goodison in January 1955, when the Blues were drawn at home to Liverpool in the fourth round. Mounted police had to disperse a vast crowd in Goodison Road when tickets ran out. The queue had stretched for over a mile, many people having waited throughout the night. Sadly, Everton crashed 4-0 to their arch-rivals.

of the ground. The towers, the tallest in the country, could accommodate a further 18 lamps on each pylon if it was felt that the illumination generated was insufficient.

The company installing the system claimed that each lamp would last for at least 500 hours, or 330 matches! At 25 shillings (£1.25p) a time, the bulbs were not deemed to be costly and to save spasmodic replacement, the makers suggested the club install new lamps every three to four years.

The lights themselves were 1,500-watt tungsten bulbs, each over a foot long and 15 inches in diameter. They screwed into their sockets, the illumination being heightened by huge concave mirrors behind each unit.

It was claimed that the light output was the equivalent of 400 good-sized houses blazing away with every light they had. The towers themselves were built to withstand hurricane-force winds of up to 120 mph. They could take a three-inch sway at the top, but the people who had scaled the towers during the weeks building up to the big switch-on claimed it felt more like three feet when a gust struck a pylon.

In truth, they were rock-solid, soaring so high that they were visible for miles around. Merseyside and North Wales Electricity Board officials had to build a special transformer sub-station to provide the necessary 6,000-volt load.

Everton cashed in on the system to electrically heat the water for the players' baths as well as installing an electric laundry. Would the team now provide some electrifying football?

All was revealed when the Blues entertained Liverpool on the big night for what was an extra-special occasion. It was not a League game, but rather a first leg of the Liverpool County FA Anniversary Cup.

The Reds dominated in the opening half hour, but their finishing was erratic. They missed the all-round ability of Billy Liddell in the middle and the ball-control and scheming of Jimmy Melia. Equally, they had the misfortune of having a goal disallowed on the stroke of half-time for offside. Rowley looked 'on' when Molyneux booted the ball into the penalty area from the halfway line. The forward rounded Donovan and flicked the ball into the net, almost out of the hands of goalkeeper Dunlop.

But the flag was up and it meant Everton took advantage. They grabbed a two-goal lead early in the second half, both goals being scored by young Eddie Thomas who came on as a substitute for Fielding.

To add insult to injury, Liverpool claimed Everton's second goal was well offside, surrounding the referee and holding up the restart for over a minute. Hickson was yards 'off' when the movement began, but he was played on when the pass to him struck Byrne. Hickson ran on 20 yards before squaring the ball to the in-running Thomas to slot home.

The night was significant in as much as Liverpool gave a debut on the left wing to a young local boy, John Morrissey. He was their best forward in the first period, sending over some first-class centres. Morrissey, of course, would eventually cross the park for a bargain-fee of £10,000 in 1962 and become a firm Goodison favourite for close on a decade.

It was an illuminating night all round. Floodlit football would become part and parcel of life on Merseyside in the years that followed, but the people in Goodison Park that October night were very much in on the start of something big.

Everton: Dunlop; Donovan, Tansey, Birch, Jones, Meagan, McNamara, Temple, Hickson, Fielding(Thomas), Williams.
Attendance: 58,771

DAVE HICKSON - MILLENNIUM GIANT
1950-1960

THE 1950s were not years of milk and honey for Evertonians in the shape of trophies in the board room. Indeed, the Blues were relegated at the start of the decade for only the second time in their history and they would spend three years out of the top flight. But in a strange kind of a way, this era had a magic all of its own and the fact that the 1950s were nothing less than swashbuckling and full of hope had a lot to do with the powerhouse style of one man.

Everton have always had a reputation for great centre-forwards. The fans had been brought up on the feats of Fred Geary, Alex "Sandy" Young, Bobby Parker, Dixie Dean and Tommy Lawton. When Dave Hickson came onto the scene in 1951, his sheer enthusiasm and will to win, linked a bravery that went above and beyond the cause of duty, instantly captured the hearts and minds of the fans.

Hickson had the perfect mentor. When he was in the Cheshire Army Cadets, he was actually coached by the legendary Dean whose magic rubbed off on the boy from Salford. Hickson never forget those priceless lessons in leading the line.

His potential was nurtured in non-League football in Ellesmere Port, but Everton's Cliff Britton encouraged him to move across the Mersey. It was the start of a love affair between player and fans that exists to this day.

Someone once dubbed Hickson Merseyside's Cannonball Kid. The nickname was perfect. You could see Hickson coming, but you couldn't stop him. His powerhouse style got him in trouble with more than one referee, yet off the field he was quiet and unassuming – a real gentleman. It was easy to see why he was such a crowd favourite.

The blond bomber had actually signed professional forms for Everton in 1948, but his career was interrupted by national service. His army tour took him to Egypt and effectively wiped two years off his football record, but he would soon be making up for lost time.

He scored five in a reserve game against Sheffield Wednesday, but the manager stuck with

experience during that 1950-51 season as the spectre of relegation began to creep up on the Blues. The unthinkable happened and Everton, who had previously spent just one season out of the top flight, had to face up to life in the Second Division.

Hickson set his heart on playing a key role in the Everton revival. A certain Harry Catterick would hold down the number nine shirt for the opening four games of the following season. The Blues lost one, won one and drew one but Catterick, later to become a Goodison legend down a different route, failed to score.

Hickson was called up for the visit to Leeds, a 2-1 win. He got his first goal in a 3-3 home draw with Rotherham and would go on to make 31 League appearances, hitting the net 14 times. The striker was naturally delighted to be up and running, but bitterly disappointed that the club failed to bounce back at the first time of asking, finishing seventh.

The following year proved sensational, but on the FA Cup front rather than in the League. Dave's exploits in a chase to the semi-finals are dealt with in detail in the "Blood And Thunder" chapter elsewhere in this book.

For now, I will simply note that Hickson was the spark that ignited the great Everton revival. He played in 40 games in the 1953-54 promotion campaign and his 25 goals, alongside the 31 scored by the equally prolific John Willie Parker, put the Blues back where

they belonged. He said: "On the night we came back, we all vowed that Everton would never go down again. Thankfully, this has been the case."

Because he went in where others feared to tread, Hickson had his moments with officials, but it was mainly for dissent rather than foul play. He took as many knocks as he gave, saying: "I was a winner. I played for the fans and for the club. I was sent off three times, but only once for a tackle. That was during my time with Liverpool and we were 3-0 up at the time! It was just a retaliatory thing that happened in the heat of the moment."

Just to mention Hickson in the same breath as "Liverpool" was painful to Evertonians. It was bad enough when he was sold to Aston Villa in in 1955 for £20,000, later moving to a Huddersfield Town side managed by Bill Shankly. There was joy and elation when he returned to Goodison for £6,500 in July 1957, but although he notched a goal every other game over the next two and a quarter

seasons, the Everton hierarchy caused a storm by agreeing to sell him to . . . the Mersey Reds!

Everton had signed Alan Shackleton from Leeds and certain members of the board felt that Dave was expendable. The story dominated the

FACTFILE

Born Salford: 1929.
Everton appearances: 243.
Everton goals: 111.
Everton honours:
Second Division runner-up: 1953-54.

headlines in the Liverpool Echo and one report said: "Never in the history of football in this city has there been such a rumpus about a player from one club joining neighbours and rivals. Everton fans have written that if Hickson goes, they will go with him. Liverpool have received warning that if Hickson arrives, some of their most loyal fans will depart! It remains to be see if these factions are as good as their word."

Royal blue letters flooded in, all saying the same thing. How can you sell a Goodison icon, especially one who remains a goal machine? Liverpool still clinched the deal for £12,000 and on November 7, 1959, the unthinkable happened.

Hickson pulled on a red shirt and stepped out at Anfield in front of 50,000 people who had previously looked on him as the devil incarnate. He partnered a young Roger Hunt and proved that Roy of the Rovers is alive and well and wearing the biggest blond quiff in the business, scoring both goals in a 2-0 win, a left foot drive and a typical diving header.

On the same day Everton crashed 8-2 at Newcastle, but Dave Hickson would take no satisfaction from that. He would go on to play for Tranmere Rovers – becoming one of the only people ever to star for all three Merseyside clubs. But his heart always remained at Goodison Park and he is back amongst the memories and the supporters who idolised him, working behind the scenes these days in a public relations capacity on matchdays as well as acting as a guide for the popular stadium tours.

Dave has some stories to tell. He was a superstar before the phrase was invented and no one would deny him the right to be called an Everton Millennium Giant – one of the great Goodison number nines.

Carey Takes A Taxi Ride And The 'Millionaires' Take Centre Stage

WHEN an Everton manager is under threat, you will hear the Goodison fans talking about the possibility of him 'taking a taxi'. This phrase will totally bemuse outsiders, but Blues' fans are very much aware of its significance. In the summer of 1961, boss Johnny Carey travelled to London for a routine Football League meeting in tandem with club chairman John Moores.

Carey had been at the helm since 1958, a former Manchester United player who had learned the managerial ropes at Blackburn Rovers. Carey knew his football, of that there was no doubt. He brought the likes of Billy Bingham, Jimmy Gabriel, Roy Vernon and Alex Young to Goodison and in 1960-61 achieved fifth position in the First Division, the club's best placing since the war. The manager was on the right lines, but the man at the top, chairman Moores, was impatient for success. Head of the Littlewoods Organisation and Everton's chief shareholder, Moores was ready to use his vast fortune to help the Blues live up to their motto: 'Only The Best Will Do'.

Carey was calm, assured and extremely likeable, but the chairman wanted a strict disciplinarian at the helm, someone who would move ruthlessly in the transfer market to give the Blues that extra lift towards the top. And so when he left that fateful League meeting with Carey in tow, he chose to use the taxi journey to the station to inform the manager that his services would no longer be required.

To this day, struggling Everton managers dread the cry from the terraces of 'Take a taxi'. Carey took the 'sacking' decision with dignity, but it was nevertheless a shattering blow. Moores now appointed Sheffield Wednesday's Harry

An intriguing photograph of Everton manager Harry Catterick and chairman John Moores with a group of Everton apprentice professionals in November 1962, all schoolboy internationals. Left to right: Ken Griffiths, Aiden Maher, Geoff Harcombe, John Hurst, Gerry Humphreys, Geoff Barnett and Gerry Glover. All except Griffiths and Harcombe would play for the first team. It was said that Catterick only wore a tracksuit when Moores was about to make a visit. The 'Cat' obviously had advance notice on this day!

Catterick to the hot seat, a man who had played centre-forward for Everton in the late 1940s and 1950s without setting the place alight. But if Catterick was only an average player, he was most certainly an outstanding manager.

With Moores' full support, he won the League Championship in his second season with a side packed full of riches. Everton were known universally at that time as 'The Millionaires'. It was a tag which was fully justified because Catterick made a string of big-money buys. But the end justified the means because the Blues would also win the FA Cup in 1966 before the manager went off on a fresh tangent,

building a new Championship side around home-grown players in 1969-70.

Throughout this period, Moores influence was considerable. He was chairman twice, 1960-1965, and 1972-73. His success – first and foremost as a highly successful businessman and secondly as a leading figure in the world of sport (he also owned the old Liverpool Stadium boxing venue and was a leading shareholder in Liverpool Football Club) – earned him civic and national recognition. Moores was made an Honorary Freeman of the City in 1970, awarded the CBE in 1972 and was knighted in 1980, not least for his charitable services. In the same way that it is impossible to write about Everton without making mention of the likes of George Mahon and Will Cuff, those early Goodison guiding lights, it is impossible to talk about the modern Blues without making due reference to Sir John Moores. He exerted a very different type of influence, but it was nevertheless a crucial involvement, coming at exactly the right time.

Obviously, success is all about having the right players, but if a club has not got leadership from the top, mediocrity will always prevail. On the subject of managers, Everton's first recognised 'boss' was Theo Kelly, appointed to the post in 1939. Prior to that time, team selection was a matter for directors, specially appointed committees and senior coaches. Kelly had been club secretary for some years prior to being offered the new title of team manager. He would retain the position for seven years. He found himself in charge of a team playing wartime regional football in the first instance. Seemingly reluctant to move in the transfer market unless it was absolutely vital, he angered the fans by selling Tommy Lawton to Chelsea in 1945 and the restless Joe Mercer to Arsenal. Some felt that his administrative background as secretary made him too careful in a financial sense.

He was finally replaced by Cliff Britton in 1948. Britton had been a stylish and highly respected wing-half with the club, gaining an FA Cup winners' medal alongside Dixie Dean and the rest in 1933. He had gained managerial experience with Burnley, taking them from the Second Division to the First as well as reaching an FA Cup Final.

An easy going, yet confident man, he took Everton to the 1950 FA Cup semifinal, a bitter losing experience against Liverpool. Things now took a sharp downwards turn and despite signing Harry Potts from Burnley and Jock Lindsay from Glasgow Rangers, the Blues suffered the indignity of being relegated for only the second time in their history in 1951. Britton now set about the challenge of restoring the club's top-flight status and after finishing seventh and 16th. Everton finally bounced back in 1953-54 as Second Division runners-up.

Britton stepped down in 1956 and for two years, the Blues had Ian Buchan operating, not as a manager in the true sense, but rather as first-team coach. Buchan was a fitness fanatic and he marshalled the Blues well in this respect, but he was no tactician and no one was surprised when Johnny Carey took over in 1958. Carey's rise and fall has been described earlier in this chapter, likewise the arrival of Catterick. 'The Cat' would put Everton back on the map in no uncertain terms with players of the calibre of Gordon West, Tommy Wright, Howard Kendall, Colin Harvey, Brian Labone, John Hurst, Johnny Morrissey and Joe Royle, to name just a few. Catterick won two Championships and the FA Cup between 1961 and 1973 when he 'moved upstairs' in an advisory capacity after suffering a heart attack. The great Everton manager died at Goodison Park after watching an FA Cup quarter-final against Ipswich Town on 9 March 1985.

Everton, having won the title in 1970 with what should have been the team of the decade, now inexplicably fell from grace. They went 13 long years without a major trophy, even though Billy Bingham, in the first instance, and then Gordon Lee would both go tantalisingly close. But John Moores, all those years earlier, had emphasised that he wasn't

interested in Nearly Men. And so Howard Kendall accepted the call to Goodison in 1981 to become the most successful Everton manager of all time. Kendall was a class act as a player, a man whose powerhouse tackling and superb passing qualities helped to inspire that famous 1970 Championship success. Now, after a tense settling in period, he would win two titles in his own right, the FA Cup, the European Cup-winners' Cup and two Manager of the Year awards. He shocked the fans by leaving the club after the 1987 title success to join Athletic Bilbao with his right-hand man, Colin Harvey, taking charge. The old partnership was restored when Kendall returned in 1991, via Manchester City,

with the joint aim once again to put the Blues back on top.

However, Kendall would leave on a point of principle when the board refused to sanction the purchase of Dion Dublin. He was replaced by Mike Walker from Norwich who failed to spark a long-overdue revival. Everton turned to Joe Royle whose early reign promised much with an FA Cup Final success over Manchester United. But when Royle's team began to struggle, he too stepped aside, leading to Kendall returning for an unprecedented third spell at the helm.

Walter Smith, the vastly-experienced former Glasgow Rangers boss, would lead Everton into the new Millennium.

Johnny Carey was Everton manager between 1958 and 1961. He was sacked in a famous incident in the back of a taxi after leaving a League meeting in London with chairman John Moores. This photograph was taken in August 1959, Carey watching Dunlop, Ashworth, B.Harris, Tansey and Jones go through their paces at Bellefield. Managers in those days, of course, wore suits, not tracksuits.

Derek Temple's famous 1966 FA Cup Final goal against Sheffield Wednesday earned him a place in the Everton Hall of Fame. But Derek was rattling them in for the Blues long before that. He is pictured here in October 1957, rifling home the equaliser in a 1-1 draw with Burnley.

May 1960 and Peter Farrell figures in his last game as player-manager of Tranmere Rovers in the Liverpool Senior Cup Final at Goodison. Farrell had been an influential Everton captain in the 1950s. He is applauded on to the Goodison pitch he had graced so many times.

Harry Catterick inherited some good players from the sacked Johnny Carey in 1961. Billy Bingham, Bobby Collins, Alex Young, Roy Vernon and Jimmy Fell are pictured in training.

The Golden Vision in full flight. Alex Young leaps over the despairing challenge of Cardiff City centre-half Danny Molloy in April 1961. Everton won 5-1, Young scoring two and Bobby Collins a hat-trick.

Opposite page: A nice action shot of goalkeeper Albert Dunlop, who made 231 appearances between 1956 and 1963.

Everton's 'Little General' Bobby Collins was a bundle of dynamite for the Blues in 147 appearances, scoring 48 goals. He left Goodison for Leeds in 1962 and is seen here waving goodbye at Lime Street Station. He proved as inspirational at Elland Road as he had been at Goodison, being named Footballer of the Year in 1965.

Three heads are better than one ...Brian Harris, Jimmy Gabriel and Brian Labone leap in the snow during a 1961 training stint.

ALEX YOUNG – MILLENNIUM GIANT
1960-1970

WHEN fans look back on glory days past, it is easy to get misty-eyed about so-called heroes and legends. Sometimes, their real ability seems to grow in stature with every passing year as memories fade while imaginations become more intense.

When I was a young boy, the legend of the immortal Dixie Dean had reached such fever pitch that I was told by my father that the great man could head the ball into the opposing area from the halfway line. Dean was, without doubt, the undisputed king of the air and a genuine Roy of the Rovers figure, but no one could head the ball that distance, even if he had wanted to. I use the the example to demonstrate that there is a fine line between fact and folklore.

I therefore try to keep a sense of reality when people ask me about great players who I was fortunate to see in action at their peak. One of these was Alex Young - the Golden Vision. His nickname is enough to conjure up images of a

FACTFILE

Born: Loanhead, 1937.
Everton appearances: 271.
Everton goals: 87.
Everton honours:
Football League Championship winner: 1962-63.
FA Cup winner: 1966.
Charity Shield winner: 1963.
Full Scotland caps: 8 total (2 with Everton).

magician in a football jersey, weaving his spell in front of his adoring fans.

But just how good was he? When the question is asked, I answer it in a simple terms, but I trust it gets the message over. I don't have to remember individual games and particular goals to revel in the memory of Alex. It is enough to recall in broader terms his impact during the 1962-63 Championship winning season in which he was an ever-present and scored 22 goals.

I can remember as a 14 years old standing on the Gwladys Street terraces with my Evertonian pal Mal Smith, the pair of us mesmerised by the skill and – dare I say it – the vision of this blond genius. We would look at each other after an instinctive moment of genius and tears of sheer joy would be in our eyes. Yes, we were at an impressionable age. Yes, we were like disciples of a religious sect, wanting to be brain-washed by the sheer quality of our number one soccer hero. But for a player to inspire such emotion tells you instinctively that he was a true great.

Everton have possibly had better players. They might have had more consistent individuals. Those being constructively critical would point out that Alex saved his best for hallowed ground at Goodison, but didn't travel particularly well. They might have been correct. But that simple fact that Young inspired me like no other Everton player before or since, albeit in fleeting moments of unmatchable skill, earned him my Millennium Giants vote for the 1960s.

Young was signed from Hearts on November 23, 1960 in a £55,000 deal that also brought full-back George Thompson to Goodison. Johnny Carey was the manager who secured his signature, significantly beating off overtures from Preston North End's Cliff Britton who was a former Everton player and manager!

Alex immediately won over the fans with his guile and class. After his debut against Spurs on December 17, 1960, the Echo reported: "Young is a thoroughbred, a great mover with the ball, fast, active and razor sharp in his reactions. For his size, he is a good header of the ball. He is artistic, clever and can score goals."

Thus, Alex Young was summed up perfectly. His first goals for the Blues, a well-taken double, came in March 1961 at Blackburn (who said Alex couldn't play away!). Roy Vernon scored the other goal that day in an emphatic 3-1 win. Here was the perfect partnership, all movement and subtlety, masking the fact that when a chance arose, either player could strike with the speed of a cobra and the accuracy of a slide rule.

Carey would soon be replaced by Harry Catterick, but the team building would go on as chairman John Moores demanded a side capable of winning Championships and Cups. The Blues had a tremendous keeper and character in Gordon West, a rock-solid centre-back in Brian Labone, true grit and sheer inspiration in the midfield areas in the shape of Jimmy Gabriel and Tony Kay and great wingers in Johnny Morrissey and Alex Scott (who replaced another great wide man in Billy Bingham).

But Alex was the folk hero. He once told me: "I drew my inspiration from the crowd. There were times when I had out-of-this-world games, matches in which everything I attempted turned to gold, duels in which, with a minimum of effort, I ran rings around defenders and laid on goals for my colleagues in the Everton attack."

Just as quickly the honesty which was also a part of Young's make-up leads him to admit: "There were other times when I exasperated myself and must have stretched the patience of manager Harry Catterick."

Star player and strict disciplinarian boss never really hit it off. Young simply made up his mind to play for the supporters – and what a relationship that was.

It is impossible to write about Alex without explaining his famous nickname. On Wednesday, 13 April 1968, the Liverpool Echo's television page declared: "Tonight is Everton night, so Blue you might even think you have colour television. The Golden Vision will unfold on your screens. Written by Neville Smith in partnership with ITN newscaster Gordon Honeycombe, the BBC1 production covers a week in the life of Everton FC, its players and fans. The Golden Vision is Alex Young and the play centres on the men whose chief obsession is football in general and Everton in particular.

"They eat, sleep and drink football and their wives and girlfriends are inexorably involved in the endless soccer discussions and preparations for Saturday."

Incredibly, even as The Golden Vision was being broadcast, Alex Young had played his last ever game at Goodison Park although we didn't know it at the time. Three days later he would return to the side after a 12-game absence for a clash at Sheffield Wednesday, a goalless draw.

He would be left out at home to Chelsea, come on as a substitute in a defeat at Nottingham Forest, drop out again against Manchester City and Stoke and then make his last ever appearance in the royal blue – fittingly wearing the number nine – at West Ham. It was a 1-1 draw, Jimmy Husband getting Everton's goal.

When the Blues played their final game of the season, at home to Fulham, supporters were bitterly disappointed that Young was again sidelined. We would never see him again.

In the August of 1968, at the age of 31, Alex became player-manager of Irish club Glentoran. Ironically, I had achieved a personal ambition that very same day when, as a young journalist working for a local weekly paper, I interviewed him at Bellefield for the first time. He told me about his great memories, his frustrations at losing his place, his dreams of one day becoming a manager. What he couldn't tell me was that he had already signed the Glentoran contract and was waiting for it to be made official.

"I found out the following day as I was heading home, my interview about to go to press. I saw an Echo billboard outside Central Station declaring: EVERTON TRANSFER GOLDEN VISION.

" I had to race 15 miles to my office to change the story and managed it with minutes to spare. Alex would later apologise and explain that he simply couldn't reveal the full details of his impending move at the time, although he went some way by emphasising his managerial dreams."

I simply shook his hand and thanked him for everything he had done for the Evertonians who adored him. His Irish sojourn would last just two months. He would finish his career in the unglamorous surroundings of Stockport's Edgeley Park.

I preferred to remember this football aristocrat in royal blue, inspiring journalists to wax lyrical in his honour. One scribe declared: "Not for Young the storm-tossed battles of brawn and ill-will. He brought a fluency, grace and charm to football, but for all that he possessed a vicious shot and a heading ability way above average."

Hail the Golden Vision.

Alex Young wasn't very tall, but he had a tremendous spring. Here he challenges Manchester United goalkeeper Gaskell for a high centre in April 1962, a 1-1 draw.

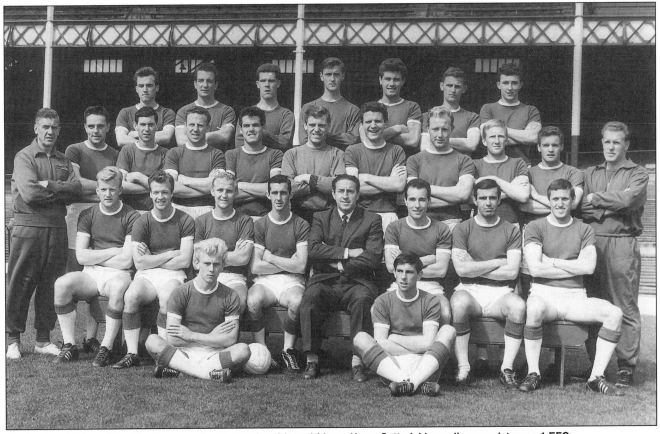

September 1962, and the Everton squad with genuine title ambitions. Harry Catterick's car licence plate was 1 EFC.

The title beckons in May 1963. Everton beat Bolton 1-0 at Goodison with only three games left. Roy Vernon, the scorer, is seen testing Eddie Hopkinson who managed to deflect this shot wide.

Vernon Makes It V-Day

Saturday, 11 May 1963
Everton 4 Fulham 1

MANAGER Harry Catterick picked up an interesting Christmas present in December 1962. It was a new licence plate with the legend 1 EFC.

It was his way of saying that there was only one team in the country worth following in the ensuing months. Harry knew what he was talking about. Because on Saturday, 11 May 1963 the Blues stood on the verge of their first League Championship success since season 1938-39.

Fulham arrived on Merseyside like lambs to the slaughter. Everton needed two points to make certain of that title

crown and nothing was going to stop them in that final game of the season.

Tottenham, chasing the Blues all the way, had sent a message to their London rivals suggesting that a little bit of capital pride would not go amiss. But the Merseysiders – and skipper Roy Vernon in particular – were to prove unstoppable.

Naturally, there was a certain amount of tension before the kick-off. Full-back Alex Parker recalls that Tony Kay tried to hide his nerves by singing as loudly as he could. Vernon was cracking jokes non-stop, while Alex Young just sat there saying absolutely nothing.

Catterick's men had finished the season at a sprint. Prior to the Fulham

clash they had won six of their previous eight games, drawing the other two at home. In doing so, they had overtaken Tottenham and Leicester in the race for the line. Now they stood just 90 minutes from glory.

Fulham, though, could not be ignored. Their side featured top-class goalkeeper Tony Macedo, England's first £100 a week footballer Johnny Haynes and former England international wing-half Bobby Robson. As it turned out, all the stars on the day were wearing royal blue shirts.

Liverpool Echo reporter Michael Charters summed up the scenes at Goodison perfectly in the wake of a resounding 4-1 victory, inspired by a Vernon hat-trick. He wrote: *Has there ever been an atmosphere, an excitement, a thrill sportswise in Liverpool to equal that at Goodison?*

Old-timers, having seen the great football moments in this city over the past four decades, say there has been nothing like it since Dixie Dean broke the goalscoring record in 1928 in the last match of the season on the same pitch.

Over 60,000 delirious fans saluted the Blues on the final whistle and there were roars of laughter when a loudspeaker announcement, in giving the results of the Tottenham and Leicester games, commented: "Now let's see who could be the runners-up!"

Everton won the game with an outstanding first-half display. They were two up inside eight minutes, thanks to the accurate shooting of the matchless Vernon. The first came when he won possession on the edge of the area, speeding on to draw out Macedo before beating him with his swerve and pace – slotting an angled shot into the back of the net.

Fulham were soon reeling. Vernon chased an Alex Parker clearance with defender Mullery ahead of him and favourite to touch the ball back to his goalkeeper. Instead, the player struck the ball too hard and it rebounded off the 'keeper into the path of the marauding Vernon. He drew Macedo over to the right before scoring from almost the same position as the first goal.

Alex Young, Everton's acclaimed Golden Vision, was having a wonderful match. His heading, distribution and artistry had the visitors in all kinds of trouble. But Fulham

Everton's 1963 Championship triumph was wrapped up with a memorable 4-1 triumph over Fulham, inspired by a Roy Vernon treble. The elated Gwladys Street faithful roar themselves hoarse.

Harry Catterick left the Championship celebration dinner in 1963 to drive north of the border and capture Partick Thistle's Sandy Brown for £38,000. Brown played in every position for the Blues, even taking the goalkeeper's jersey on one occasion when Gordon West was sent off. But Sandy scored a famous own-goal in a derby game against Liverpool and even now local Sunday League players are likely to refer to an 'og' as a 'Sandy Brown'.

How the title was won. This 1963 *Liverpool Echo* cartoon strip tells the story of the final day.

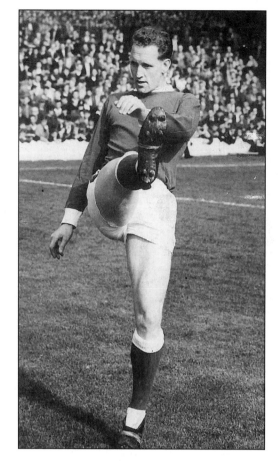

managed to reduce the arrears when Haynes and Robson linked superbly to enable outside-right Key to volley past Albert Dunlop, an end of season deputy for the injured Gordon West.

But with Tony Kay and Jimmy Gabriel moving forward at every opportunity to support the attack, Everton were soon pounding the Fulham defence once more. Dennis Stevens had the ball in the net from a clever Young header, but the referee had blown moments earlier for a foul by Keetch on Young.

It didn't matter because the Blues promptly scored from the resulting free-kick. Vernon's initial shot rebounded to Alex Scott and his low shot struck a Fulham player en-route to the back of the net to make it 3-1. The fans were breathless, having witnessed four goals in 28 minutes. It would be five minutes from time before Fulham were finally finished off.

A long clearance from Dunlop was headed through by the immaculate Young. Vernon once again beat Mullery in a close challenge for the ball, drew Macedo to the right and then sent an angled shot through the narrow gap into the corner of the net. The Championship celebrations now began in earnest.

A ring of policemen ensured there would be no wholesale pitch invasion. It meant the team could make the traditional lap of honour, cheered every inch of the way. The *Liverpool Echo* reported that it was shattering, ear-shaking approval for the Everton team and management who had come through in the home straight to take 20 out of the last 24 points.

Having saluted the players, the fans now turned their attention to the directors' box, chanting: 'We want John Moores.'

The chairman had lost his hat when he threw it high in the air after Everton's second goal. He acknowledged the cheers and then the players joined him in the Main Stand, still in their playing strip, but clutching bottles of champagne. Tony Kay, all dash and power and aggression on the pitch, was puffing on a giant cigar, the kind Winston Churchill would have been proud of.

The Cup that cheers… Everton director Mr Holland Hughes formally receives the 1963 Championship trophy at the League's annual meeting in London.

The crowd were delighted and only calmed down long enough for skipper Vernon to make a short speech. The mutual respect between players and fans was there for all to see. It was time for everyone to wend their way home, manager Catterick climbing into his car, registration number 1 EFC.

It was a four-wheeled League table, a Champion Chariot. The 'Cat' was the proudest man in England.

Everton: Dunlop; Parker, Meagan, Gabriel, Labone, Kay, Scott, Stevens, Young, Vernon, Temple.
Attendance: 60,578

Above: Everton's 1963 Championship captain Roy Vernon with another Goodison title-winning skipper, the legendary Dixie Dean.

Top: Tony Kay was a red-haired tiger who cost Everton £55,000 when they signed him from Sheffield Wednesday in November 1962. He immediately helped to inspire a Championship success, but found himself caught up in a major soccer bribes scandal in 1965, linked with his Hillsborough days. He was subsequently banned for life.

Right: The 1962-63 title is in the bag and Harry Catterick toasts the crowd in champagne from the Main Stand. Tony Kay, by his side, is smoking a big cigar. The rest celebrate in a more straightforward manner, including Jimmy Gabriel, Derek Temple, Albert Dunlop (deputising for the injured Gordon West), Brian Labone, Alex Parker, Alex Scott and Alex Young.

Everton crushed
Manchester United
4-0 at Goodison to
take the FA
Charity Shield in
1963 with goals
from Gabriel,
Stevens, Temple
and Vernon. A
delighted Vernon
holds up the
Shield with John
Moores.

Dennis Stevens
was an ever-
present in the
1962-63 title
success. He is
seen scoring in
the subsequent FA
Charity Shield
victory over
Manchester United
at Goodison.

Milan Maestros Hit Town

Wednesday, 18 September 1963
Everton 0 Inter-Milan 0

EVERTON played in the Champions Cup for the first time in 1963 after an outstanding title-winning campaign on the home front. Their first opponents in the European Cup were famous Italians, Inter-Milan, who came to Goodison suggesting that their first-leg tactics would be based on out-and-out defence.

Legendary coach Helenio Herrera said as much in his pre-match Press conference, but it was nothing more than a clever confidence trick.

Milan stepped out in front of 62,000 fans to play a superb attacking game in the first half and while they packed their defence when they needed to, the emphasis was on swift and decisive attacking breaks that thrilled the crowd.

The Italians were precise in everything they did. Everton were never allowed to gain the upper hand and the resulting goalless draw suited the visitors down to the ground.

Inter had a magnificent centre-back in Guarneri and he overshadowed home favourite Alex Young, helped by deep-lying left-half Picchi. The numbers on the backs of the visiting defenders were meaningless. They move around fluently, plugging gaps and playing themselves out of trouble with a calm assurance and genuine skill. It was a highly impressive display.

World-renowned inside-left Suarez collected the ball from his defence and sent crisp, accurate passes cutting through the home defence. This free-flowing player stamped his authority on the game and earned the admiration of the appreciative Goodison fans. But the biggest danger came from flying winger Jair, who got more shots in than any other player. Brian Harris did well to contain him as much as he did.

For their part, Everton's forwards struggled to break down the solid Inter defence. The normally influential Roy Vernon failed to make an impact on the proceedings, shadowed constantly by right-half Tagnin. At the same time, wingers Derek Temple and Alex Scott were well-marshalled by Faccetti and Burgnich.

Everton met Italian giants Inter-Milan in the first round of the European Cup in September 1963. Roy Vernon goes close in the goalless first leg, but is thwarted by goalkeeper Sarti.

Inter Milan goalkeeper Sarti leaps high to deny Alex Young as he tried to reach a Jimmy Gabriel centre during the European Cup, first-round, first-leg game at Goodison in 1963. There was a major selection surprise in the return when a San Siro Stadium baptism of fire was handed to a young Colin Harvey. The Blues lost 1-0, but a famous Goodison career was under way.

Everton's only success story on the night was in defence where Brian Labone and Alex Parker played particularly well.

To be fair, Parker had no winger to mark and so effectively had the freedom of the field on the right. He was able to push well forward and produced Everton's best shot of the night. Jimmy Gabriel moved into the attack in the second half, but even his heading ability and thrust failed to trouble the Italians too much.

Tony Kay was full of fire and his tackling was ferocious at times. He had his name taken, apparently for treading on Suarez's hand.

Inter were given an ovation from the crowd at the end. They had almost stolen victory at the death when Suarez sent Jair racing through with a 40-yard pass. Only a last-ditch tackle by Harris saved the day.

Everton's failure to snatch a goal meant that the return in the imposing San Siro Stadium was virtually a foregone conclusion. But the Italians were quick to salute the Goodison crowd. One report said: The way they sportingly applauded the Milan players at the end stamped them as real gentlemen.

Everton: West; Parker, Harris, Gabriel, Labone, Kay, Scott, Stevens, Young, Vernon, Temple.

Attendance: 62,000

Factfile: Inter-Milan duly won the return 1-0. From Everton's point of view, the night was significant for one thing. A youngster named Colin Harvey was thrust into the San Siro cauldron and acquitted himself superbly. It was the start of a famous career for one of Goodison's favourite sons.

As the 1963-64 season drew to a close with a home game against West Ham, there was once again no place in the side for Goodison idol Alex Young. 'Sack Catterick, keep Young', was the message from one supporter who is led away by a policeman. Catterick seemed to be vindicated when Fred Pickering, wearing the Golden Vision's number nine shirt, scored twice in a 2-0 win. But 18 months later there would be a more serious sequel when Catterick was kicked by fans in a disgraceful incident at Blackpool after once again overlooking Young's claims. This time he had given a shock debut to a 16-year-old local boy, Joe Royle. Young would bounce straight back and go on to help Everton win the FA Cup that year, but it's worth noting that Royle eventually became one of the greatest Everton centre-forwards of all time.

Far left: Roy Vernon goes in to challenge Leeds United goalkeeper Gary Sprake at Goodison in 1964.

Left: Fred Pickering was a powerhouse centre-forward, signed by Everton from Blackburn in 1964. He scored a hat-trick on his England debut against the United States in a 10-0 victory, but was involved in a sensation in 1966 when he was left out of Everton's Cup Final side. As it turned out, the man who replaced him, Mike Trebilcock, proved to be a two-goal Wembley hero.

Below: It looks as if Liverpool's giant skipper Ron Yeats has delivered a karate chop to fell Everton's Alex Scott in this derby clash in February 1964. In fact, Scott had just shot narrowly wide in a 3-1 victory.

Roy Vernon was a lethal penalty-taker as Manchester United goalkeeper David Gaskell found to his cost in 1963-64.

The man signing out is Mick Meagan, bound for Huddersfield in July 1964. The man on the way in, standing, is England's Ray Wilson, who went on to play for England in the 1966 World Cup Final. He was possibly the greatest left-back Everton have ever had.

Little and Large, but no laughing matter The clock shows 3.40pm and rival skippers Brian Labone and Leeds United's ex-Blue Bobby Collins walk from the Goodison pitch after the referee stopped an explosive game. Everton's Sandy Brown had been sent off after only four minutes. An Evertonian encroached on the pitch and had to be restrained by Johnny Morrissey as he exchanged angry words with Billy Bremner and Norman Hunter. Sanity eventually prevailed and play resumed, Leeds finishing 1-0 winners.

Everton chairman Mr Holland Hughes met the players prior to the 1965-66 season and asked them to 'snooker' all-comers in the year ahead. Alex Young, Jimmy Gabriel and Brian Labone look on.

Opposite page, top: Jimmy Gabriel leaps above teammate Jimmy Husband to head Everton's equaliser in a 2-2 draw with Blackburn in October 1965.

Opposite page, bottom: An early goal from Jimmy Gabriel, Everton's powerhouse wing-half, helped inspire a 3-1 win over Spurs in October 1965.

Everton beat Nuremberg 2-1 on aggregate in the first round of the 1965-66 Inter-Cities Fairs Cup. The team are pictured leaving for the airport from Goodison for the 1-1 first leg. Left to right: Fred Pickering and Johnny Morrissey (on the bus), Dennis Stevens, Sandy Brown, Jimmy Gabriel, Derek Temple, Gordon West, Andy Rankin, Tommy Wright, Colin Harvey, Ray Wilson and a pipe-smoking Brian Harris. Note the ground entry price of four shillings (20p).

Brian Harris raises his arms in delight as he sees Derek Temple's goal give Everton a 2-0 lead in the fifth-round FA Cup tie against Coventry at Goodison in 1966.

Cup training in January 1966, prior to the third-round clash with Sunderland. Leapfrog partners are Alex Young, Colin Harvey, Brian Harris, Brian Labone, Alex Scott, Sandy Brown, Derek Temple and Fred Pickering.

On the rails to FA Cup glory in 1966. Manager Harry Catterick and coach Tom Eggleston head for London with the team for the Final battle with Sheffield Wednesday.

Everton's FA Cup Final appearance in 1966 inspired this reunion of members of the 1933 Cup-winning side. Back (left to right): Jimmy Stein, Albert Geldard, Billy Cook, Jock Thomson. Front: Tommy White, Ted Sagar and Dixie Dean.

The FA Cup has been won in 1966 and the players parade the trophy along Scotland Road in an open-top bus.

World-Class Memories of Pelé, Eusebio And Gallant North Korea

WHEN the World Cup Finals came to England in 1966, it went without saying that Goodison Park would be one of the venues. Brazil, Bulgaria, Hungary and Portugal featured in Group Three matches on Merseyside, and Goodison also staged a truly sensational quarter-final clash in which the gallant North Koreans played their part and the semi-final between the Soviet Union and West Germany.

These were exciting times for the soccer-mad public of Liverpool with legendary stars like Pelé and Eusebio treading a very impressive Goodison stage. The old Main Stand, with its vast standing enclosure below was an awe-inspiring sight when it was packed.

A feature that hits you when you view aerial pictures from 1966 is the presence of the two D-shaped safety rings behind each goal which prevented missiles being launched the way of unsuspecting goal-keepers. In the first instance there were three matches, each with a very special appeal.

World Champions Show Their Age

12 July 1966
Brazil 2 Bulgaria 0

BRAZIL, the pride of South America and the World Champions, were given Goodison Park as their base for their three opening matches, but the famous team was beginning to show its age.

Two stars of the 1958 World Cup winning team had been recalled in Orlando and Bellini. They joined vastly experienced individuals like Djalmar Santos and Garrincha in a side that was a strange mix of men possibly past their best linked with thrilling new talent. Of course, Pelé was a class act and there were others with wonderful ability, like Tostao, Gerson and flying winger Jairzinho.

No wonder the Merseyside fans flocked in their thousands to Goodison to see Brazil begin with a clash against Bulgaria. Alas, the cynicism of the Bulgarian defenders helped to ruin the game as a spectacle. Pelé was involved in a running battle with his marker Zhechev.

Instead of concentrating on his own

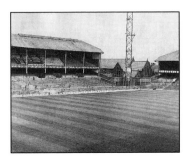

strengths, the Brazilian ace allowed himself to be side-tracked and he was guilty of one or two niggling fouls of his own. In this tit-for-tat atmosphere, the Bulgarian was always going to have the final say and he cut down his opponent with a tackle that infuriated the 5,000 Brazilians in the crowd. Pelé, writhing in agony on the Goodison turf, would now miss the next match through injury.

Earlier, he had scored the first goal of the 1966 tournament when he bent a superb free-kick wide of Bulgarian 'keeper Naidenov. It was an historic moment, the player becoming the first player to score in three successive tournaments.

Garrincha was also playing in the Finals for the third time and he increased Brazil's lead after 63 minutes, also with a swerving free-kick. But despite their winning start, it was clear that this was not the Brazil of previous years.

Brazil: Gilmar; D.Santos, Bellini, Altair, Paulo Henrique, Denilson, Lima, Garrincha, Pelé, Alcindo, Jairzinho.

Bulgaria: Naidenov; Shalamanov, Vutzov, Gaganelov, Penev, Kitov, Zhechev, Yakimov, Dermendyev, Asparoukhov, Kolev.

Attendance: 52,847

Hungary's first goal against Brazil at Goodison in 1966. Goalkeeper Gilmar is grounded, well beaten by Bene's shot.

Goodison Glory For Magical Magyars

15 July 1966
Hungary 3 Brazil 1

BRAZIL kicked-off their second Goodison game without Pelé, but they were able to replace him with the talented Tostao. The stylish Gerson also came into the side. The rain poured down on an overcast Merseyside afternoon, but the football was of the highest class.

Hungary's display was said to be reminiscent of the glory years of 1953 when they had the likes of Puskas and Hidegkuti in their ranks, players who had helped crush England for the first time at Wembley. The new Hungary had a real star in Florian Albert, whose running and passing had the Brazilians in all kinds of trouble.

Brazil were down after only three minutes when Bene claimed a loose pass,

176

Brazil's Jair tries a flying header at the Hungarian goal, but his effort is saved by goalkeeper Gelei.

Farkas of Hungary raises his arms in delight after scoring his side's second against Brazil in a shock 3-1 victory in the 1966 World Cup.

racing through to claim a fine goal. Tostao equalised after 14 minutes when a Lima free-kick rebounded to him, but Hungary carved open a superb chance after 63 minutes when Albert found Bene and the winger crossed for Farkas to volley home.

Ten minutes from time, Meszoly converted a penalty to make it 3-1 and inflict upon Brazil their first World Cup defeat since 1954. The fans had turned up to Goodison to marvel at the Brazilians, but they went home saluting Albert & Co, and the magical Magyars.

Hungary: Gelei; Kaposzta, Matrai, Sipos, Szepesi, Mathesz, Meszoly, Bene, Albert, Farkas, Rakosi.

Brazil: Gilmar, D.Santos, Bellini, Altair, Paulo Henrique, Lima, Gerson, Garrincha, Alcindo, Tostao, Jairzinho.

Attendance: 57,455

The Black Pearl Crushes Brazil

19 July 1966
Portugal 3 Brazil 1

BRAZIL now made no fewer than nine changes in a bold bid to stay in the competition, giving World Cup debuts to seven players. It was the ultimate gamble, not least because Pelé was not fully fit.

The experienced Gilmar was replaced in goal by Mangar and Portugal, inspired by the man they called the Black Pearl, stormed into a 2-0 interval lead. Eusebio of Benfica displayed pace, power and class, while Pelé was reduced to a limping passenger, once again hacked out of it by some vicious tackles.

Portugal swept in front after 14 minutes when Manga pushed a Eusebio cross straight to Simoes, who headed home. Eusebio himself made it 2-0 when he headed home a Coluna free-kick, glanced on by Torres.

Rildo reduced the arrears after 72 minutes, but the unstoppable Eusebio rifled in a shot from a corner five minutes from time to take his side into the quarter-finals.

The disenchanted Pelé suggested that he never wanted to play in another World Cup game because of the disgraceful tackling of some of his rivals, but four years later he would produce the best football of his career in Mexico.

Portugal: Pereira; Morais, Baptista, Vicente, Hilano, Graca, Coluna, Augusto, Eusebio, Torres, Simoes.

Brazil: Manga; Fidelis, Brito, Orlando, Rildo, Denilson, Lima, Jairzhinho, Silva, Pelé, Parana.

Attendance: 62,204

Goodison World Cup Classic

23 July 1966
Portugal 5 North Korea 3

THE fans at Goodison Park were now party to a quarter-final tie that captured the imagination of the whole world. The Koreans, playing in Group Four, had caused a sensation at Ayresome Park, Middlesbrough, by beating Italy 1-0.

Now they faced Portugal at Goodison Park, still the underdogs, but with their confidence soaring. The people inside the Everton ground that day were left open-mouthed as the Koreans stormed into a 3-0 lead with the game only 22 minutes old.

Pak Seung-zin scored in the opening minute with a left-foot shot from the edge of the box. Dong-woon tapped in the second after Pereira misjudged a cross. Seung-kook grabbed the third and Eusebio and his teammates looked down and out.

But the great man now took charge himself to launch a remarkable revival. Eusebio made it 3-1 after 27 minutes, then reduced the arrears further from the penalty spot.

Ten minutes into the second half he completed his hat-trick with a cracking shot from the edge of the six-yard box. And with the crowd on their toes, he put Portugal in front for the first time with his second penalty.

The brave Koreans were finally beaten 12 minutes from the end when Augusto turned home a corner-kick, inevitably swerved in by Eusebio. It had been a day the fans inside Goodison would never forget. The atmosphere was thrilling, the action spell-binding and the occasion as colourful as you will get.

Portugal: Pereira; Morais, Baptista, Vicente, Hilano, Graca, Coluna, Augusto, Eusebio, Tores, Simoes.

North Korea: Chan-myung; Zoong-sun, Yung-kyoo, Yung-won, Yoon-kyung, Seung-zin, Seung-hwi, Bong-jin, Doo-ik, Dong-woon, Seung-kook.

Attendance: 51,780

One of the most famous images of the 1966 World Cup — Eusebio is sent sprawling against the North Koreans. This famous picture was taken by award-winning *Liverpool Echo* photographer Stephen Shakeshaft.

Beckenbauer At His Magical Best

25 July 1966
West Germany 2 Soviet Union 1

GOODISON staged the semi-final between West Germany and the Soviet Union but it lacked the excitement of the thrilling Portugal-North Korea quarter-final.

The Russian defence was solid and famous goalkeeper Lev Yashin was in fine form, but Haller opened the scoring for the Germans a minute before the interval, following a fine cross from Schnellinger.

The Russians then had Chislenko sent off and were reduced to nine fit men for much of the second half with Sabo injured.

Beckenbauer provided the killer touch after 68 minutes with a shot that deceived Yashin and, although Porkuan reduced the arrears, the Germans were now set for a Final date with England.

West Germany: Tilkowski; Lutz, Weber, Schulz, Schnellinger, Beckenbauer, Halle, Overath, Seeler, Held, Emmerich.

Soviet Union: Yashin; Ponomarev, Shesterniev, Veronin, Danilov, Sabo, Khusainov, Chislenko, Banichevski, Malafeev, Porkujan.

Attendance: 43,291

Famous Russian goalkeeper Lev Yashin dives out to block a shot from West Germany's Uwe Seeler in the World Cup semi-final at Goodison, a 2-1 win for the Germans.

The Ultimate Trophy Parade

Roger Hunt and Ray Wilson show off the World Cup at Goodison in 1966.

13 August 1966
Everton 0 Liverpool 1

THIS Charity Shield confrontation was significant, not so much for the match itself, as the fact that three of the game's most famous trophies were paraded the length and breadth of Goodison Park, not least the Jules Rimet Trophy which had been won so gloriously by new World Champions England just two weeks earlier. Over 63,000 supporters, bedecked in blue and red, converged on Goodison Road to salute Merseyside's Big Two.

They were party to a remarkable lap of honour that took place 20 minutes before the kick-off. England teammates Ray Wilson of Everton and Roger Hunt of Liverpool carried the World Cup between them or rather the solid gold statuette that was named after a former FIFA president.

Blues' skipper Brian Labone paraded the FA Cup and Reds' captain Ron Yeats the League Championship trophy. It was a truly remarkable sight and one which emphasised that the city of Liverpool was undoubtedly the soccer capital of England.

When the action finally got under way, the men from Anfield looked that little bit sharper and they grabbed the lead after five minutes through Hunt. Thompson started the move in the inside-right channel, feinting to deliver a shot and then edging the ball a few yards to his teammate. Hunt hammered the ball into the top corner of the net to make it 1-0.

Soon afterwards, a glorious pass from Alex Young played Alex Scott in, but although the winger got the ball past the 'keeper, he lost his footing and the visitors cleared.

Liverpool gave their opponents few opportunities to bounce back.

It meant the game was never a classic, although Young, Everton's Golden Vision, made a tremendous run down the right in the closing stages before hoisting in a centre that was claimed by Tommy Lawrence. In the end, Liverpool were good value for their victory.

The occasion is worth recalling from an Everton point of view, simply because of the ultimate Goodison Park trophy parade. It really was a sight to savour.

Everton: West; Wright, Wilson, Gabriel, Labone, Glover, Scott, Young, Trebilcock, Harvey, Temple.

Liverpool: Lawrence; Lawler, Byrne, Smith, Yeats, Stevenson, Callaghan, Hunt, St John, Strong, Thompson.

Attendance: 63,329

The FA Cup holders Everton and Champions Liverpool met in League action at Goodison in August 1966. Alex Young slips past Tommy Lawrence, only to shoot wide. The Blues still managed a 3-1 victory with two goals from Alan Ball and another from Sandy Brown.

Above: Jimmy Gabriel drives the ball between Newcastle 'keeper Marshall and right-back Craggs to earn Everton a 1-1 home draw in October 1966. Gabriel was a fierce competitor who always liked to go forward.

Opposite page: A unique trophy parade delighted the fans watching the FA Charity Shield confrontation at Goodison in August 1966. Everton's Brian Labone lapped the pitch with the FA Cup alongside Liverpool skipper Ron Yeats carrying the Championship trophy. England's Roger Hunt and Ray Wilson followed behind with the Jules Rimet World Cup Trophy .

Left: June 1969 and half of the old Main Stand has been demolished to reveal the houses behind. These properties were standing in 1892 when the ground was opened and were a familiar sight to the early Goodison pioneers.

Goodison snow scene in February 1968. The fifth-round FA Cup tie against Bristol Rovers had to be called off. Ironically, the sun was shining down in Bristol.

Everton played in the European Cup-winners' Cup in 1966-67, beating Aalborg 2-1 on aggregate in the first round. Alan Ball is pictured cracking home a close-range winner at Goodison. The Blues lost in the next round to Real Zaragoza.

A 1966 view of Everton's original undersoil heating system of wires. It caused drainage problems and had to be lifted.

Everton cracked open the champagne after an Alan Ball goal at Goodison knocked Liverpool out of the FA Cup fifth round on 11 March 1967. Back row (left to right): Tommy Eggleston, Ray Wilson, Johnny Morrissey, Colin Harvey, Alex Young, Derek Temple. Front: John Hurst, Brian Labone, Ball, Tommy Wright, Jimmy Husband and manager Harry Catterick. Howard Kendall, having just signed in from Preston for £80,000, watched the tie from the stands. Sadly, the side lost 3-2 to Forest in the sixth round.

Howard Kendall on his Everton debut against Southampton in March 1967. What an influence he would become over the next few years.

Opposite page, top: Jimmy Husband chases a loose ball against Chelsea at Goodison in 1967-68. Nicknamed Skippy because of his distinctive running style, Husband became one of the most unorthodox strikers in the League and scored 55 goals for Everton.

Opposite page, bottom: Everton have had few better servants than Colin Harvey, seen here scoring past Stoke City's famous England 'keeper Gordon Banks in a 2-1 win in October 1968.

Great pals, magnificent teammates. . Brian Labone and goalkeeper Gordon West team up for a Bellefield wheelbarrow race in the late 1960s.

Brian Labone was a model centre-half with the added ingredient of being one of the biggest Evertonians in the business. He played for the Blues over 15 seasons, an outstanding captain, a quality England international and as dedicated a club man as you will get with 530 Everton appearances under his belt between 1957 and 1972.

Johnny Morrissey was a skilful winger with a touch of real steel. Defenders were actually scared of him, not the other way round. Johnny's face says it all as he gives two Southampton defenders a tough time in December 1968, John Hurst inspiring a 1-0 home win.

A dramatic night shot, taken through the framework of the Main Stand when the new floodlights were tested in August 1970.

Champions And Entertainers

Wednesday, 1 April 1970
Everton 2 West Brom 0

EVERTON clinched the Championship in style in a game in which they ran the show from midfield, inspired by the legendary Ball-Harvey-Kendall triumvirate. One could only feel sorry for Albion, who had to try and make a game of it in the emotion-charged atmosphere of Goodison Park.

The Blues performance was full of the brilliance that had mesmerised teams the length and breadth of the country in the preceding months. It was fitting that they should clinch the title in the last home game of the season, handing out a football lesson to their unfortunate rivals.

Everton produced two goals on the night, but it could so easily have been a bagful. John Osborne in the Albion goal had a splendid match, which was just as well for the outclassed visitors.

Harry Catterick's men took 13 minutes or so to settle down, clearly feeling the tension of the occasion. But they soon moved into overdrive and never looked back.

With total control in midfield, the Blues dominated for 90 per cent of the game. Johnny Morrissey, strong and direct on the left, had one of his best games of the season and ripped the Albion defence to shreds.

Alan Whittle defied his comparative inexperience with another dashing display of front running, getting on the scoresheet for the sixth successive game. Joe Royle, a centre-forward in the finest Everton tradition, also played his part. Here was a team with class in every department.

November 1969, and Everton already lead the table with just one defeat in 17 games. They extended the run with a 1-0 home win over Forest. Jimmy Husband makes a spectacular leap over the fallen Hennessey. The ball rebounded off the Forest man and Tommy Wright plundered the match-winner.

Goodison Park during the 1969-70 season.

Roger Kenyon was commanding at centre-back, doing a tremendous job in the continued absence of injured skipper Brian Labone. Tommy Wright and Sandy Brown were also comfortably in control on those rare occasions when Albion threatened.

Goalkeeper Gordon West, always a crowd favourite, only had one save to make, dealing superbly with an effort from Len Cantello. West was as much a spectator as anyone in the 58,523 crowd - the highest attendance of the season. This

would be Everton's seventh successive win, giving them an unassailable nine points lead at the top of the table.

The game was played to a continuous roar of appreciation. It was a classical display of football, speedy, accurate and incisive. Colin Harvey almost scored in the opening moments, but Osborne, produced the first of a series of quality saves.

But he had no chance when Whittle broke the deadlock after 20 minutes with his 11th goal in 15 League games. Harvey

Osborne helpless. What a goal to clinch the title.

The scenes on the final whistle as Everton celebrated their seventh League Championship triumph were remarkable. Manager Catterick was first on to the pitch, throwing an arm around each player in turn as they headed for the dressing-room. With the volume of noise increasing by the second, the players returned for a lap of honour.

Labone, a reluctant spectator during the game itself, now joined his teammates on the pitch and there was a special cheer for the injured skipper. Hundreds of fans now spilled onto the pitch despite appeals for them to remain on the terraces.

The players disappeared to the safety of the dressing-room once more, but soon reappeared in the directors' box where Louis Edwards, chairman of Manchester United and a member of the League Management Committee, presented the trophy which had been collected in a secret trip to Leeds a couple of days earlier. Alan Ball, captain in Labone's absence, received the trophy from Mr Edwards.

Ball had been an inspirational figure throughout a memorable campaign, his competitive spirit, skill and never-say-die approach winning him an army of admirers.

This was the team that should have dominated English football for the next five years. That the side broke up without winning another major trophy remains one of the great mysteries of modern football.

But in 1969-70, Ball & Co reigned

tried to get in a shot from the edge of the area, but mis-hit the ball. Whittle seized control and kept a cool head, unleashing a fierce shot that struck a defender on the way into the roof of the net.

Harvey settled it midway through the half with one of the great goals of the season. The *Liverpool Echo* reported: *He collected the ball way out, took it down the left, turned back in his tracks and lost two of his shadowers at the same time. He brought the ball into the middle and cracked in a shot from 25 yards which left the airborne*

The 1969-70 Championship is won and two captains celebrate after the victory over West Brom. Alan Ball is in contemplative mood and settles for a celebration cup of tea. The injured Brian Labone, who missed the run in through injury, is in more bubbly mood.

supreme, and on that April night, Goodison Park was the stage on which the finest team the Evertonians had seen for many a long year demonstrated that there is no substitute for class.

Everton: West; T.Wright, Brown, Kendall, Kenyon, Harvey, Whittle, Ball, Royle, Hurst, Morrissey.

Attendance: 58,523

Happiness is an FA Charity Shield victory over Chelsea in August 1970. Colin Harvey leads the celebrations after a 2-1 won. Howard Kendall and Alan Whittle were the scorers.

A famous Goodison moment in the European Cup in November, 1970. Goalkeeper Andy Rankin punches the air after denying Borussia Mönchengladbach's Muller in a tense penalty shoot-out. His teammates leap for joy and the ground erupts with 42,000 celebrating victory.

Germans Crushed In Penalty Shoot-Out

4 November 1970
Everton 1
Borussia Mönchengladbach 1
(Everton won on penalties)

EVERTON went into this European Cup, second-round return against Borussia Mönchengladbach, determined to prove their worth as English Champions, despite their disappointing form on the home front.

They had swept to the League Championship seven months earlier, playing football of the very highest class with the famous Ball-Harvey-Kendall midfield combination an inspirational force.

Harry Catterick's men now had the perfect opportunity to re-emphasise their quality on a European stage, having held the German Champions to a 1-1 draw in the away leg with a crucial goal from Kendall.

Prior to this match, the legend persisted that the greatest game ever seen at Goodison was the 6-4 FA Cup replay victory over Sunderland on 30 January 1935. After a thrilling Champions Cup tie, there was a powerful school of thought that this game was the greatest of them all, certainly in terms of drama and nail-biting excitement.

The 42,744 fans lucky enough to be present witnessed a magnificent duel which ended with a thrilling penalty shoot-out in which Everton goalkeeper Andy Rankin was the hero of the hour. The Blues won the spot-kick battle 4-3 after the game had been drawn 1-1 (aggregate 2-2) after 30 minutes of extra-time.

The match began as sensationally as it finished with Morrissey claiming a goal after just 24 seconds. Borussia 'keeper Kleff completely misjudged an orthodox cross from the left winger, the ball skidding off the wet turf and finding the back of the net with the visiting defenders totally stunned.

It was the perfect start, but while Everton had most of the play, carving out chance after chance, the German 'keeper now made a mockery of his schoolboy error by producing a string of world-class saves.

Kleff made two spectacular back-breaking saves to deny Royle in the first half and his goalkeeping wizardry continued when he left Kendall, Morrissey, Husband and Harvey all cursing their luck.

Rankin had been little more than a spectator, but he lost possession after making a fine save from a Laumann header after 34 minutes and the German followed up to equalise on the rebound.

Everton now produced a great team display to try to find a way through with Kendall outstanding in terms of his tackling and passing, Royle brilliant in the air and Hurst sound in central defence.

Everton's European Cup campaign in 1970 began with a home game against no-hopers Keflavik, who took a shock lead. But Alan Ball led a storming revival, claiming this cool equaliser and eventually completing his hat-trick in a 6-2 win. Royle (2) and Kendall also scored and a 3-0 away win increased the aggregate score to 9-2.

Joe Royle was first to go in the shoot-out and Andy Rankin spared his blushes as Everton went through 4-3 on penalties.

Brown and Husband were brought on for the tiring Newton and Whittle to add some fresh zest in the final 30 minutes, but Borussia held on and the whole stadium held its breath as the penalty shoot-out now unfolded.

It started badly for the Blues. Royle, such a force in normal play, saw his kick saved by the inspirational Kleff, who had more than made amends for his earlier blunder. Sielhoff put the Germans ahead, only for Ball to make it 1-1.

Laumann, Borussia's goal hero, now held his head in his hands after pushing his penalty well wide and Everton were back on course. Morrissey put them in front, Heynckes made it 2-2 and Kendall, Koppel and Brown all converted to make it 4-3 with just one kick left.

By now the atmosphere was unbelievable. The whole ground was buzzing and the Goodison roar reached a crescendo as Muller, a great figure in the German defence, stepped up with the thankless task of trying to keep his side in

Factfile: The Blues had beaten Keflavik in the first round, 9-2 on aggregate. They went out in the third round to Greek Champions Panathinaikos on the away goals rule with the aggregate score 1-1.

the game. He hit the ball hard enough, but Rankin dived to his right to push the shot away and he was immediately engulfed by delighted teammates.

The fans were singing in the rain, ecstatic that their side had moved into the third round.

It had been a truly wonderful night and while it's nigh on impossible to say which was the greatest Goodison occasion of them all, this match would certainly take some beating in terms of a fever-pitch finish.

Everton: Rankin; Wright, K.Newton (Brown), Kendall, Kenyon, Harvey, Whittle(Husband), Ball, Royle, Hurst, Morrissey.

Gordon West was a brilliant shot-stopper and a magnificent character to have in the dressing-room. The Everton 'keeper is pictured in action against Sheffield United in August 1971.

Class on the field and a pretty smart team off it. Joe Royle, Henry Newton, Howard Kendall, Brian Labone and John Hurst attend a function in April 1971.

Alan Ball suggests to the photographers that the Blackpool goalkeeper's agony had absolutely nothing to do with him in a goalless draw, April 1971. Ball was a marathon man, a top-class goalscorer, a firebrand and an inspirational leader. Remember the famous white boots, mud-splattered in this instance.

Opposite page, top: Everton crushed Southampton 8-0 in a remarkable Goodison clash in November 1971. The Blues were snow kings for the day, not least Joe Royle who scored four. David Johnson got a hat-trick and Alan Ball completed the rout. Royle is seen causing havoc in the Saints' goal.

Opposite page, bottom: A fine action shot showing the shooting power of Howard Kendall as he scores in a 2-2 draw with Wolves in March 1972.

Colin Harvey had all the qualities of a top-class midfielder. He was supremely mobile, had vision and never shirked a tackle.

BOB LATCHFORD – MILLENNIUM GIANT
1970-1980

THE 1970s were famous for many things. Flared trousers, colourful tank tops, Slade, glam rock and Everton's arch-rivals Liverpool taking Europe by storm.

For the Blues it was a decade that promised everything and provided nothing on the trophy front.

Everton began this ten year period as Champions of the Football League, seemingly on the brink of another golden era. They finished it with nothing else to show for their efforts, other than an appearance in the League Cup Final in 1977. Even that was a losing experience against Aston Villa.

Future generations scanning the record books might believe that there was nothing to cheer the Goodison faithful during this spell. Statistics can't lie, can they?

I'm not going to attempt to try and bull up a spell that was often full of frustration for the Mersey Blues, but at the same time I'm not going to knock it.

There were simply too many good players trying to get the club back on track. Howard Kendall and Colin Harvey were still very much around at the start of this period. The versatile John Hurst was heading towards close on 400 games for the Blues. Joe Royle was still in the picture. Keith Newton and namesake Henry were England players.

Mike Lyons was that rare breed who could play centre-half and centre-forward with equal power and passion. Roger Kenyon was another solid centre-back and John Connolly a skilful winger. Midfielder Martin Dobson, bought for a British transfer record fee of £300,000, was a class act. Andy King scored some memorable goals and fostered a

remarkable relationship with the fans while Mick Pejic arrived to show what tackling was all about. Another rock-solid acquisition was Bruce Rioch who arrived in tandem with a bundle of magic called Duncan McKenzie.

Everton finished fourth in 1975, were beaten in the League Cup Final in a replay against Villa in 1977 and just weeks later were denied a second Wembley appearance of an eventful campaign after controversial referee Clive Thomas inexplicably ruled out a perfectly valid Bryan Hamilton FA Cup semi-final winner against Liverpool at Maine Road, a tie that is now part of Mersey soccer folklore. Everton improved to third in the League in 1978 and fourth in 1979.

The Blues were always so tantalisingly close to reliving the glory game, but inconsistency was their biggest enemy. One man rose above it all to become the definitive hero of this period, significantly an individual who wore the famous number nine that for generations had been the jersey of legends.

Bob Latchford was quite simply one of the leading goalscorers of his generation. Everton might not have secured any silverware in the 1970s, but they captured a 'trophy' that just about every team in the top flight coveted. That 'trophy' was Latchford.

He was signed from Birmingham City in 1974 in a deal worth £350,000. Sadly, in capturing a giant, Everton had to part with one. The great Howard Kendall, still skipper and a major influence on the side, went in the other direction, along with the lesser known Archie Styles.

Although not particularly tall for a traditional centre-forward, Latchford was strong and always in the right place at the right time.

FACTFILE

Born: Birmingham, 1951.
Everton appearances: 289.
Everton goals: 138.
Everton honours:
League Cup runner-up, 1977.
England caps: 12.

He was the top League scorer in his first four seasons at Goodison, a blitz that reached its peak on Saturday, April 29, 1978, when Latchford became the first top flight player for six years to reach the 30 League goal mark – a feat that won him a £10,000 jackpot prize from the Daily Express.

He would ultimately score 138 goals in 286 starts, grateful for the pinpoint service from another great Blues acquisition, Dave Thomas.

When you think of Everton in the 1970s, you instinctively think of Bob Latchford. He actually made his Football League debut for Birmingham alongside Fred Pickering, ironically a former Everton centre-forward of some note. The date was March 21, 1969.

Later Bob would learn the ropes alongside that great pro Bob Hatton while that Birmingham side also featured a young Trevor Francis who would develop into a world class star and win the European Cup with Nottingham Forest.

However, when Everton offered a fee that would smash the British transfer record with Kendall as part of the deal, Birmingham couldn't say no.

During an eventful Goodison career, Latchford might not have clinched the silverware his brilliant front play deserved. At the same time, no one will ever forget his moment of personal glory – the day Bob literally hit the jackpot in 1978 against Chelsea.

The Blues did not win a Championship or a Cup that day, but the wall of sound that swamped the players in the wake of of the final home game of the season against Chelsea said it all.

Latchford had reached the 28 League goals by mid-April. With three games left, the fans were confident that he would pass the magical 30 barrier. But in the end, it was all on the final Chelsea clash at Goodison. Bob's sensational day is dealt with elsewhere in this book.

It's enough here to say that the Goodison goal machine would not be denied. Bob Latchford lit up the 1970s for Everton. Most of his goals came from close range, the sign of a truly natural goal poacher. He was deceptively quick over short distances and, like Joe Royle before him, had this knack of hanging in the air to meet high crosses.

He was also brave and diving headers were his speciality, meeting the cross at the near post and flicking the ball into the opposite corner.

Latchford lay second only to the legendary Dixie Dean in the all-time Goodison scoring charts until another famous number nine, Graeme Sharp, powered onto the scene to claim that title.

There was an ironic twist to the Bob Latchford story. The wheel would turn full circle in 1981 when Kendall, the player involved in the swop deal that brought Bob to Goodison, returned triumphantly – as manager. The striker was the first to leave as a famous rebuilding job began.

Latchford deserved to be an integral part of a highly successful, trophy-winning set-up. It remains a crying shame that his Blues' career did not have a silver lining, but he still left his undoubted mark on Evertonians everywhere. He gave us all a tremendous amount of pleasure.

They used to say Mike Lyons would run through a brick wall for Everton. He never gave less than 100 per cent in over 400 appearances, switching comfortably between centre-half and centre-forward. He is pictured celebrating at David Webb's expense after scoring in a 2-0 win over Queen's Park Rangers in 1972.

Former Goodison right winger Billy Bingham returned as manager in the summer of 1973, faced with a major rebuilding job. He is pictured with chairman John Moores discussing the challenge.

Joe Harper joined Everton in December 1972, hailed as a new breed of striker. Only 5ft 6in tall, the former Aberdeen star relied on his sharpness in the box. He celebrates after scoring in a 3-0 win over Ipswich at the start of the 1973-74 season, but returned to Scotland after only 14 months at Goodison.

Gordon Lee left Newcastle United to replace Billy Bingham as Everton manager in January 1977. Lee was dedicated and hardworking but, like Bingham, failed to bring a major trophy to Goodison. He was replaced by Howard Kendall in 1981.

It looks as if Goodison has been bombed. In fact, it is a major demolition job to remove the remainder of the old Main Stand so that the new structure could be completed in 1971.

Talking business. two of the finest Everton centre-forwards of all time. Dixie Dean, the acknowledged daddy of them all, discusses the finer points of putting the ball into the back of the net with Bob Latchford, whose 30 League goals in 1978 was exactly half of Dean's record-breaking 1928 tally.

Latchford's £10,000 Jackpot

Saturday, 29 April 1978
Everton 6 Chelsea 0

EVERTON finished the 1977-78 season with nothing to show in terms of silverware. But the final game of the season was an unforgettable occasion and not just because the Blues crushed Chelsea 6-0 in front of an ecstatic crowd of 40,000 people. It was also the day when Bob Latchford became the first top-flight player for six years to take his seasonal League tally to 30 goals.

The Evertonians turned up in force to see him plunder a memorable double and claim a £10,000 prize put up by the 'Daily Express' newspaper. The bounty added to the occasion, whipping the fans up into a frenzy every time the home side moved on to the attack.

Latchford, a bustling centre-forward who was deadly in the box, will never forget the afternoon when Goodison Park went goal crazy and he was the toast of Merseyside.

He said: "There was quite an atmosphere that day, considering there wasn't very much on the game itself. The pitch was dry and bobbly, but the goals soon started to flow."

The one drawback was that the home side powered into a 3-0 lead without Latchford finding the net. Would he miss out on that lucrative cash bonanza? Bob provided the answer with a second half header that produced a deafening roar from the royal blue army, but he was still one goal short of his target with the clock ticking away.

Everton conjured up goal number five,

Above, top: A typical Bob Latchford goal, plundered inside 90 seconds in a 4-0 win over Spurs in March 1977.

Above: Bob Latchford was at his best, poaching from close range. This is his 26th League goal of the season in his highly successful 1977-78 campaign, scored against Derby County.

The bearded Bob Latchford was an instant hit with the Evertonians in 1974. He is saluted here by the Goodison fans after scoring twice in a 4-1 win over his old club, Birmingham City. He scored an impressive 138 goals in 286 full appearances for the Blues.

but the scorer was Mike Lyons, who vividly recalls the crowd's reaction.

He said: "I tucked the ball into the bottom corner and turned away to celebrate, but because I had failed to knock the ball back to 'Latch', who was in a great position, everybody just stood and looked at me. It's the only time I've scored at Goodison and felt sick about it!"

But the man of the moment would not be denied his finest hour. His moment of glory came from the penalty spot and when the ball flew into the back of the net, the place erupted. He said: "It was a terrific moment, a fantastic way to end a season."

Naturally, everybody thought Latchford was in the money. In reality, his bank balance was boosted, only to the tune of £192. Part of the deal was that half of the £10,000 would go to the Football League and Professional Footballers' Association Benevolent Fund. Bob decided to share the rest with all of the players who had

helped him achieve his 30-goal total. Hence, £10,000 became the princely sum of £192.

Even then, the story had a sting in the tail. Latchford was taxed on the basis that he had received a £5,000 bonus and it took him three years to sort the wrangle out with the Inland Revenue.

Still, Bob had taxed the resolve of defenders up and down the country during that free-scoring campaign. The only disappointment was that Everton only managed to finish third in the table when many people felt they were good enough that year to have gone all the way.

For the record, the goals against Chelsea that memorable April day were scored by Latchford (two), Dobson, Lyons, Robinson and Wright.

Everton: Wood; Robinson, Pejic, Lyons, Wright, Buckley, King, Dobson, Latchford, Telfer, Thomas.

Attendance: 39,504

CONGRATULATIONS BOB
ON YOUR 100TH
LEAGUE GOAL

An Evertonian Pizza Parlour manger, known locally as Rocco, was so convinced that Bob Latchford would score his 30th League goal of the 1977-78 season at West Brom in the penultimate game that he said he would shave his head if it didn't happen. A bald Rocco is pictured looking distinctly glum. Latchford produced the goods a week too late to prevent this hair-raising story.

Duncan McKenzie was Everton's Mr Magic for two seasons in the late 1970s. Signed from Anderlecht, he had tremendous skill and was a real crowd pleaser.

Everton had the measure of archrivals Liverpool in this fourth-round FA Cup tie in January 1981. The Blues won 2-1 with goals from Peter Eastoe and Imre Varadi. Ray Clemence is in a tangle in the net as Varadi celebrates his goal.

Everton 1983-84; The team finished seventh that year, but reached the Milk Cup Final and won the FA Cup.

In Goodison Place for the first time. Andy Gray joined Everton in November, 1983 and made an immediate impact.

Peter Reid was a combative, inspirational figure for Everton in the 1980s. He is pictured here speaking on behalf of the injured Adrian Heath against Luton Town in April 1984.

Andy Gray scored spectacular goals. He is seen netting with a diving header in a 4-1 home win over Sunderland in 1985.

Below: A touch of class. Mrs Maguerite Murphy used to watch every single game at Goodison, first team, reserves and youth side. She also had a regular Monday lunch date at the Royal Blue Restaurant and got the surprise of her life in September, 1984, when her lunch companions turned out to be the FA Cup, Youth Cup and Charity Shield. She was absolutely delighted.

Right: The 1985 Everton Toffee Girl, Joanne Francis.

June 1980 and a brand new underground heating system with miles of piping is laid. It remains highly effective.

Happiness . . .
Crushing Manchester United!

27 October 1984
Everton 5 Manchester United 0

THIS wasn't so much a victory over Ron Atkinson's highly-rated Manchester United as a summary execution. Five goals flew past the bemused Gary Bailey as Everton produced a performance worthy of potential League Champions.

Prior to this game, there were still those outside of Merseyside who were refusing to take the Blues seriously as genuine title candidates!

But in the wake of a sensational triumph, the bookmakers had no choice but to slash the odds on Howard Kendall's men. Here was a game in which Everton's football ranged from outstanding to exhilarating. One passing movement out of defence inspired the instinctive roar of Olé from the crowd as the ball was sprayed accurately from one player to another.

It was the day when goalkeeper Neville Southall was surplus to requirements. He could have watched the game from the terraces, so superior were Everton to their rivals from Old Trafford. The supporters knew instinctively that it was going to be one of those days when Kevin Sheedy

Adrian Heath (number eight) slots home Everton's third goal against Manchester United and the massacre is well under way.

A player's view of Graeme Sharp's fifth goal for the Blues in a crushing victory over Manchester United.

began the rout in the fifth minute – with a header!

In doing so, he clashed heads with United's Kevin Moran and went off immediately to have three stitches inserted to a wound to the forehead, returning six minutes later.

Moran was less fortunate. He was taken to hospital suffering from double vision.

There was nothing wrong with Sheedy's eyesight. He moved on to an Adrian Heath through ball to clip home the second goal with outstanding precision. Heath grabbed the third from close range after 35 minutes with the crowd warming to a potential massacre.

Alan Brazil got in United's first shot - after 81 minutes! The crowd applauded politely and then exploded when Gary Stevens hammered home his side's fourth from 20 yards out. Graeme Sharp was soon pouncing at the near post to head

home a Heath corner and the victory was complete.

That famous Old Evertonian Joe Mercer couldn't contain his excitement. Everything about them was right said Joe – from the goalkeeper right through the team. It was the best performance by any Everton team I can remember.

Joe's enthusiasm was possibly a little bit over the top, bearing in mind the fact that he had played with the legendary Dixie Dean and had witnessed many a golden moment at Goodison down the decades.

But no one was arguing on the day. Everton had indeed hit the heights and the rapturous applause was thoroughly deserved.

Everton: Southall; Stevens, Van den Hauwe, Ratcliffe, Mountfield, Reid, Steven, Heath, Sharp, Bracewell, Sheedy (Gray).

Attendance: 40,769

The Pride of Germany Blitzed

24 April 1985
Everton 3 Bayern Munich 1

IT will go down in history as the greatest Goodison Park cup clash of modern times: Everton 3 Bayern Munich 1 – let the scoreline roll off the tongue and feel the passion of that never-to-be-forgotten night in 1985 when Everton blitzed the pride of Germany, to power into their first ever European Final.

Down the years, football enthusiasts had suggested on more than one occasion that the Goodison faithful were a 'watching crowd'. In other words, they revelled in, and appreciated class, but very rarely let their hair down.

Some had gone so far as to suggest that the make-up of the stadium, with its high stands and wide open spaces, didn't lend itself to the proverbial cauldron of excitement.

This myth was exploded into the night air as the Blues marched to the final frontier in the Cup-winners' Cup, having already disposed of University College Dublin, Slovan Bratislav and Fortuna Sittard.

Everton gave one of the greatest club sides in Europe a one-goal start in this finely balanced second leg and then battered them into submission with a breathtaking display of power that left the visitors reeling.

Goodison Park exploded as goals from Graeme Sharp, Andy Gray and Trevor Steven broke the hearts of Bayern Munich. The West German League leaders thought they had the tie in the bag when Dieter Hoeness squeezed them in front after 37 minutes.

But Everton, inspired by 11 heroes on the pitch and 49,000 never-say-die supporters on the terraces, hit back with a vengeance.

The courage, determination and commitment that inspired the triumph and

Bayern Munich are on the run and the Everton players rush to congratulate Andy Gray, scorer of the crucial second goal.

earned a Final clash with Rapid Vienna was epitomised in the displays of the three goalscorers. Sharp and Gray gave the Germans a pounding with as bold a display of front running as you will see. It was the very best of British in terms of aggressive centre-forward play. They were rewarded with a goal apiece in the second half when Bayern were on the rack and on the run with the Evertonians roaring their men forward.

If that wasn't enough, Steven brought

the house down four minutes from time like some latterday Bobby Charlton, racing clear and unleashing an unstoppable shot from the edge of the box that flew past Belgian international 'keeper Jean-Marie Pfaff.

On the final whistle, skipper Kevin Ratcliffe rushed across to throw his arms around his Welsh international teammate Neville Southall and every single player received a standing ovation from fans who were breathless with the excitement.

"You are all crazy men", said Bayern coach Uli Hoeness. "No," said Andy Gray and Graeme Sharp, "We are winners!"

Last off was Gray. He thrust his fists high into the air and the final cheer must have rattled the Bayern dressing-room door as they sat disconsolate, reflecting on a remarkable game.

German coach Uli Hoeness, shell-shocked by the powerhouse tactics Everton had employed, waited in the tunnel and spat out a frustrating aside to Gray.

"That was not football. You are all crazy men," Hoeness declared. What he really meant was: "We've been played off the park by one of the best teams in Europe!"

Gray said: "I will never ever forget that night. It was 0-0 after the first leg and then the Germans grabbed that early goal at Goodison, but I always knew we would fight back. Graeme Sharp got the equaliser after I knocked on a long Gary Stevens throw-in.

"The place just erupted and as soon as the ball hit the back of the net you could see the opposition visibly cracking. I grabbed the lead 15 minutes from time when I scooped the ball home from close in after Pfaff had failed to deal with another long throw and Trevor Steven finished them off."

Meanwhile, coach Hoeness was still full of mixed emotions. He told the waiting scribes that Everton were 'the best team in Europe' but added: "Gray should be playing rugby, not football." The Goodison front man, a truly inspirational figure, had been involved in a couple of bruising confrontations. But the man who led the royal blue revival with all the subtlety of a Viking warrior was totally unrepentant.

"The lads were determined to show they were as good as anything in Europe," he said. "And that's just what they did!"

Howard Kendall's pre-match battle plan had worked a treat. The Everton manager said: "We decided before the game to bomb them. We felt the best way to approach the tie was to put them under immediate pressure and not get involved in the patient, slow build-up routine. I felt that if we moved forward slowly from the back, it would be playing right into their hands. It was a case of cashing in on our strengths and it paid off"

It is now history that the Blues went on to beat Rapid Vienna in Rotterdam to secure the Cup-winners' Cup. That was quite an occasion as well, but for sheer mind-blowing excitement, the Bayern triumph will live forever in the minds of the Evertonians who were lucky enough to be there.

Everton: Southall; Stevens, Van Den Hauwe, Ratcliffe, Mountfield, Reid, Steven, Sharp, Gray, Bracewell, Sheedy. *Attendance: 49,782*

We Shall Not Be Moved

6 May 1985
Everton 2 Queen's Park Rangers 0

AFTER 15 long years, the League Championship trophy finally returned to Goodison Park following a solid 2-0 victory over Queen's Park Rangers.

It left Howard Kendall's royal blue dream machine unassailable leaders of the First Division with five games to go. The FA and European Cup-winners' Cup Finals were still to come, but for now it was enough to revel in the ultimate domestic prize.

And what a day it was. The news had spread before the game that goalkeeper Neville Southall was the new Footballer of the Year. When he appeared on the pitch before the kick-off to do a radio interview with teammate Peter Reid, the fans roared their delight... the shape of things to come.

The party atmosphere increased when manager Howard Kendall emerged to receive his Manager of the Month award, a dress rehearsal for the ultimate accolade that was soon to follow – Football League Manager of the Year.

It was to be a fairy-tale day in every sense. Even the rain made way for sunshine skies as the players emerged from the dressing-room with the stadium heaving to the sound of 50,000 ecstatic Everton voices.

Rangers were nothing more than a supporting act to an all-star Everton cast as the Blues set about the job in hand with the kind of relentless determination that had been the hallmark of their season.

They took just 24 minutes to break the deadlock and who better to send the Gwladys Street faithful wild with delight than Derek Mountfield, a player who once stood on that famous bank of terracing, himself a devoted Evertonian.

Reid forced a corner with a bold run

Graeme Sharp shows his delight after scoring the goal against QPR that clinched the 1985 Championship. Andy Gray looks pretty pleased, too!

The title is back at Goodison and a fan ties a blue scarf around the neck of Sir John Moores. The grand old man of Goodison was as elated as anyone by the Championship success.

The 1985 League Championship is in the bag and Howard Kendall, amid the debris of celebration, steals a quiet moment with another challenge now looming — a trip to Rotterdam to face Rapid Vienna in the European Cup-winners' Cup.

into the box. Kevin Sheedy swerved in the cross and both Andy Gray and Pat Van den Hauwe got a touch before Mountfield hammered his shot into the back of the net, the ball striking both the underside of the crossbar and the 'keeper on its way in.

It was the centre-half's 12th goal of the season, a record that would have pleased many strikers.

Rangers were now on the run. Graeme Sharp had a bullet header tipped over the top, going even closer soon after with a shot that struck the right-hand post. The Scot was then booked before he rounded

Tears were mingled with cheers when Everton beat QPR in May 1985 to bring the Championship back to Goodison for the first time in 15 years. While the fans continued their celebrations on the terraces, two men had mixed emotions in a dressing-room littered with the tools of battle. Adrian Heath had been the club's leading scorer in December 1984, when injury suddenly wiped out his season. The blow came only weeks after former skipper Mark Higgins announced his retirement at the age of 26 because of a niggling pelvic problem. The emotion and frustration at missing out on a big title day is etched on both faces. Heath, finally heading back to fitness, puts a consoling arm around the shoulder of his old skipper.

off an eventful afternoon with the goal after 82 minutes that effectively clinched the Championship.

It was his 30th of the season and one that all the great Everton centre-forwards of yesteryear would have been proud of.

Paul Bracewell linked with Van den Hauwe, whose cross from the left was perfect. Sharp rose like a Dixie Dean, Tommy Lawton or Joe Royle to power a header into the roof of the net.

The old battle hymn of 'We Shall Not Be Moved' echoed around the ground. Everton were home and dry and tears of relief and emotion flowed in all corners of Goodison.

Sir John Moores, millionaire former chairman, said: "I never thought I'd live to see another League Championship come to Goodison. It's great to feel free of the domination of Liverpool."

As the grand old man of Goodison spoke, a fan tied a royal blue scarf around his neck, summing up the atmosphere of togetherness.

On the pitch manager Howard Kendall was dancing a little victory jig as the players ran to hug him. "There's only one Howard Kendall," roared the fans – following it up immediately with "Champions, Champions."

The title was in the bag, but the season was far from over.

Everton: Southall; Stevens, Van den Hauwe, Ratcliffe, Mountfield, Reid, Steven, Sharp, Gray, Bracewell, Sheedy.

Factfile: Everton went on to win the European Cup-winners' Cup with a 3-1 win over Rapid Vienna. They might have claimed a famous trophy treble, but tiredness overcame them in the FA Cup Final with a Norman Whiteside goal giving victory to Manchester United.

Everton, having clinched the 1985 title by beating QPR, paraded the trophy before the next home game, a 3-0 romp against West Ham United.

226

Record-Breaking Champions

23 May 1985
Everton 1 Liverpool 0

EVERTON wound up the 1985 Championship season in style by completing their first League double over arch-rivals Liverpool in 20 years. At the same time they took their points total to the highest figure ever achieved in the First Division.

With two games still to play they had amassed 90 points to pass the 87 accumulated by Liverpool three years earlier, although they were not in a position to match Liverpool's best-ever record which had been achieved under a different points system in 1979.

The derby match produced a somewhat unexpected hero. Graeme Sharp was on international duty with Scotland and newcomer Paul Wilkinson stepped up to score the only goal of the game.

The newly-crowned Champions had enjoyed a magnificent season, but few games gave them more satisfaction than this lone goal triumph over the old enemy. For Wilkinson, only recently captured from Grimsby Town, it was a day to savour.

Liverpool created enough chances to have won the game fairly comfortably against opponents featuring half a dozen reserves, but the Blues were in defiant mood.

Wilkinson's dream strike came in the 68th minute after Andy Gray had headed a Gary Stevens cross into his path. The England Under-21 international drilled the ball home with his right foot and neither side spared themselves in the cut

Everton wrapped up the 1985 title campaign in the best way possible — by beating Liverpool. Here Neville Southall goes down to deny the Blues' 'Public Enemy Number One', Ian Rush.

Well done mate …Andy Gray congratulates Neville Southall on keeping a clean sheet against Liverpool in May 1985.

and thrust finale that followed.

In the final reckoning all the smiles were on the faces of the blue and white army. These were heady times for the Class of '85.

Everton: Southall; Stevens, Bailey, Ratcliffe, Van Den Hauwe, Harper, Richardson, Atkin(Wakenshaw), Sheedy, Wilkinson, Gray.
Attendance: 50,000

Everton's most successful skipper. Kevin Ratcliffe with the European Cup-winners' Cup and the 1985 League Championship trophy.

Extreme right: This tiled picture; believed to be an Everton star of the last century, was found during renovation work on the Picture House theme pub in Anfield (formerly the Sandon where the Blues changed during their days at Anfield). Bill Bentley of the Tetley Walker brewery presented the picture to Howard Kendall and it now hangs at Goodison Park. The Picture House pub would become derelict but thankfully it was painstakingly restored in 1997 and re-named the Sandon to recapture the famous footballing links with the past.

229

Lineker's Goodison Swansong

5 May 1986
Everton 3 West Ham United 1

EVERTON wrapped up the 1985-86 season with a crushing 3-1 victory over West Ham United, inspired by a Gary Lineker double.

The fans in attendance that day could not have realised that they were watching the free-scoring striker in action in a blue shirt at Goodison Park for the very last time.

He would play and score in the FA Cup Final against Liverpool just days later, taking his tally for the season to 40 goals.

He would then head for Mexico with England for a World Cup challenge that would catapult him into an international spotlight and draw admiring glances from a whole array of foreign clubs.

Amongst them were Barcelona, who would soon tempt Everton to accept a £2.7m offer that brought to an end a brief, yet action-packed Goodison career for the man with the golden boots.

Lineker had struggled to impress the

Evertonians early on, but once the goals started to flow, they very quickly began to appreciate his special qualities in front of goal.

As the season drew to a close, he was attempting to become only the second Goodison player since the war to score 30 League goals.

He needed two against West Ham to match Bob Latchford's 1977-78 feat and got off the mark after 43 minutes, lashing home from close range after Paul Wilkinson had knocked on a Gary Stevens free-kick.

Kevin Sheedy almost broke the cross bar at the Stanley Park End with a thundering effort on the stroke of half-time. And three minutes into the second half, Lineker pounced on a Stewart error to clip his second goal past the advancing Parkes.

The Hammers were on the rack and Wilkinson sent a header against the post before forcing Stewart to concede a penalty. Lineker had the opportunity to take it and claim his hat-trick.

A third League goal would have seen

him equal the 31 goals scored by John Willie Parker for Everton in the 1953-54 Second Division season. But Lineker shunned the opportunity to bag his second treble in three days to allow Trevor Steven to slot home from the spot and make it 3-0.

West Ham's consolation goal came in the final minute, scored by a player who would eventually be signed by the Blues - Tony Cottee. But the applause on the final whistle was very much for Lineker & Co as they looked forward to their Wembley confrontation with the old enemy. Sadly,

Gary Lineker had one memorable goalscoring season at Goodison Park, finishing with 40 goals. He is seen here in acrobatic action against Nottingham Forest in 1985-86.

The fences came down at Goodison in April 1989, 11 years after they were erected. This followed immediately after the Hillsborough Disaster which claimed the lives of 96 Liverpudlians.

Gary had glittered for the last time at Goodison.

Everton: Mimms; Stevens, Van Den Hauwe, Ratcliffe, Billing, Richardson, Steven, Lineker(Aspinall), Wilkinson, Heath, Sheedy.

Factfile: Everton's decision to sell Lineker, a man who had scored 40 goals in total for the Blues, caused some controversy, to say the least. But manager Howard Kendall's decision proved justified the following season when the Blues regained the Championship they had lost to Liverpool. The scoring load was spread around instead of being dominated by one man. And yet the debate about the sale of Lineker inevitably continues, simply because over the following seven years he remained a goalscorer with few equals. But managers cannot concern themselves with what might have been. It's enough to say that the England star was given a top-class stage at Goodison Park, a ground he still regards as one of his favourite venues.

An aerial shot of Goodison in October 1986, looking towards the Gwladys Street End. The famous terraces are clearly visible. The land cleared behind the Gwladys Street Stand is now occupied by new houses. Fittingly, one road is named Mere Green, reflecting the fact that Goodison Park itself was previously called the Mere Green Field.

The first of two Trevor Steven penalty successes against Luton Town as the Champions celebrate with a 3-1 win.

Two Title Trophies In One Day!

Saturday, 9 May 1987
Everton 3 Luton Town 1

THE sun shone on Goodison Park to welcome home the newly-crowned League Champions. Luton Town provided the opposition for this final game of the 1987 season, but it was not so much a football match as a carnival.

Five days earlier, amidst incredible scenes of jubilation at Carrow Road, Everton had stormed to a title-clinching victory over Norwich City, courtesy of an unlikely goal hero, Pat Van Den Hauwe.

He was an intimidating full-back who bristled and battled his way through matches with a fierce glare that put the fear of God into opponents. At Norwich, he suddenly took on a new persona. It was the day that 'Psycho Pat' picked up a new nickname – Pat Van Den Howitzer!

Having struggled for 90 minutes to turn the Championship screw against Manchester City, the Blues took just 45 seconds to produce the goods against shell-shocked Norwich.

A cracking effort, straight out of the Kevin Sheedy shooting manual, exploded from the right boot of a man who was more renowned for his ferocious tackling.

The 7,000 Evertonians who had made the long trek to East Anglia, let out a deafening roar. It was only matched by the scenes of unbridled joy and elation at Goodison when Luton came to town, bit players in a Champion production.

It began with Kevin Ratcliffe leading his teammates out to collect not one, but two title trophies. The Football League had been sponsored by the 'Today' newspaper and their award was soon being passed between the delighted Everton players while skipper Ratcliffe paraded the more familiar and historic League Championship trophy.

Flags and banners were waved and there was even a mini tickertape reception. A special cheer was reserved for injured right-back Paul Power.

But would Luton play ball and give the new champions an easy ride? It became clear that they had not read the script

Trevor Steven is bundled off the ball against Luton, but he had the last laugh, scoring from the resulting penalty.

when Mark Stein blasted them into the lead with a fierce shot. Inspired by the combative Peter Reid, Everton now swept forward, virtually camping inside their opponents half. It all went wrong for the visitors just before the break.

Goalkeeper Les Sealey took a kick in the face from Graeme Sharp and was concussed. For a tense moment, there were fears that he had swallowed his tongue and was struggling to breathe, but after a lengthy delay the 'keeper climbed to his feet to warm applause and resumed between the posts.

Factfile: Everton's celebrating fans were soon caught up in a management sensation when Howard Kendall decided to accept a Continental challenge with Spanish club Athletic Bilbao. The board had no hesitation in handing the vacant Goodison hot-seat to Kendall's highly respected assistant Colin Harvey.

Sealey was not the happiest man in the ground at that moment in time and his frustration bubbled over in the 52nd minute when Everton secured a deserved equaliser. Reid showed great skill, beating two men on the edge of the box before chipping in a ball that came back off the bar.

Johnson handled in the melee that followed, Sealey showing his anger at the penalty decision by hurling the ball towards the referee. Trevor Steven retained his composure, slotting home his shot before the 'keeper was booked for booting the ball away.

Minutes later Steven repeated the act after he had been fouled by North. All hopes the Hatters had of salvaging a point disappeared when Nicholas was sent off after tangling with Reid.

The carnival had turned into something much more combative, but Everton provided the perfect finale when Sharp turned in Gary Stevens' drive to illustrate the Blues' superiority and make it 3-1.

After the match, the trophy-laden

Thanks fans... skipper Kevin Ratcliffe leads the applause as the 1987 Champions bask in the glory at Goodison after the Luton game.

Ratcliffe led the players on a lap of honour to the euphoric chant of "Champions, Champions". As manager Howard Kendall and coach Colin Harvey watched from the sidelines, no one in the ground could have envisaged the upheaval that would soon follow. But for now it was a case of soaking up the glory and enjoying every single second.

Everton: Southall; Stevens, Watson, Ratcliffe, Van Den Hauwe, Steven, Snodin, Reid, Harper, Heath, Sharp. Substitute: Adams.

NEVILLE SOUTHALL – MILLENNIUM GIANT
1980-1990

NEVILLE Southall, like one of his great goalkeeping predecessors Ted Sagar, was an Everton marathon man with unbelievable staying power. He began his Goodison Park career in October 1981 and was still at the club in November 1997.

I have no doubt whatsoever that at his peak in the mid-1980s, the down-to-earth Welshman was the best in the world and on a par with past British giants like Gordon Banks and Pat Jennings. This is the greatest tribute I can pay him.

Southall became a legend in his own playing lifetime, a super hero without an ego. He looked on all opposing forwards as the enemy, whether they were rivals coming at him in top flight action or team mates trying to beat him in training.

I well recall watching Neville during a pre-season training session in Holland when the Blues were in their pomp. Manager Howard Kendall was actually putting the strikers through their paces. The keeper should have been cannon-fodder as forwards drilled shots in unchallenged from the edge of the box.

Kendall declared that no one would leave the field until they had scored one final goal against the giant keeper. You could see the glint in Southall's eye. It was the training session that I thought would never end. The keeper wasn't just stopping the shots, he was batting them with his giant gloves almost back to the halfway line.

The players would have to retrieve the balls as Neville screamed abuse at them, defying anyone to beat him. Ultimately, I recall that it was the strikers who were last to leave. He saved his best for them. It was symbolic, his way of proving that he was the best.

Of course, he would never lay claim to being a goalkeeping superman. Whenever Nev would make a spectacular save in a game and you questioned him about it, he would shrug and say: "It was nothing, It just hit me."

Of course, nothing was further from the truth. Who could forget his amazing reflex tip over the top from a Marc Falco header at Tottenham in 1985 or his desperate touch around the post from Sheffield Wednesday's former Everton striker Imre Varadi that same season, a save that was shown so often by the BBC in their opening credits to *Match of the Day* that it won him a National Fan Club as well as the Freedom of Goodison Park.

The mark of a true giant is that he can play in different eras and still look very special. Southall was the rock on which Kendall built his great side of the 1980s, the most successful Blues' team of all time. He was still the master in 1995, defying Manchester United at Wembley to secure his second FA Cup winners medal.

FACTFILE
Born: Llandudno, 1958.
Everton appearances: 751, a club record.
Everton goals: 1 (in a penalty shoot-out in a Full Members Cup-tie against Charlton Athletic).
Everton honours:
League Championship winner: 1984–85 and 1986–87.
FA Cup winner: 1984 and 1995.
European Cup-winners' Cup winner: 1985.
Charity Shield winner: 1984, 1985, 1987 and 1995.
FA Cup runner-up: 1985 and 1989.
Milk (League) Cup runner-up: 1984.
Simod Cup runner-up: 1989.
Zenith Data Systems Cup runner-up: 1991.
Footballer of the Year: 1985.
Wales caps: 92 (a record).

No one worked harder than Neville Southall on the training ground. He would be first into Bellefield in the morning and last out in the afternoon. More than that, he was always looking to put something back into the game that gave him so much.

During his testimonial season he asked to see me at Bellefield. He asked if I would help him with a community project. He wanted to work in schools all over Merseyside to raise money for charity. Nev's challenge to the youngsters and their parents was simple. He would go to a school after training and take part in a question and answer session. He would never duck a single question.

After that he would go out onto the school field and stand between the posts to give the youngsters – and their dads – the chance to take a penalty against him. He was fantastic with the younger kids and really went for his saves against the older ones because he knew they would relish that challenge. The youngsters themselves were asked to make a contribution to charity for every penalty taken. It didn't matter how much. It was the thought that mattered to Neville, but the success of this amazing year-long venture was that a tremendous amount of money was raised. Modern players are often criticised for taking everything out of the game and putting nothing back. No one could ever level that accusation at Neville Southall.

I know that he made hundreds of personal appearances during his spell at the top, not least in his native North Wales. He was proud to be the lad from Llandudno who knew what hard work was all about.

Neville's working life had an explosive start. He worked for the local council, helping to blow up and knock down many of the gun emplacements which had been built during the war to deal with enemy planes heading for Merseyside.

Later he would work at the Ritz, not the famous London hotel but a Llandudno cafe. Then he became a hod carrier and even a bin man, hardly the glamorous life style you associate with professional footballers. Almost certainly, this is why Neville Southall never forgot his roots and why he never took success for granted.

His football career began in earnest when he was selected for Caernarfon Boys, both as a goalkeeper and a centre-half. He would soon concentrate on his talents between the posts, playing in the Welsh League for Llandudno Swifts, a youthful side who were often out of their depth at this level. Neville can recall picking the ball out of the net 16 times in one game, but he put it all down to experience and progressed with Bangor City and Winsford.

His big Football League chance came with Bury where coach Wilf McGuinness, the former Manchester United boss, took him for extra afternoon sessions. It was the work ethic raising its head again. This was his first experience of specialist coaching and he improved rapidly. Typically, he will tell you: "Everything I did was instinctive – or luck!"

No such thing. Howard Kendall saw something special in the Welshman and immediately offered £125,000 for his services. Early on he would compete for the number one jersey with Jim Arnold, a talented and intelligent player who followed Kendall from Blackburn Rovers to Goodison. It would be the 1983-84 campaign before Neville finally began to emerge as Everton's main man.

Boss Kendall would always tell you: "Nothing can be won without a class goalkeeper." In Southall he had the best in the world, without a doubt. Having won the FA Cup in 1984 and the Championship and Cup-winners' Cup in 1985, disaster struck the following year when the keeper suffered severe dislocation of his his ankle and ligament damage while playing for Wales against the Republic of Ireland.

It was such a bad injury, that some doubted if he would ever get back to his best. Bobby Mimms played in the 1986 FA Cup Final against Liverpool and the Charity Shield. Fifteen games into the 1986-87 campaign, after seven months out, Southall returned as focused and as defiant as ever.

He would be inspirational as another title was secured. His record-breaking appearance record would now unfold with an FA Cup winners medal in 1995 to add to his collection.

When Neville received the definitive football salute in 1985, the Footballer of the Year award, I went to a famous source to ask just how great the Everton goalkeeper really was. Pat Jennings, the legend of White Hart Lane and of our greatest ever custodians, told me: "He doesn't seem to have any weaknesses as a goalkeeper. He is brave, agile, has got good hands and gets on with the job. I couldn't pick anyone ahead of him in the country."

Praise indeed from one legend to another. But perhaps the biggest tribute you can pay him is that he was judged to be Everton undisputed Millennium Giant for the 1980s – the most successful era in the club's long and distinguished history. There were so many other superb candidates, but they all would have voted for big Nev, given the chance.

As it was, Graeme Sharp was their spokesman on the panel and he had no doubts about the choice. After all, he had suffered at Nev's hands every day in training for years. What better judge of a great goalkeeper than a great striker. Enough said!

Peter Beardsley opened the scoring for Liverpool, the first of eight goals on a remarkable Goodison Cup night. Beardsley would become an Evertonian and win over the fans with his great skill, one of that select band who have graced both Anfield and Goodison.

The Match Of A Lifetime

Wednesday, 20 February 1991
Everton 4 Liverpool 4

THIS FA Cup fifth-round replay between soccer's greatest rivals was to turn into a remarkable three-match marathon that included a clash, described by all those lucky enough to see it, as the 'Game of a lifetime!'

Senior fans would still argue that the 1935 FA Cup replay against Sunderland, a 6-4 bonanza in the Blues' favour, was the greatest Goodison encounter of all time.

But this modern Cup classic surely rivalled it for sensational goals and breathtaking action. And the fact that it was a 'derby' game of epic proportions added to the magic of the 1991 battle.

It will also be remembered as Kenny Dalglish's Liverpool swansong. Within days, he had resigned his position as manager in the most sensational of circumstances, claiming he could not cope with the intense pressure of being in one of the hottest seats in the business.

It meant that the Reds had to go into the second replay with a caretaker boss in the shape of that old Anfield veteran Ronnie Moran. Everton would win a nail-biting Goodison tie 1-0, but at times it was the soccer equivalent of Custer's Last Stand!

When the teams first came out of the hat together, no one could possibly have envisaged the drama that lay ahead. The first game, played at Anfield, was controversial enough. Howard Kendall and Colin Harvey plotted an audacious coup that might have come off if referee Neil Midgley had not denied the Blues what appeared to be a clear penalty.

Gary Ablett, ironically a man who would join Everton the following season, pole-axed Pat Nevin as the winger broke into the right of the box. Not only did Midgley refuse the spot-kick appeals, he made it patently clear that if Nevin 'dived' again, he would be sent off.

The Evertonians, not surprisingly, were furious. The match finished up 0-0, but that incident served to fire up the Blues for the replay.

The same official was in charge at Goodison Park. When he emerged prior to the kick-off to be photographed receiving the official match ball, a home fan leapt forward and put a red scarf around his neck. The experienced Bolton

Graeme Sharp pounces to score his first goal on a night of Cup passion.

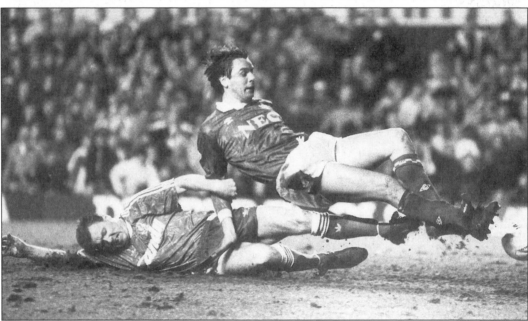

Graeme Sharp's second strike had Steve Nicol grounded and in trouble.

referee, a man with quite a reputation for his after-dinner speeches, saw the funny side and almost certainly used it at his next speaking engagement.

In the meantime, he concentrated his thoughts on this cup return, Dalglish inspiring the Liverpudlians by naming Peter Beardsley up front alongside Ian Rush. There had been much controversy across the park about the manager's apparent reluctance to give the Geordie star a regular place, even though he was a firm favourite with the fans.

This would eventually culminate in Beardsley accepting a surprise offer from Howard Kendall to join Everton. But for now, he was very much a Kop idol.

And he had the visiting fans on their feet after just three minutes with a swerving drive that was parried by Neville Southall, the goalkeeper recovering to snatch the ball away from the marauding Rush.

Liverpool finally went in front after 32 minutes when Kevin Ratcliffe was dispossessed by Rush, who sped goal-wards to draw Southall and shoot towards an unguarded net. Incredibly, defender Andy Hinchcliffe cleared off the line, only for the alert Rush to nod the loose ball to Beardsley who scored.

The Reds continued to hold sway with Jan Molby lording it in centre midfield. Now Kendall replaced the unhappy Ray

Sharp turns away to celebrate with his fellow Scot, Pat Nevin, in an amazing FA Cup replay.

Atteveld with Stuart McCall and two minutes after the interval, Everton equalised. Hinchcliffe curled in a left-wing cross and Graeme Sharp arrived to power in a header which Bruce Grobbelaar could only push on to the inside of the post, the ground erupting as the ball found the back of the net.

The Blues now took control with Sharp ready to fight for every ball and every situation. Nevin scooped over and Mike Newell volleyed wide, only for Beardsley to respond with a cracking left-foot shot after 71 minutes that restored his side's lead.

But no sooner had the visiting cheers died away, when Sharp lifted Everton's spirits with a vital equaliser following a misunderstanding between Grobbelaar and Steve Nicol. Liverpool now demonstrated their Champion spirit by going ahead for the third time after 77 minutes, when Molby's cross was nodded home by Rush.

Few people in the ground thought Everton would recover from this body blow, but their resilience on the night was quite remarkable. Only 60 seconds were remaining when Tony Cottee, an 85th-minute replacement for Nevin, raced on to McCall's pass to score a clinical

equaliser that forced the tie into extra-time.

At this stage, the fans were as exhausted as the players. Liverpool went for the early knockout blow in the extra period, but the

Factfile: Everton lived extremely dangerously in the third encounter, played at Goodison after the Blues won the toss for venue. They managed to take the lead for the first time in 222 minutes of Cup football when centre-back Dave Watson cashed in after a moment of panic in the Liverpool area.

The game was 12 minutes old when an Atteveld free-kick was flicked on, first by Sharp and then by Watson. Nicol tried to clear, but he could only glance the ball backwards and Martin Keown was able to get in a shot that Grobbelaar saved with an outstretched boot. The ball dropped at Molby's feet and the Dane somehow allowed it to squirm through his legs. A grateful Watson hammered it home from close range and Everton would now dig in to claim victory.

superb Southall claimed a cross-shot from Barnes, a Rush header and a point-blank range effort from Barry Venison.

But even the famous Welsh international 'keeper had no chance when Barnes curled home a superb right-foot shot from the edge of the box after 102 minutes.

It meant Liverpool were in front for the fourth time. It was all or nothing for Everton and they came up trumps with Cottee proving a real 'super sub'. With six minutes left, he fired in a shot that found the net through Grobbelaar's legs after Glenn Hysen had allowed Molby's attempted backpass to run on into the box.

It was 4-4 and when Midgley finally called an end, both teams received a memorable standing ovation. The only snag was, they had to go through it all again the following Wednesday. Could the players and the supporters last the pace? This was now the million-dollar question.

Everton: Southall; Atteveld(McCall 46), Watson, Keown, Ratcliffe, Hinchcliffe, Nevin(Cottee 85), McDonald, Ebbrell, Sharp, Newell.

Cottee plunders his second and Everton's fourth as a remarkable game reaches its climax.

It's 4-4... and Liverpool goalkeeper Bruce Grobbelaar just cannot believe it.

Gwladys Street's Last Stand

Saturday, 4 May 1991
Everton 1 Luton Town 0

THIS was the day when I put my reporter's notebook to one side, turned my back on the Press Box and joined the faithful on the Gwladys Street terraces for an afternoon of nostalgia.

It was the day supporters stood on that famous bank of terracing for the very last time prior to seats being installed. As a kid, I'd been a fully paid-up member of this section, first cheering on Dave Hickson and later saluting the likes of Bobby Collins, Roy Vernon, Alex Young and the rest.

It was the first time I had stood on the Gwladys Street for over 20 years, but it was fascinating to climb on to the famous shelf, that slightly elevated section of terracing, to reclaim my old 'spec' in the company of my own two boys, Colin and Peter.

Maybe you look back on things through rose-tinted glasses, but I seemed to remember the support being that much more raucous and passionate. But it wasn't the greatest of games and the supporters ran hot and cold.

The sun came out and things began to look up with Robert Warzycha and Tony Cottee playing their part. It was Cottee who scored the only goal of the game, seizing control after Stuart McCall had blocked an attempted clearance.

Cottee rounded 'keeper Alec Chamberlain and gleefully slotted home his 22nd goal of the season.

It was enough to secure victory, but here was a day when the result was irrelevant. The old ground would never quite be the same again for those supporters as they wended their way away from the Gwladys Street terraces. It was now just a part of Goodison folklore.

Everton: Southall; Ebbrell, Hinchliffe, Ratcliffe, Watson, Atteveld, Warzycha, McCall, Newell, Cottee, Beagrie.
Attendance: 19,909

The new Gwladys Street roof began to take shape in the summer of 1987.

The crash barriers are removed in readiness for seats installed in May 1991.

Enter Peter Beardsley — The Geordie Genius

Saturday, 21 September 1991
Everton 3 Coventry City 0

THE summer of 1991 was a tricky one for Everton manager Howard Kendall. He had pursued Derby County striker Dean Saunders for months, only to be disappointed at the last possible moment when the Welsh international chose to sign for arch-rivals Liverpool.

But this was not to be the end of the story. Saunders' arrival at Anfield marked the beginning of the end for Kop favourite Peter Beardsley. One of the game's great entertainers inexplicably found himself struggling to nail down a regular place in season 1990-91.

Kendall, seeing his chance, offered Liverpool £1 million for a player who had been a thorn in Everton's side on more than one occasion in derby battles. Graeme Souness, having invested over £4m on Saunders and his Baseball Ground teammate Mark Wright, decided to accept

the bid and one of the most remarkable deals of recent years was completed with the Blues' boss delighted to have captured such a class act.

There were those at Anfield who thought Beardsley would not have the 'bottle' to maintain his high level of performance across the park and that the transfer, at such a late stage in his career, might backfire on the talented Geordie. He would soon prove that there is no substitute for star quality.

Beardsley demonstrated clearly that it's not the colour of the shirt that is important, but rather the ability and character of the man wearing it. The Evertonians took to him from the moment he made his League debut against Nottingham Forest on 17 August, 1991.

The campaign itself would prove highly frustrating for the Blues. They began so brightly, showing skill and flair to earn special salutes from a host of rival managers, not least Brian Clough (Forest),

Alex Ferguson (Manchester United) and Dave Stringer (Norwich). But as the year progressed, Everton somehow lost their way.

It was left to Beardsley – backed up by men like Dave Watson and Martin Keown – to try and keep the fans smiling through a difficult spell.

The Geordie star would finish with 20 goals, his First Division return proving superior to Saunders, the man who replaced him at Anfield. This, in itself, had to be a source of satisfaction to the Evertonians.

One of the highlights was Beardsley's Goodison Park hat-trick against Coventry City. There was an element of good fortune about the first goal, scored after 40 minutes. Former Everton defender Brian Borrows, in attempting to clear a Mike Newell cross, succeeded only in playing the ball against the legs of the in-running Beardsley. The ball richochetted towards the corner of the net and while goalkeeper Steve Ogrizovic got a hand to it, he couldn't prevent a goal.

But there was certainly nothing lucky about the Geordie's second after 61 minutes. Robert Warzycha's testing cross was only half cleared and Beardsley crashed it home with venom from the edge of the box. Manager Kendall later suggested it was exactly the kind of goal the player used to score on derby day against the Blues!

The hat-trick was completed 15 minutes from time. Neil McDonald, a second-half substitute for Kevin Sheedy, sent Mark Ward racing into the box. He appeared to be fouled by the luckless Borrows, but the referee initially ignored the spot-kick appeals. It was only when he spotted a linesman's flag did he finally stop play.

Beardsley, completely unruffled by the Coventry complaints, stepped up to fire the penalty hard and low into the bottom corner. The home fans celebrated with a chant that would echo around Goodison Park all season: "There's only one Peter Beardsley!"

Everton: Southall; Atteveld, Hinchcliffe, Ebbrell, Watson, Keown, Warzycha, Beardsley, Newell, Sheedy (McDonald), Ward. Substitute: Cottee.
Attendance: 20,542

Peter Beardsley celebrates with his teammates after scoring against Crystal Palace.

Farewell to 1991-92. Peter Beardsley and Neville Southall salute the fans after the final game against Chelsea.

Factfile: Howard Kendall's second spell at the Goodison Park helm would end in controversial circumstances. He quit on 4 December 1993, following an abortive attempt to sign Manchester United's Dion Dublin for £1.7 million.

The Everton board refused to sanction Kendall's bid for the big centre-forward and the manager felt this made his position untenable. It was ironic that Dublin, as a Coventry player, would go on to play for England against Chile at Wembley in February 1998. The Blues not only missed out on a quality striker. They also lost – albeit temporarily – an outstanding manager.

With Kendall gone, coach Jimmy Gabriel was forced to take the helm in difficult circumstances. Everton did not score a single goal for seven matches and a mighty challenge awaited new boss Mike Walker when he arrived from Norwich City in January 1994.

Walker had done well at Carrow Road, but he had no experience of managing a club of Everton's size and stature. His first signing was striker Brett Angell from Southend, a player whose goal return at a lower level was unquestionable, but who failed to make the grade at Goodison.

One great signing by Walker was battling midfielder Joe Parkinson who was captured from Bournemouth for a bargain £800,000. To provide the skilful element to the midfield, Anders Limpar arrived from Arsenal for £1.6 million. Gary Rowett was a squad signing from Cambridge for £300,000.

More significant was a double summer swoop for midfielder Vinny Samways from Spurs for £2.2 million and the popular signing of striker Daniel Amokachi from FC Bruge for £3 million. Walker can also take the credit for negotiating a loan deal for giant Scottish centre-forward Duncan Ferguson whose subsequent impact on the Goodison faithful would be immense. No one questioned the Glasgow Rangers player's ability. It was his disciplinary record that had worried possible buyers.

Walker in the first instance and then Joe Royle had tremendous faith in the big man whose love affair with the Evertonians blossomed from the word go.

Walker's Everton would have their moments, but he failed to spark the kind of revival the club craved. Everton finished 17th at the end of the 1993-94 campaign and two worrying – some would say terrifying – relegation campaigns followed, culminating in that famous last-gasp survival battle on 7 May 1994 which is featured in the next chapter. Walker's days were numbered.

The Great Escape! A Day For True Blue Patriotism

Saturday, 7 May 1994
Everton 3 Wimbledon 2

ASK any Evertonian to name the most sensational Goodison Park clash of all time and contrasting answers will come thick and fast.

This theatre of dreams has produced the lot in its time, great team performances, remarkable moments of individual magic, record breaking achievements and emotional Championship days that are part of Everton folklore.

You will have read about many of these landmark occasions in previous chapters. But what would get your vote as the most remarkable Goodison occasion of all time?

Senior fans will naturally recall that unforgettable day in 1928 when the immortal Dixie Dean scored his 60th League goal of the season in a breathtaking clash against Arsenal.

Others will talk about the goal-packed clash of 1935 when the Blues beat Sunderland 6-4 in the FA Cup, rated by many as the finest tie ever seen at Goodison.

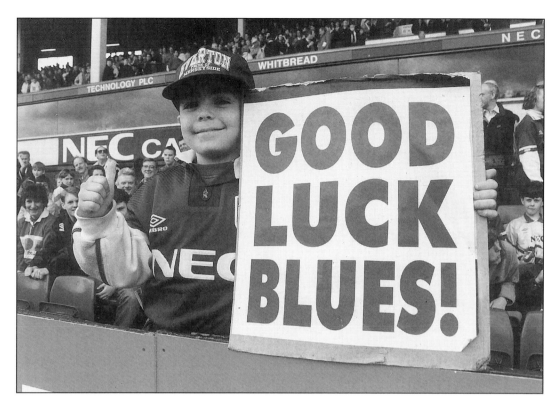

In the glorious 1980s, during the most successful period in the club's history, Everton's European Cup-winners' Cup demolition job on Bayern Munich is often spoken about as the the club's most unforgettable moment, not to mention that pulsating 4-4 derby FA Cup deadlock with Kenny Dalglish's Liverpool in February 1991.

Outsiders might therefore find it strange that the most sensational, heart stopping, tear-filled clash of them all was …against WIMBLEDON!

Need I say any more. This was the day, in May 1994, when the Blues came to within a few seconds of being relegated for the first time in 43 years.

It was unthinkable, it was little short of terrifying for the Goodison faithful, but it was a distinct possibility when the battling

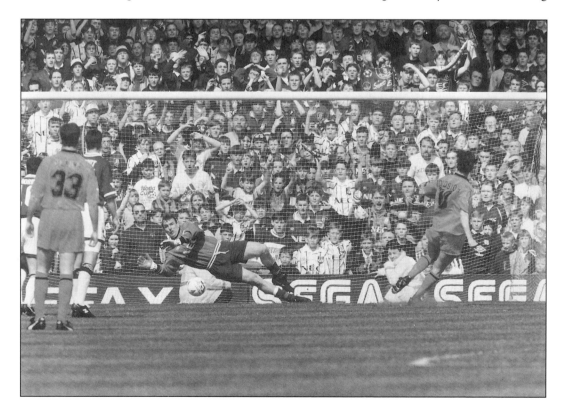

Goodison silenced …as Dean Holdsworth just manages to beat Neville Southall from the spot to open the scoring for Wimbledon.

Mr Cool ...Graham Stuart edges Everton back into the game from the penalty spot.

Londoners arrived on Merseyside for the final game of the season.

Nothing less than a win was going to be good enough, especially for chairman-elect Peter Johnson who was on the brink of concluding a takeover deal with a promised investment of around £20 million.

Johnson's dreams and ambitions were in danger of being torpedoed before his very eyes. Previously, he had successfully influenced Tranmere Rovers fortunes. But this was the big time with all the participants playing for big stakes. For instance, opposite number Sam Hammam ensured Wimbledon would not lie down by offering his players an all-expenses paid holiday to Las Vegas should they win this game and claim their highest-ever top flight placing.

It was therefore an occasion for Everton bravehearts, super optimism and blind

Barry Horne's 25-yard piledriver flies into the top corner of the net for a sensational equaliser against Wimbledon. "Who needs Cantona when we've got Barry Horne?" was the most popular post-match chant.

The goal that kept Everton up ...scored by Graham Stuart, hidden behind Tony Cottee.

faith. It was a day when grown men would cry and children would realise, perhaps for the first time, just what it really meant to be a True Blue.

When the unthinkable happened and Wimbledon surged into a two-goal lead inside 20 minutes, it was if the world had caved in.

The relegation roulette wheel was spinning wildly and that silver ball looked as if it would win The Dons their Vegas bonus. What happened next is something that Evertonians will never forget.

This was an afternoon when I could not bring myself to watch from the Press Box. It was not a day to be dispassionate and businesslike. Too much was at stake.

I sat in the Directors' Box, although not as a guest of the directors. I was with a party of loyal Evertonians who had taken over the mini sponsor's lounge near the Main Entrance, a tight gathering of a dozen or so Goodison fanatics who lunched together and talked together about happier days at the School of Soccer Science.

We were all graduates of that Academy, brought up with a Golden Vision of how

football should be played. Yet here we were, caught up in this all or nothing scrap with the Bash Street Kids. Would we survive or would we be part of one of the most calamitous days in the history of Everton Football Club?

This was clearly not a day for taking any chances. An old schoolfriend of mine, George Rice, had been lucky at the races a couple of days earlier. Drawing on this good fortune, he refused to change his clothes in the build-up to the Wimbledon showdown, even down to his underwear. Who were we to argue? A magician had actually been booked to entertain us (and calm us) in that tense hour before kick-off.

It was all very symbolic. We knew we might need a few tricks to outwit the battling Dons and we desperately wanted the magic to rub off on the players as they prepared just a few yards away in the home dressing-room.

As the seconds ticked away to 3pm, we reflected on the pre-match words of skipper Dave Watson who had declared: "This is the biggest game in the club's history. Everything is at stake. We simply

Hero of the hour. Fans rush on to mob two-goal hero Graham Stuart who proudly clutches the matchball.

must win and hope other results go our way. Everything is on the line against Wimbledon."

Manager Mike Walker popped his head into the sponsor's room to speak to us. It was our equivalent of the pre-match team talk. "We'll be alright," he said. "We'll win. Don't worry."

Trying to be equally positive, we offered him our conjurer friend as a genuine attacking alternative to Rideout, Cottee or Limpar. "You should see some of his tricks, Mike. He's just magic!"

Walker smiled and disappeared towards his inner sanctum, presumably to fill his players' heads with with the same optimistic thoughts that he had just dispensed in our company.

We headed into the stand, to be enveloped by a roar that signalled the arrival of the gladiators. Two weeks earlier, Crystal Palace boss Alan Smith had described Goodison as 'a great stadium, but not exactly hostile'.

This was a different ball game. The wall of sound lashed Wimbledon full in the face for three explosive opening minutes, at which point Everton – or should I say Anders Limpar – inexplicably put his finger, or rather his hand, on the self destruct button. The Swede recklessly handled Elkins' early corner kick and

Dean Holdsworth silenced the Goodison roar from the penalty spot.

After 20 minutes, more defensive chaos saw Gary Ablett deflect the ball into his own net to leave Everton's hold on the Premiership hanging on a thread.

Within 60 seconds of the restart, Limpar made amends when he won a penalty at the other end which Graham Stuart confidently converted.

The second half would be like the last round in a heavyweight championship fight. Everton were on the ropes. It was all or nothing.

Wimbledon goalkeeper Hans Segers parried a powerful Stuart shot a minute after the restart. Stuart was then a hero at the other end when he blocked a Holdsworth header on the goal line.

With only 23 minutes left a miracle was needed and it came in the shape of a thunderous 20 yards drive from Barry Horne that flew over Segers into the roof of the Wimbledon net to make it 2-2.

The stadium was now rocking as the fans urged one last push for safety. Fittingly, it was man-of-the-match Stuart who brought the house down, squeezing an 18-yard shot past Segers who really should have done better with this last-gasp effort on the 81st minute mark.

Who knows, maybe our magician

These faces tell the story ...we're safe!

255

friend had cast a spell as the ball left Graham's boot. No one cared. The final whistle couldn't be heard amidst the bedlam and the noise. We knew it was over when we saw Stuart grab the ball and run towards the tunnel, only to be swamped by fans as they invaded the pitch.

There were tears as well as non-stop cheers. I recall a young fan dropping to his knees in the middle of the pitch as chaos unfolded all around him. He had his head buried in his hands in sheer relief.

I hugged my pal George Rice, his face beaming. I wasn't sure if it was the victory or the relief that he could finally go home and change his 'lucky' underwear.

This truly had been the Great Escape, summed up perfectly at the end of the *Liverpool Echo* match report, penned by my colleague David Prentice.

Saturday was wonderful, but never again . . . please.

Everton: Southall, Snodin, Ablett, Watson, Unsworth, Stuart, Ebbrell (Barlow 80 minutes), Horne, Limpar, Cottee, Rideout. Subs not used: Angell, Kearton. *Attendance: 31, 297*

DAVE WATSON – MILLENNIUM GIANT
1990 -2000

WHEN Howard Kendall tried to sign giant centre-half Dave Watson from Norwich City in August 1986, he knew instinctively that he was on a winner. It wasn't any in-depth scouting report that persuaded the Everton manager that the defender was a gem. It was the response from his opposite number – Carrow Road boss Ken Brown.

The Norwich chief initially turned Kendall down flat with the words: " I can't sell him to you. It would be like losing an arm."

These words, intended to shun Kendall, only made him absolutely committed to capturing the Merseysider who began his career with Liverpool before making a massive impact on East Anglia.

FACTFILE

Born: Liverpool 1961.
Everton appearances: 523 (up to end of 1999-2000 season).
League Championship winner 1986-87.
FA Cup winner: 1995.
F.A. Cup runner-up: 1989.
Charity Shield winner: 1987 and 1995.
Simod Cup runner-up: 1989.
Zenith Data Systems runner-up: 1961.
England caps 12 (6 with Everton).

This was the campaign after the controversial sale of Gary Lineker to Barcelona who had captured the imagination of the Spaniards with a tremendous World Cup after amassing 40 goals in what proved to be his only season with the Blues. That goal haul had still not been enough to win Everton their second successive title in 1986 and the plan was to return to the tried and trusted battle plan that had secured the Championship in 1985.

It had been a bold decision by Kendall to release Lineker, but he felt the Blues were knocking too many high balls down the centre to exploit the England star's explosive pace. The manager was prepared to gamble and seek to exploit the wide midfield players more with goals coming from a variety of sources instead of being reliant on one striker, admittedly a very special one.

The fans were therefore paying particular attention to the subsequent summer signings – expecting the club to replace one superstar with another, especially with £2 million in the bank. Behind the scenes, the manager wasn't actually planning to make any major signings, but was rather looking to provide cover in several key positions.

As it turned out, the biggest amount of money he spent was £900,000 – for Watson. While no one doubted that the player had real ability, it was not looked on in the same light as a move for a glamorous striker or a skilful midfielder. Of course, Kendall didn't see it that way.

Ken Brown's words kept spinning around in his mind. "I can't sell you the lad. It would be like losing an arm."

In the end Norwich relented and Watson was heading back to familiar Merseyside territory. Derek Mountfield had been struggling with a recurring injury and Ian Marshall was the only other recognised centre-back of note. Mountfield had played his part in the 1984 FA Cup victory over Watford and the famous 1985 double winning season that brought the title and European Cup-winners' Cup to Goodison. He had also scored a string of crucial goals along the way.

It meant that Watson was not only the big investment after Lineker, but also coming in for a man who had become something of a crowd favourite. Dave found it hard to gain acceptance in those testing early days. There was also the expectation level of a crowd with their sights firmly on another title.

After two months the new man was left out as a fit Mountfield returned, but Kendall in his apt autobiography *Only The Best Is Good Enough* recalls: "I never once feared that Dave would give up the battle – he's not that sort of person – and after forcing his way back into my plans in early December, he not only became a permanent fixture but a firm crowd favourite. Very few players in English football can match Dave Watson for determination, courage and determination."

I would add another quality. Consistency. Watson would become a man mountain in the heart of the Blues' defence and the title was regained in 1987 – without Lineker. Dave made 35 League appearances that season. Success was sweet, not least because the Blues claimed the crown back from arch-rivals Liverpool – Dave's first club.

It's one thing for fans and journalists to wax lyrical about soccer stars, but when a fellow professional pays a very special tribute it suggests the individual on the receiving end has outstanding qualities. Watson's early partner and club skipper Kevin Ratcliffe described him as "the best centre-half I have ever played with."

Ultimately Kevin would pass the skipper's armband to Dave as the big defender powered on towards a Goodison playing career that would see him breaking the 500 game barrier with ease.

Watson had won his first international cap as a Norwich player in 1984 when he played in the famous Maracana Stadium against Brazil. He would win 12 caps, six of them with Everton and his last international appearance was in 1988. Most Evertonians believe he should have won many more and Dave made a personal point on that score in the build up to Euro 96 which was staged in this country.

The Everton skipper led a Hong Kong Select X1 against Terry Venables' England. It was meant to help ease the international side's way into those crucial Championships, but Watson is not a man to step aside in any situation. His team, made up of Hong Kong club players and veteran Premiership stars, embarrassed a star-studded England outfit.

Venables still didn't get the message, even though Watson had held aloft the FA Cup the previous summer after a sensational Wembley victory over Manchester United. Joe Parkinson, who played in front of Watson that day in a battling midfield, describes Watson as the perfect captain. He said: "Waggy would go around the dressing room before every game and let everyone know what was expected. He would make sure you got the first tackle in."

Evertonians will never forget that 1995 moment when Watson climbed the steps of the Royal Box to collect the Cup. The beam on his face when he thrust it high into the air was a sight to behold. It was a warrior revelling in a wonderful moment.

If I was asked to describe Dave Watson as a player I would simply say rock solid, no nonsense and inspirational. When under pressure, Dave would never take a chances with any fancy stuff. It was Row Z and let's get back into position for the next threat. This approach was simplistic but highly effective. In this respect he was the antithesis to T. G. Jones, Everton's Millennium Giant for the 1940s who would side-step a forward and slip a pass back to his goalkeeper. Both were supremely effective, but I think Dave would have enabled his manager to sleep more easily at night.

When you add the 250 appearances he made for Norwich City to the 520 plus appearances he made for Everton, you can see that Dave Watson has been an immovable object, both to rivals forwards and team mates hoping to usurp his position.

He has been an exemplary captain who had no hesitation in leading the club as caretaker boss during one tricky spell between managers. These days Watson's influence is growing on the backroom staff.

I suspect if Walter Smith was asked to part company with his veteran defender, even now, some familiar thoughts would go through his mind. "It would be like losing an arm!"

It is no surprise that Everton's Millennium Panel and the fans handed him the honour of being the club's last Millennium Giant of the century. Servants don't come any bigger.

Mike Walker would be sacked by Everton's new chairman Peter Johnson three months into the 1994-95 season. It was time to appoint a man steeped in Goodison tradition. Enter Joe Royle from Oldham Athletic in November 1994 to fulfil a boyhood dream.

Royle, of course, had enjoyed outstanding success as a player at Goodison. He had been a key member of the 1969-70 Championship side, had played for England and had served a solid managerial apprenticeship with the Latics.

His hour had come and Royle was determined to seize the opportunity. The big man would save Everton in another relegation-haunted season and lay the foundations for a revival that looked as if it had been ordained in a royal blue heaven.

Big Joe would inspire a sensational FA Cup triumph over Manchester United at Wembley in 1995. The following season, the club finished an encouraging sixth in the Premiership. The platform was there to power on with a good squad of players. The pacey and skilful Andre Kanchelskis was signed from Manchester United for £5 million after marathon negotiations.

Nick Barmby, with dreams of building a solid England career, arrived from Middlesbrough for £5.75 million. Solid centre-back Craig Short was captured for £2.65 million and outstanding Leeds United midfielder Gary Speed breezed in for £3.5 million, declaring he was 'coming home' to the club he had supported as a boy.

Speed would subsequently join Newcastle United in acrimonious circumstances in February 1998, but at this stage he was looking an extremely valuable acquisition.

Royle was undoubtedly a shrewd operator who wanted the very best for Everton. His team building included the purchase of goalkeeper Paul Gerrard from his former club Oldham and Royle also paved the way for powerful defender Slaven Bilic to join the Blues from West Ham for £4.4 million, although he was never able to name the Croatian star in one of his line-ups.

The player gave a commitment to Everton, but chose to finish the 1996-97 season with relegation-haunted West Ham. By the time he eventually arrived in the summer, Royle had upped and left after feeling, like Howard Kendall before him, that he no longer had the total backing of the board.

Royle's Everton had started that 1996-97 season well enough, but the side had a worrying run over the Christmas period. Despondency replaced previous high expectations and Royle's answer was to try to sign two Norwegian players in the shape of big striker Tore Andre Flo and the lesser known Claus Eftevaag.

Chairman Johnson, unconvinced and increasingly disenchanted, vetoed the signings. It would lead to the parting of the ways. Royle's last game was in March 1997 when Everton lost 2-0 at Goodison to Manchester United. It was all so ironic when you reflected on the glory that was Wembley 1995 when Royle's Dogs of War overshadowed the Red Devils underneath Wembley's twin towers.

There is no doubting Joe Royle's passion for the Everton job and the club that had always been his number one. Both manager and fans were left wondering about what might have been. The one thing they can never do in football is take your memories or your successes away. Royle's feat in managing an Everton FA Cup winning side as well as playing in a famous Championship outfit means he will forever remain a part of Goodison folklore.

He had helped to inspire some great moments at Goodison, not least against the old enemy Liverpool. He held a remarkable Indian Sign over the club's arch-rivals. One of those great derby victories will be highlighted in a later chapter. But first, the battle for Goodison Park itself, and how a revealing newspaper headline heralded the start of a major fight for control of one of Britain's greatest clubs.

Everton For Sale!

The inside story of Goodison's greatest power struggle

WHEN Peter Johnson crossed the River Mersey from Tranmere Rovers to finally be installed as the new owner of Everton, on 26 July 1994, Evertonians were looking forward to a bright new Goodison Park era after months of uncertainty.

At an extraordinary general meeting of shareholders, a resolution to double the existing capital of 2,500 shares was

The Cup that cheers ...Peter Johnson won his takeover battle in 1994 and was able to parade the FA Cup at Goodison the following year, after the victory over Manchester United.

approved by 1,659 votes to 22. Johnson's election as a director was unanimous. He was now the power behind the throne and immediately after the AGM was installed as chairman. Team manager Mike Walker suddenly found himself with £10 million at his disposal to use in the transfer market.

The ambition of the new regime was clear as Johnson declared: "I promise that I will be passionately committed to returning this great club to its former glory. I am absolutely delighted to be here. Everton can now get on with the job of winning some trophies again."

Johnson added: "This is an opportunity for me to help revive a great club. I love my football and I would not have gone outside of my home city for anything."

Johnson had fought a long battle for control with world famous theatre im-

presario and long standing Evertonian Bill Kenwright, but when the dust settled there was an encouraging show of togetherness.

Kenwright retained his place on the board and a key member of his consortium, Arthur Abercromby, joined him as a director along with John Suenson-Taylor, grandson of the late Sir John Moores.

Two of Johnson's own lieutenants from his Park Food Empire, Clifford Finch and Richard Hughes – both long-standing Evertonians – were also co-opted as directors.

There was great relief amongst supporters that the club now appeared to be moving forward at full steam after all the uncertainty of the previous year – and what a year it had been!

I found myself at the centre of the great Everton takeover debate, almost from day one. In May 1993 I broke the story on the

front page of the *Liverpool Echo* that would focus the minds of the fans for the next 14 months. The bombshell lead headline stated the unthinkable: "EVERTON FOR SALE."

The *Echo* had gained information that one of the big merchant banks in London had been instructed to seek ways of refinancing the Goodison outfit. At that time, a spokesman for Sir John Moores vigorously denied that the 97-year-old head of the Littlewoods organisation had any intention of selling his shares.

However, the 'Everton For Sale' exclusive WAS correct and it drew the whole affair out into the open. It actually helped the Everton board at the time because it had been working in something of a vacuum.

It would not be long before the battle lines were drawn up between Bill Kenwright and Peter Johnson. Kenwright showed his hand first and had the early backing of the fans who recognised his long-standing passion for the Blues. When Johnson, the ambitious chairman of Tranmere Rovers, threw his hat into the ring, it was felt that he had the wealth and the will to push the club ambitiously towards the 21st century.

At one point it looked as if there would be a debilitating internal war between the Park Foods chief and the rival consortium whose principal players were Kenwright and Arthur Abercromby, backed up by Tony Tighe, Tom Cannon and Mike Dyble.

Fans suddenly had to remind themselves of the history behind the Goodison power game. For years, Everton had been under the influence of the powerful Moores family. John Moores, the man who dreamed up the football pools and later became head of the powerful Littlewoods empire, was one of the most influential figures in the history of the club.

In the 1960s and early 1970s, the club was known as 'The Millionaires' as the chairman helped to inspire League and FA Cup glory while developing Goodison Park as a club stadium second to none in Britain.

But as age took its toll and Sir John became frail and unable to exert his influence in a meaningful way, it became increasingly difficult for the board to operate in a football world in which the Stock Market was beginning to walk hand-in-hand with the transfer market.

If the Everton club was to retain its position in English football's recognised top six – and if it was to compete with the Manchester Uniteds, the Liverpools and the increasingly influential big guns from the capital – there was no alternative but to generate new funds with a major injection of new money.

A young Sir John Moores would have acted with all of his time-honoured decisiveness and ambition for his beloved Blues. He still held the power in the shape of his majority shareholding, but his age and his frailty meant he was now confined

Peter Johnson's dream team, pictured in front of the new Stanley Park Stand on 20 August 1994 (from left to right): The Hon John Suenson-Taylor, (Lord Grantchester) Sir Philip Carter, Arthur Abercromby, Keith Tamlin, Clifford Finch, Peter Johnson (chairman), Mike Walker (manager), David Newton, Bill Kenwright, Richard Hughes and Jim Greenwood (chief executive). Missing board members are Dr David Marsh and Sir Desmond Pitcher.

to his home in Formby – a proud old man contemplating his final days, not the 21st century challenge that now faced Everton.

There is no doubt that he had talked about the future needs of the club to his two sons, John Jnr and Peter, but neither came close to having his passion for football in general and Everton in particular.

It is ironic in the extreme that the club Sir John Moores loved was being stifled by the circumstances of his fading health.

There was a growing need for Everton to be sold – and it all came to a head when the grand old gentleman of Goodison died peacefully in September 1993.

John Jnr and Peter, now held the controlling interest in Everton, but neither of them appeared ready or willing to pick up their late father's mantle and drive the club forward.

Both men, while steeped in Littlewoods tradition, had other business and recreational passions. John Moores Jnr, a Freeman of the City of Liverpool and Chancellor of John Moores University, was a successful farmer.

Peter, a colourful character, launched the Peter Moores Foundation in 1964 to support the arts and became a trustee of the Tate Gallery. *Who's Who* lists his pastimes as opera, shooting and fishing. No mention of football.

The Everton board now needed to act to get some movement. Some people on the outside questioned why there was a need for a financial revolution.

After all, had not the club enjoyed

League, FA Cup and European success just a few years earlier in the mid-1980s under the outstanding leadership of then chairman Sir Philip Carter who was still an active board member?

The cold truth was that times had changed. Landmark decisions in the early Nineties were becoming increasingly difficult to action without massive funds at your disposal.

The opportunity was finally there for someone to seize overall control and spark an ambitious new era, but who would pick up the gauntlet.

In the first instance, Kenwright was convinced that he was the man for all Everton seasons. His priority was to win the support of the Moores, a move he felt would smooth his path to victory and clinch his Goodison takeover dream.

He was therefore elated when, just before Christmas 1993, he met Peter and John Moores Jnr along with their sister Lady Grantchester and obtained a signed document, backing his takeover bid. Kenwright was convinced these official Heads Of Agreement were enough to win the day, but there was an unexpected twist in February 1994, when John Moores questioned the validity of a statement regarding his father's will. It was suggested that Sir John had declared that the new owner of Everton should be "selflessly devoted to the club and a 'safe pair of hands'".

The interpretation of this was that a only a 'True Blue' should own the club These words seemed to undermine Peter

Johnson's chances because of his former passion for rivals Liverpool FC .

Peter Moores had passed on his Everton inheritance to his sisters, Lady Grantchester and Janatha Stubbs. This effectively made John Moores Jnr the club's largest single shareholder with just under 21.2 per cent. He now declared that Sir John had not been specific about the future ownership of Everton.

He said: "My father himself had been a keen Manchester United supporter until his interest in Everton developed. He left no instructions at all in his will about his Everton shares. They were simply left to my brother and me. During his lifetime, my father discussed with me on several occasions his wishes for the future of the club and hence his shares.

"He urged me to use the shares to ensure that Everton was kept on a sound financial basis and above all achieve success. At no stage did he mention to me a 'safe pair of hands' or a 'True Blue'.

This statement was music to the ears of Peter Johnson, but left Bill Kenwright in a state of confusion. He still had the Heads of Agreement , signed in the presence of John and Peter Moores and Lady Grantchester, but it appeared that John Moores was now opening a clear route to the Goodison board room for Kenwright's big rival from Birkenhead.

At the same time, the Everton directors were now turned on a point of order, raised by Sir Desmond Pitcher. He stated it was not in the board's remit to favour one candidate over another and that they had no alternative but to accept the best offer on the table for the benefit of the shareholders. As Peter Johnson was now talking about £4,000 a share, double his original offer, Kenwright was blown out of the water.

In a financial nutshell, there were 2,500 shares in Everton FC prior to the takeover battle. As chairman-elect, Johnson was now prepared to underwrite the issue of a further 2,500 shares at £4,000 each, boosting the club's coffers by £10 million

and giving him a clear majority in the boardroom.

So it was that the greatest off-field battle ever fought at Goodison came to its conclusion. For his part, Kenwright declared: "Peter Johnson knows that I love Everton more than anything in the world. I wanted to check out his commitment, above and beyond the money side of it. Some people will suggest that all the delay has affected the team's performance, but this cannot possibly be true. Mike Walker has been given everything he has asked for.

"What people don't understand is that the buying and selling of a club as big as Everton involves a tremendous amount of legal work and accountancy. Because of my stand, Peter Johnson vastly improved his original offer and that can only be good for the Blues."

The new chairman was ecstatic at his success, pledging to do everything in his power to make Everton great again.

The revitalised board would kick-off the new 1994-95 campaign posing for a team picture of their own in late August, standing proudly on the lush Goodison Park pitch in front of the impressive new Stanley Park Stand which was very much a symbol of a new beginning.

For years, the previous wooden structure had been the domain of away supporters. It was decided that the giant new stand, built at a cost of £2.3m and capable of holding 6,000 supporters, would be filled with home fans. Indeed, this section would soon be rivalling the famous Gwladys Street as a base for some of the club's staunchest supporters.

There is no doubt that the move to fill both goal stands with passionate and committed Evertonians has helped to improve the atmosphere at this famous stadium. The volume can now be turned up to intimidate opponents from all sides.

Everton were back in business, on and off the pitch, and determined to play the GOODISON GLORY game once more.

Flying Scot ...Duncan Ferguson rises from the pack to head Everton into the lead against the old enemy.

Duncan Goes To War and Royle Is In His Own Blue Heaven

Monday, November 21st 1994
Everton 2 Liverpool 0

JOE Royle's return to Goodison in November 1994, boosted flagging spirits and inspired a wave of expectancy amongst the fans, even though Everton had won only once in 16 outings and were rock-bottom in the Premiership.

Royle's first challenge was to select a team to take on arch-rivals Liverpool in the 156th Merseyside derby. The occasion proved a shock for Graham Stuart, the man whose goals had kept Everton up at the end of the previous season in that sensational game against Wimbledon. Stuart was axed and Vinny Samways was another surprise omission. Samways had been Mike Walker's last acquisition for Everton prior to the parting of the ways. The midfielder had been signed from Spurs for £2.2 million during the summer.

Recalled for the Blues was John Ebbrell, named as part of a battling midfield quartet which included Barry Horne, Joe Parkinson and Andy Hinchcliffe. It was a clear sign of Royle's early thinking.

He urged his players to fight for the right to win the game by competing forcefully in every area. The Dogs of War were being let off the leash, the shape of things to come, although it should be emphasised that the side, on its day, could play good football as well as out-power opponents.

Former skipper Brian Labone, now one of Everton's greatest fans, backed up his old playing partner in the hours before the derby with a clear statement of intent when he said: "You can forget all about the School of Science. This game is all about getting at least one point. We won't be playing any fancy stuff, but you can be sure we will be challenging all the way."

The fans studied the League table,

aware that victory would lift the Blues up to third from bottom above Leicester City and Ipswich Town. However, the opposition were quietly confident to say the least. Tommy Smith, Labone's old 1960s adversary, was supremely optimistic, bordering on the cocky when it came to the big match predictions.

The Anfield Iron declared: "It's not like me to be so positive on these occasions, but I can't see anything other than a Liverpool victory. Everton DO have one mighty weapon …the Goodison Park crowd. They have been absolutely magnificent this season, week in, week out.

"But I can see the final margin being as much as 3-0 in our favour."

Smithy would not just be forced to eat humble pie by the end of the evening. he would choke on his bold prediction.

Everton would storm to a 2-0 success to give their new boss the perfect start. Just as significant was the sight of Duncan Ferguson's name on the scoresheet, his first strike for the club. After six games without a goal, big Duncan rose powerfully in the 56th minute to place a deft header past David James in the Liverpool goal.

Paul Rideout, who had replaced the injured Matt Jackson at half-time, netted the second in the final minute from eight yards out after James had failed to deal with Hinchcliffe's testing cross.

The visiting fans had taunted their rivals with chants of "You're Going Down" before the kick-off. They were now stunned and silent. Liverpool – vibrant, creative and lively in previous matches – had been out-tackled, outwitted and out-passed by opponents who were driven by a desperate need to move off the bottom rung of the Premiership ladder.

Royle summed up the performance perfectly when he said: "We went to war to get this result. I couldn't have asked for anything more – a clean sheet, two goals by the strikers and a local derby win against the old enemy."

It was a night for the Goodison strikers and streakers! Local man Mark Roberts bared all as he strode, stark naked, out of the Bullens Road Stand. Roberts ran the full length of the pitch, heading for goalkeeper Neville Southall, while play went on uninterrupted.

He had words of protest against Brian Clough painted across his back and

Joe Royle had every confidence in Duncan Ferguson. In the manager's eyes the big striker was number one, as Liverpool found out to their cost.

Factfile: Some Goodison derby folklore...

■ The first Goodison league derby took place on 13 October 1894. Everton were top of the table with seven wins from seven games and with a goal difference of 27-7. They beat Liverpool 3-0 to prove that the form book CAN count in these big confrontations..

■ The first player to score four times in a derby was Alex 'Sandy' Young, at Goodison Park on 1 April 1904. Everton won 5-2. Young was famous for wearing a 'snake' belt to hold up his baggy shorts.

■ The fans established their own derby record on 18 September 1948, when 78,299 of them turned up at Goodison Park. Everton were bottom of the old First Division at the time, but upset the form book to hold the old enemy to a 1-1 draw. Did the rival captains also achieve a record that day? Everton's Alex Stevenson was 36 and Jack Balmer of Liverpool was 32.

■ On 11 March 1967, the unmistakable sound of derby match cheers could be heard simultaneously on BOTH sides of Stanley Park! Goodison was the setting for an FA Cup fifth round clash, but the demand for tickets was so great that Liverpool arranged for closed circuit TV to relay black and white images to eight giant screens at Anfield. So it was that a 'new' derby record attendance was set of 105,000 with 68,851 fans at Goodison and 40,149 at Anfield! This remains the highest ever attendance for an FA Cup tie outside of Wembley.

■ Everton won 1-0 with a great goal from Alan Ball. The night was memorable for the gale force winds as well as the action. The organisers of the Anfield 'matinee' realised what a gamble it had all been when two of the screens blew away, half an hour after the final whistle. By then the fans were either on their way home or in the pubs which had been granted a late licence for the night.

* This was also the night when a 20 years old Evertonian, desperate for a Goodison ticket, put an advert in the *Liverpool Echo* offering his 1957 Ford Consul, complete with MoT certificate, for a 'passport' to the big game. Paul Gray was contacted by a man from Bootle and subsequently handed over the keys for a ground ticket, valued at just five shillings or 25p in modern terms.

■ In December 1969, the most famous own-goal ever scored in a derby found the back of the Everton net at Goodison. Sandy Brown was the unfortunate Blue who sent a bullet header past his own keeper, Gordon West as the home side crashed 3-0. Even now, all own-goals scored on Merseyside are referred to as a 'Sandy Brown'.

■ On 28 October 1978, Everton's derby hero Andy King suffered the indignity of being 'sent off' by a policeman at Goodison after scoring a famous winner against Liverpool. King was about to be interviewed by BBC commentator Richard Dukenfield for *Grandstand* on the final whistle. As the TV man began to ask his first question, a giant figure loomed behind them, grabbed them both by the collar and frog-marched them off the pitch. It was the police inspector in charge of that area who barked at the startled Dukenfield: "My instructions are that nobody is allowed on the pitch at the end of the game – and that means nobody!" And here was Andy thinking he had done a great job for the Boys In Blue!

The blue streak ...bare faced cheek or a genuine protest? A fan races towards Neville Southall as the derby action continues. He was protesting about Hillsborough comments made by Brian Clough.

Duncan. He gives us good options and makes such a difference."

Skipper Dave Watson backed up the plea to the new boss, saying: " The big man was on fire against Liverpool. He won everything in the air and caused them all kinds of problems."

Royle, of course, would put his faith in Ferguson in every way and it would prove one of Everton's most significant signings in years.

The Blues would soon be putting their relegation fears firmly behind them and embarking on a famous FA Cup run that would take them all the way to Wembley. The Dogs Of War were barking ever louder. Would this be the start of something big?

backside. Clough, writing about the Hillsborough Disaster, had made derogatory remarks about the Liverpool fans. Roberts was later fined £150 for baring all, his solicitor saying he had raised £250 for a children's charity after collecting sponsorship in pubs.

But the main headlines the next day were all about that sensational Everton victory. The back page of the *Liverpool Echo* declared: "BUY FERGUSON QUICKLY JOE."

It was fellow forward Paul Rideout who was urging the manager to make the powerful Scot his first signing. The £4 million Rangers striker had been on loan at Goodison for two months. Rideout said: "It would be great if we could keep

Everton: Southall, Jackson (Rideout 45), Ablett, Unsworth, Watson, Parkinson, Horne, Ebbrell, Hinchcliffe, Ferguson, Amokachi (Limpar 77). Substitute not used: Kearton.

Liverpool: James, Jones, Bjornebye (Redknapp 63), Babb, Ruddock, Scales, McManaman, Molby, Barnes, Fowler, Rush. Substitutes not used: Clough and Stenssgaard.

Attendance: 40,000

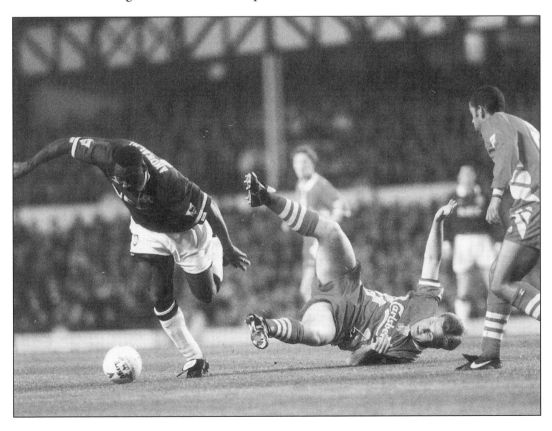

Fall guys ...Everton's Daniel Amokachi and Liverpool's Jan Molby collide in the heat of the derby battle.

Nil Satis Nisi Optimum – Goodison Park Faces a 21st-Century Challenge

WHEN Everton left Anfield in the summer of 1892 and made the short, but historic journey across Stanley Park to take up residence in their new Goodison Park home, it seemed as if stadium technology could be improved no further.

Goodison was described as *magnificently large, rivalling the greater American baseball pitches. One of the finest and most complete grounds in the whole kingdom.*

The fans stood on the raised cinder banks and marvelled at the sheer size of the place. The ground was enclosed by a high wooden fence. A covered grandstand had been built on the Bullens Road side of the pitch and – as the Everton directors ambitiously sanctioned further work – there was soon cover on all four sides.

This, for Victorian supporters, was a football paradise and as they moved rapidly towards the 20th century it seemed that Goodison Park, like some Roman amphitheatre, would stand for ever and a day – a proud testimony to the vision of chairman George Mahon and his pioneering fellow directors.

The Roman symbolism is perfectly apt. Mahon was the Emperor, taking his legions on a march to conquer new territory. Goodison was 'captured' and civilised. It was a temple to the god football and the Emperor and his subjects, quite naturally, would chant its praises in Latin.

Nil Satis Nisi Optimum – Only The Best Is Good Enough.

No one is quite sure when the famous motto was first used. But there is no doubting the fact that it summed up perfectly the club's powerful ambitions, on and off the pitch, at that time.

When it came to innovation, Goodison

Park was always one step ahead of the rest. No expense was spared, whether it was replacing a perfectly adequate stand with a spectacular new version, installing the latest floodlights, experimenting with undersoil heating or fitting an escalator to transport supporters to their seat in the gods, the directors of Everton FC have always lived up to the club's maxim.

Nil Satis Nisi Optimum. Yes, the great stadium would stand the test of time. Or would it? Goodison Park seemed as safe as the Bank of England.

When new chairman Peter Johnson arrived in 1994, it was business as usual. Like his ambitious predecessors, he wasted little time in sanctioning further improvements. The Stanley Park End had been completely rebuilt. A vast amount of upgrading took place all over the ground in the shape of new lounges, refreshment areas and better seating arrangements. Even the famous old entrance was given a new look.

More significantly, Johnson insisted that the interior decoration would now reflect the history of the club. Many of the lounge areas and function suites were previously packed with the kind of paintings and images that would have seemed more appropriate on your living room wall. On entering these rooms, you felt as if you were in a large hotel rather than a famous football club.

I have no doubt that someone had taken this decision constructively somewhere down the line as the stadium became a venue for conferences, wedding receptions and evening functions. As tasteful as it was a Football club as prestigious as Everton needs to focus on its proud past.

To his credit, Peter Johnson immediately grasped the importance of revelling in a glorious history. At Tranmere Rovers, he had named many of the bars after famous players. Ironically, Rovers had the Dixie Dean Lounge while Everton had the mundanely named 300 and 500 Clubs.

Johnson quickly put that right with the development of the luxury Dixie Dean Platinum Suite and the Alex Young and Joe Mercer Lounges. Suddenly we were talking Legends and a bar of the same name, containing some fascinating memorabilia, was opened in the Stanley Park Stand. Meanwhile, the hotel foyer art was at last replaced with powerful images of all the Everton greats. This work was pushed through energetically by Johnson's right-hand man Clifford Finch who was the new director responsible for the commercial side of the club.

Finch was not a salaried employee of Everton. His main role was on the board of directors at Johnson's Park Foods empire. When things began to go wrong for the club, and the chairman retreated into his shell, Finch annoyed many fans who thought he was simply too vocal and too powerful. They did not want to hear him speaking like a manager and were unhappy with his perceived influence on transfer talks. But he was a driving force at this time as projects like *The Evertonian* magazine and Radio and TV Everton began to take shape. Goodison Park appeared more vibrant than ever although there was definitely two factions within the board … the Johnson men and the rest, the latter including Bill Kenwright, Sir Philip Carter, Arthur Abercromby and Keith Tamlin, men who would ultimately become part of the new way forward.

But this was all for the future.

For the first time in over a century, new stadiums were being built and not just in the top flight. Huddersfield's McAlpine Stadium was both futuristic and impressive. Sunderland moved from their historic Roker Park home to the Stadium of Light. Middlesbrough left Ayresome Park for the purpose-built Riverside Stadium. Bolton Wanderers' Burnden Park ground, which in 1933 had attracted a crowd approaching 70,000 people for a League game against Manchester City, was bulldozed to the ground and replaced with the sweeping lines of the new Reebok Stadium. Derby County left their famously cramped home at the Baseball Ground for pastures new at Pride Park.

Therefore, a perfectly reasonable question was asked of Everton chairman Johnson in February 1998 during a TV interview. Would Everton ever consider leaving Goodison Park? The Blues chief didn't say yes, but then he didn't say no. The traditionalists took a deep breath. The *Liverpool Echo*, not surprisingly, pressed the chairman further.

On 19 February 1998 – 105 years and six months after the Goodison turnstiles had rattled for the first time – a banner headlined posed a straight question to the ambitious Mr Johnson: *Playing Away?*

Columnist Philip McNulty revealed that Everton were considering the long-term possibility of quitting Goodison Park, but reassuringly added that the fans would be consulted first.

Johnson admitted that relocation of the famous old stadium was an option under review, claiming it had become outdated in the wake of the Taylor Report that followed the Hillsborough Disaster. Clubs had been forced to go all-seater for safety reasons.

Taylor's logic was sound, but ground capacities would naturally be seriously affected. Goodison, which had once coped with crowds as high as 78,000 plus, was now jam-packed at the 40,000 mark.

Johnson said: *Our problem is that we are very much landlocked and our capacity could suffer further if we made major changes to two of our stands. That would be a problem. I'm not at all happy about the facilities that we have got behind us. I think Goodison has suffered for being so far advanced compared to any other stadium in the past. It really was a beautiful ground, but it is important that we do improve facilities and moving ground is a possibility.*

Those words, uttered constructively and honestly, were sacrilege to many fans. The chairman grasped the nettle and continued: *I can see the European Super League coming. I'm not sure what structure that would be, but I do believe it is the direction we will take.*

That is why it is so important to address the stadium issue because, when going into Europe, I think you will want the big clubs with the big grounds and the big followings. We must address that.

Johnson did not dismiss the traditionalists. He said: *I appreciate there are many people who would be concerned about any major move. We would always consider the feelings of the fans and we will certainly seek out their opinions.*

It was now out in the open and for the following two weeks, a fierce debate raged in the columns of the *Liverpool Echo* and *Football Echo*. Behind the scenes, plans were being drawn up to canvass supporters' opinions.

Johnson would live by his word and seek a mandate from the fans to take his plans a stage further, but even this unusual display of football democracy would spark controversy as an anti-move group – operating under the banner of *Goodison For-Everton* – raised objections. They were mistrustful of the way the votes would be counted and claimed Goodison Park was not beyond further redevelopment.

This was not a debate for sitting on the fence. Peter Johnson produced a glossy brochure entitled: *It's Your Move*. His opponents countered with a less sophisticated, but equally powerful offering, *Grounds For Concern*.

The battle lines were drawn.

Chairman Peter Johnson, pictured with his information pamphlet *It's Your Move*.

270

It's Your Move!
The Shape Of Things To Come

ON Tuesday, 6 May 1997 the *Liverpool Echo* took the rare step of leading its front page with a football story. It was hardly surprising as this was no ordinary soccer offering. It was an exclusive that would intrigue, surprise and stir every fan who had ever watched a match at Everton's historic Goodison Park home.

The main focus on the page was a colourful hand drawing of a futuristic 21st-century football ground – the New Goodison. It is fascinating to compare it to the simple ink drawing at the front of this book which was the first image fans had of Goodison Park, *c.*1892.

The New Goodison, although only at the visionary stage, showed four tiers of seats soaring up towards a cantilever roof. A thin line of Executive Boxes split the tiers, circling the entire stadium. This was Peter Johnson's £100 million Golden Vision of Everton's projected new home.

It was revealed that the chairman would take his ambitious blueprint to the fans in a poll, to be conducted at the final home game of the season against Chelsea.

Further drawings gave a bird's eye view of the New Goodison, complete with parking spaces for up to 12,000 cars. Johnson revealed that the new 60,000 seater stadium would be a monument to the club's past with a Visitors' Centre tracing the proud history of the club and a high profile museum in tandem with an Everton Hall Of Fame.

Fans approaching the stadium would move through a huge gate and and pass specially commissioned statues of Everton legends like Dixie Dean, Tommy Lawton and T.G.Jones.

Johnson, sensitive to the fact that many fans had scattered ashes of their loved ones at Goodison Park, proposed a Hall Of Remembrance at the new stadium where supporters could commemorate relatives.

It was made clear that this would be a football ground in every sense, not a sports stadium with a running track divorcing the crowd from the action. At the same time, themed restaurants, public houses and wide concourses would be integrated in the plans in line with the world's leading stadium designs.

Four people-carrying towers dominated the four corners of the stadium with the possibility of the famous tower on Everton's emblem being incorporated into the site. Johnson said that the club would use a top American conceptual architect as a consultant .

To publicise his plans, the chairman produced a booklet under the banner: *It's Your Move* – indicating that the fans would have the final say.

It was made clear to the supporters that the drawings were a vision and not the final draft. Johnson declared: *This is the chance of a lifetime for Everton Football Club. The designs are in the very early stages, but this will be a very special stadium because Everton is a very special club. We regard ourselves as Merseyside's club and we will be staying on Merseyside.*

This is our chance to put Everton at the forefront of European and world stadia, but the move will be ultimately decided by our fans. I want the new ground to reflect the standing and status of the club.

The chairman had visited stadia like Barcelona's Nou Camp, the San Siro in Milan and the new Ajax Arena in Holland as he considered his early plans. He said: *We want our new home to be a stadium Everton fans can relate to. It will be a football ground, first and foremost. There will be no running track and the massive stands will be located close to the pitch to recreate the intimidatory atmosphere of the current Goodison Park.*

The chairman realised that these proposals would not be welcomed by everybody. Too many glory days, packed

full of history and emotion, had unfolded at the club's spiritual home on Goodison Road to expect a simple "Yes" vote to the proposed move.

The loudest voice of dissent came from the Goodison-For-Everton group. It was right and proper that there would be serious debate because this was such an emotive issue. It was important that all views were aired.

GFE spokesman Greg Murphy, a supporter for 25 years, said: *We are not being deliberately awkward but we feel the fans should be consulted. We want to exercise the right to stay at Goodison.*

We don't deny the ground could do with improving and it is a shame the way it has been left to deteriorate. But we believe Everton should stay at its present home and the ground undergo redevelopment.

The Goodison For-Everton group said it would go public with its opposition at the home game against Arsenal in February, 1997. They declared they would organise petitions as well as holding collections to finance their opposition. Spokesman Murphy reaffirmed their total opposition to the notion of moving away from Goodison, adding: *We are not being wilfully intransigent or obstructive, We genuinely believe the club can stay at Goodison Park. Our belief is based on reason rather than nostalgic passion. We will be up and running for the Arsenal game. We want to make people aware of our existence and it is also a match against a club that has stayed at its famous old stadium, despite a reduced capacity.*

We would like to talk to the club about their plans. If Peter Johnson could prove to us there was no logistical way we could stay at Goodison, then we would accept that.

The GFE were not intent on civil war, but rather wanted an open debate. To this extent, the *Liverpool Daily Post* and *Echo*, plus the *Football Echo*, were inundated with letters from fans. This was effectively the first straw poll of how the vote might go. Having read and edited every one, my own prediction at this stage was for a 70 per cent "Yes" vote for the move. As it turned out, it would be slightly higher.

Nearly 84 per cent of the club's supporters who voted in the club's official poll supported Johnson's £100 million dream. A total of 37,000 *It's Your Move* brochures were distributed. Returned forms showed that 21,974 fans took part in the ballot with 18,374 backing the chairman's plans (83.62 per cent) while

3,600 (16.38 per cent) said "No" to the proposed relocation.

The Goodison-For-Everton group immediately declared that they were unhappy with the way the brochures had been distributed and also the manner in which the votes were counted. But Johnson had his mandate – and it was a powerful one. He immediately set the wheels in motion on an ambitious four-year project. He assured supporters that team building would not be affected by his stadium proposals and stated that he hoped the Blues would kick-off the 2001-02 season in the New Goodison, saying: *I am delighted with the overwhelming support. It is a massive mandate and our first priority is now to investigate where the site should be.*

In the lead-up to the poll, it was generally assumed that land near to Kirkby Golf Course, just four miles from Goodison Park, had been ear-marked for the new stadium. However, there was immediate opposition from golf course members and some locals. A planned inspection of the site was aborted when protesters blocked the entrance.

Peter Johnson was now forced to play his cards closer to his chest, aware that his successful poll was only the first victory. Naturally, in the absence of regular bulletins about the ground move, speculation was rife amongst supporters concerning possible venues. The South Docks were mentioned, along with the old Liverpool Airport site in Speke and even the former Cronton Colliery site near Widnes. There was now a new wave of opposition at suggestions that the club might be forced to consider options well outside the Liverpool City boundaries. Even the City Council took a stance, clearly determined to keep Everton in Liverpool.

The legendary George Mahon, the chairman who took Everton on their short but historic journey from Anfield to Goodison Park in 1892, faced up to all the same cries of suspicion and doubt before he was able to declare, in a now famous and stormy meeting at the Collegiate in Shaw Street, that he had the new ground 'in his pocket' – referring to a signed document in his possession securing the Mere Green Field on the north side of Stanley Park. This would become Goodison.

Mahon would almost certainly have related to Peter Johnson's challenge in every way. Football stadiums become second homes to loyal supporters. When the 'castle' is threatened, people pull up the drawbridge.

The great Goodison debate has shown no sign of abating. Indeed, it reared its head again in June 2000, following the sensational news from Anfield that arch-rivals Liverpool were plotting a shock move of just a few hundred yards into Stanley Park – ironically to the site of Everton's very first pitch. However, we are still focusing on the 1997-98 campaign which had just one priority for manager Howard Kendall – survival.

This would be a campaign in which the Blues would suffer the indignity of holding up the bottom of the table for an uncomfortable spell in December before climbing to safety under the astute guidance of the vastly experienced Kendall, but even the most testing of campaigns have their high spots. The Goodison story continues.

An Amazing Row, A Warning To The Stars – And Danny Boy's Perfect Derby Response

Saturday, October 18 1997
Everton 2 Liverpool 0

EVERTON'S struggling stars went into the 157th League derby with mixed emotions. On the one hand, they could look back on a string of memorable displays against an old enemy who appeared to have lost the will and the way to beat their Goodison Park rivals.

Against that, the Blues were struggling near the foot of the Premiership table and entering this big game on the back of a sensational midweek Coca-Cola Cup reversal at Coventry City where they had crashed 4-1 in bitterly disappointing circumstances. At the end of that game, incensed manager Howard Kendall stormed on to the field and appeared to tell his players to lap the pitch. Those watching in the stands interpreted this as the definitive slap across the face for Everton's rock-bottom stars. Kendall would later claim that his men had simply been told to go on a 'warm-down' jog.

Whatever the case, they were remarkable scenes as Craig Short in particular exchanged heated words with his furious manager. The players eventually trudged off, shaken and hopefully stirred.

Kendall had questioned their pride – and rightly so. While some would see it as a negative, the vast majority of fans saw it as a positive. This had been a crucial game for Everton and they had let themselves down badly with the manner of their performance.

Duncan Ferguson rises powerfully in the penalty area to beat Neil Ruddock to the ball and put Liverpool under pressure with a clever flick-on. Big Duncan would once again be a thorn in the side of the Mersey Reds as Everton claimed a sensational victory at Goodison Park.

Teenage forward Danny Cadamarteri constantly had the Liverpool defence on edge in the derby. His pace tested the resolve and experience of Neil Ruddock, beaten to the ball here by the determined Everton striker.

The manager, far from taking the heat out of the situation, subsequently threw down the ultimate challenge to his stars as a testing derby confrontation with Liverpool loomed on the Saturday. Kendall said that his players' futures were at stake following that amazing on-field bust-up at Coventry. Even chairman Peter Johnson joined the debate, saying: "I'm quite sure we will pull out all the stops against Liverpool because this is the nature of the derby. But it is a little unfortunate that the same effort has not been noticeable in our other games this season. If you could put the derby passion into our next 30 matches I think you would see us climbing the table"

Clearly, even top stars like Duncan Ferguson and Nick Barmby were under pressure as Everton, third from bottom, entered a vital three-game spell against Liverpool, Coventry again and fellow

strugglers Southampton. The vastly experienced Kendall had rattled the cage and his humiliated players were snarling. So would the manager's psychology work or would it backfire on him in the derby?

As it turned out, the Blues would not just keep up their remarkable Indian Sign over their arch-rivals. They would also kick the form book over the Gwladys Street Stand. There is no doubt about it, the Blues went into this game as the biggest underdogs for years. They ended it as Mersey Top Dogs once more, rediscovering all the passion and spirit which had deserted them at Highfield Road.

Neville Southall was making an unprecedented 41st derby appearance. Was it also to be his last? The great goalkeeper would soon be making way for young pretender Thomas Myhre and accepting loan spells at Southend United and Stoke City. Yet on this day, Southall was at his brilliant best. He looked as calm, assured and totally in control as in any of his 570 plus previous appearances for the Blues.

The defence in general looked more organised. Up front, Nick Barmby was possibly unlucky to lose his place, but the young man who was named alongside Duncan Ferguson would end up being the toast of Goodison Park by the end of an eventful afternoon.

Danny Cadamarteri's pace and enthusiasm was the perfect foil for big Duncan's flicks which caused panic around the Liverpool box. At the same time, the Scot himself was more authoritative and fired up. These matches are traditionally explosive affairs. This one was no different. Graham Stuart found himself cautioned after only two minutes. The visitors suddenly realised that form and league position are not necessarily the best guides when trying to predict a derby result.

Cadamarteri, at 18 one of the youngest players on the pitch, almost embarrassed rival 'keeper David James on the 15-minute mark. The Liverpool man dawdled over a clearance and the speedy forward raced in, almost making his opponent pay a heavy price.

Robbie Fowler and Karlheinz Riedle shot wide at the other end before Short, caught up in that amazing row with boss Kendall at Coventry, showed exactly the right response. His outstanding tackle prevented Fowler from shooting on target from 12 yards out. Everton had further chances of their own before finally rocking their rivals on the stroke of half-time.

Andy Hinchliffe's swerving corner had

Liverpool in all kinds of trouble. James, in attempting to clear, punched the ball against the unfortunate Neil Ruddock who watched in horror as it rebounded off him into the net in front of the ecstatic Gwladys Street fans. Goodison exploded and the Everton players headed for the dressing-room at the interval to the deafening sound of a standing ovation. What a difference a few days can make!

In a hectic second period, Southall would use all his experience to foil the marauding Steve McManaman, the 'keeper racing out of his area to block with his legs. Then Short made an unexpected 40-yard run out of defence before setting up the lively Cadamarteri whose shot was stopped by James. Everton survived a frantic scramble of their own when a Stig Bjornebye corner, whipped in as viciously as Andy Hinchcliffe's earlier goal-creating effort, was met by Paul Ince. The ball flew towards the net, only to strike Earl Barrett on the arm and roll along the goal-line before being hooked clear by Gary Speed.

If the incident had happened in front of the Kop, the resulting roar might have persuaded the referee to award a penalty. In truth, there was no intent by the defender and Everton escaped a nail-biting moment.

Almost immediately, the Blues would calm the nerves of their fans with a 75th-minute goal that completely flattened Liverpool's revival hopes. Defender Bjorne Kvarme learned that you cannot be anything less than totally positive in a derby. He was robbed just inside his own half by the alert Cadamarteri and the teenager sprinted away down the left before cutting inside the startled Neil Ruddock. The ball flashed from the forward's right boot into the back of the net.

Everton had secured three vital points, but in real terms

What a moment for Danny Cadamarteri as his right-foot shot flashes hard and low into the corner of the Liverpool net to seal a memorable 2-0 derby victory for the Blues. Oyvind Leonhardsen can only watch as Cadamarteri strikes from inside the box, having cut inside the helpless Neil Ruddock.

the result was much more important than that. It was the perfect platform to launch a spirited charge out of the relegation danger zone. There was also a bonus for match-winner Cadamarteri, if he needed one. His goal meant he had found the net five times in six starts for the Blues. England manager Glenn Hoddle was in the stands who no doubt made a note for the future, declaring: "Age doesn't come into it. It's quality that counts."

Veteran Everton defender Dave Watson added: "Danny doesn't have a care in the world. I've seen kids a bag of nerves before big matches, but Danny's got the headphones on and dancing around the dressing room. He's some character."

The young man himself said: "I was determined to put Kvarme under pressure and nick the ball away from him. I ran towards the area and saw Neil Ruddock moving towards me and I decided that if I pulled the ball across him, I would have a clear shot on goal. So that's what I did. I've already scored against Arsenal this season, the team I supported as a boy. But you can't top this feeling. It was absolutely magic."

That is precisely how the *Football Echo* saw it. The headline 'Cadamagic' stretched across the front page, declaring an outstanding Everton victory.

The last word had to go to delighted boss Kendall who had slaughtered his team for lack of pride and effort at Coventry just days earlier. He had a special word for the kids like Cadamarteri and fellow teenager John Oster, saying: "They have shown they can come into the side and not be affected by the big occasion."

The Evertonians walked tall out of Goodison Park. They would see their side hold the old enemy 0-0 in the return at Anfield in February, 1998. While no one could claim that this was anything less than another season of frustration for the supporters, the derby matches helped to raise the spirits and suggest that Howard Kendall's third Goodison Park reign would ultimately get the club back on track for glory.

Everton: Southall, Barrett, Watson, Short, Hinchcliffe, Stuart, Speed, Williamson, Oster (McCann 66), Ferguson, Cadamarteri (Ball 87). Subs not used: Gerrard, Phelan and Barmby.

Liverpool: James, McAteer, Ruddock, Kvarme, Bjornebye, McManaman, Thomas, Ince, Berger (Leonhardsen 55), Fowler, Riedle (Owen 50). Subs not used: Nielsen, Harkness, Wright.
Attendance: 40,112

The Relegation Nightmare That Turned Into A Fan-tastic Day

Sunday, 10 May 1998
Everton 1 Coventry City 1

EVERTON went into the final game of the 1997-98 season with their proud 44-year unbroken record in the top flight hanging by a thread.

The mathematics were frighteningly simple. The Blues' result against Coventry City at Goodison Park had to be better than that of relegation rivals Bolton Wanderers at Chelsea.

A win for the men from the Reebok Stadium would send one of football's greatest names plummeting into what was effectively English football's Second Division – now the Nationwide League's First Division – for the first time since 1954, and Bolton, buoyed by a string of end-of-season victories, had a self-belief that suggested Everton's fate was sealed.

Wanderers were further encouraged by the fact that opponents Chelsea were just days away from a crucial European Cup-winners' Cup Final against Stuttgart. The Londoners had reported a string of pre-match injuries which suggested they had their own agenda. All this – and more – played on the minds of the Everton faithful as they made their way to Goodison Park for what was billed as the 'Day Of Destiny'.

Over the previous 106 years, there had been many eventful days at Goodison Park. For tension, drama and sheer relief, it seemed that the mind-blowing survival clash against Wimbledon in 1994 would never be surpassed. But at the end of 90 nerve-jangling minutes, this life-saver against Coventry City would rival it as one of the most emotional games ever witnessed at the stadium.

Everton drew 1-1 in a clash that had more twists and turns than a *Brookside* script while Bolton lost their nerve – and their treasured place in the Premiership – after crashing 2-0 at Stamford Bridge. In the final reckoning, the two relegation rivals shared the same number of points (40) and the same number of goals (41). But Wanderers had conceded five more goals (61 against 56) and that sealed their fate.

The goal that mattered for Everton in

this clash was rifled home by Gareth Farrelly after only six minutes. The ball flew into the top corner of the net from his right boot and Goodison Park simply exploded. The royal blue army had provided remarkable support all season, making a mockery of the club's relegation plight. Now, 40,109 dedicated Evertonians switched up the volume to keep the players in the race.

All over the stadium, fans with radios kept track of Bolton's progress. This was not a day for faint hearts.

In the 73rd minute, a surreal roar went up that signalled news from Stamford Bridge. The chant that accompanied it was not for any player on the Goodison pitch. "Vialli, Vialli, Vialli." Chelsea's player-manager had rocked brave Bolton to become an adopted Everton super hero in his own right.

The gods were smiling on the Blues, who now won an 84th-minute penalty. Coventry defender Paul Williams appeared to win the ball cleanly as substitute Danny Cadamarteri tried to force his way through. Nick Barmby, Everton's undoubted man-of-the-match, was handed the challenge of beating Magnus Hedman from the spot. Somehow, the goalkeeper flew to his right to push the kick away.

Incredibly, Coventry now swept forward at the other end where the giant Dion Dublin rose to meet a David Burrows cross. The striker's header sailed through the hands of the diving Thomas Myhre. The visitors were level and every fan in the stadium knew that just one more goal from Coventry, or an equaliser for Bolton, would send Everton crashing out of the Premiership.

Instead, the only other goal came from

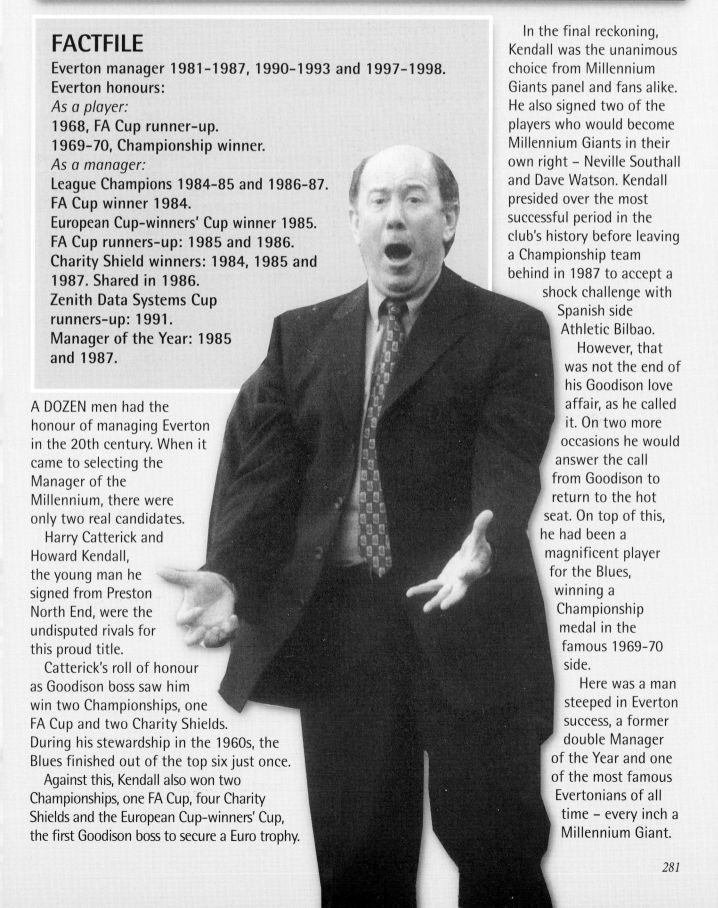

HOWARD KENDALL
MANAGER OF THE MILLENNIUM

FACTFILE

Everton manager 1981-1987, 1990-1993 and 1997-1998.
Everton honours:
As a player:
1968, FA Cup runner-up.
1969-70, Championship winner.
As a manager:
League Champions 1984-85 and 1986-87.
FA Cup winner 1984.
European Cup-winners' Cup winner 1985.
FA Cup runners-up: 1985 and 1986.
Charity Shield winners: 1984, 1985 and
1987. Shared in 1986.
Zenith Data Systems Cup
runners-up: 1991.
Manager of the Year: 1985
and 1987.

A DOZEN men had the honour of managing Everton in the 20th century. When it came to selecting the Manager of the Millennium, there were only two real candidates.

Harry Catterick and Howard Kendall, the young man he signed from Preston North End, were the undisputed rivals for this proud title.

Catterick's roll of honour as Goodison boss saw him win two Championships, one FA Cup and two Charity Shields. During his stewardship in the 1960s, the Blues finished out of the top six just once.

Against this, Kendall also won two Championships, one FA Cup, four Charity Shields and the European Cup-winners' Cup, the first Goodison boss to secure a Euro trophy.

In the final reckoning, Kendall was the unanimous choice from Millennium Giants panel and fans alike. He also signed two of the players who would become Millennium Giants in their own right – Neville Southall and Dave Watson. Kendall presided over the most successful period in the club's history before leaving a Championship team behind in 1987 to accept a shock challenge with Spanish side Athletic Bilbao.

However, that was not the end of his Goodison love affair, as he called it. On two more occasions he would answer the call from Goodison to return to the hot seat. On top of this, he had been a magnificent player for the Blues, winning a Championship medal in the famous 1969-70 side.

Here was a man steeped in Everton success, a former double Manager of the Year and one of the most famous Evertonians of all time – every inch a Millennium Giant.

Chelsea's Jody Morris. Bewildered Bolton were buried. Everton had starred in a re-run of the *Great Escape*, but the message from the most relieved fans in football was a simple one.

This must never be allowed to happen again. Manager Howard Kendall made the pledge when he emerged from an emotion-packed dressing room. He said: "I don't want to go through that again and I say now that this football club will never go through another day like that while I am manager.

"It is a great sense of relief. I think there has been doom and gloom around the place with people pointing the finger. People not involved in football management have been telling me what I have been doing wrong. The build-up to the game was disappointing, but there was never a negative thought in the heads of our fans. They were magnificent."

Nick Barmby put his penalty disappointment behind him to salute the supporters. The battling midfielder said: "I have never heard anything like that crowd before. I was lucky enough to be involved in the European Championship semi-final against Germany in 1996 at Wembley.

That was an unbelievable occasion, but the Everton crowd topped that. I can't speak highly enough of our supporters. It was unbelievable. You couldn't help but get emotional about it and I would like to thank every single one of them.

"I just hope for their sakes that they never have to go through something like that again."

The fans had swarmed on to the pitch at the end, but the mood of elation soon turned to one of anger. Chairman Peter Johnson felt the brunt of that criticism, but the supporters were soon concentrating on a night of celebration. They had earned it. Everton had been the relegation-haunted club with the champion fans.

Everton: Myhre, O'Kane, Short, Watson, Tiler, Ball, Hutchison, Barmby, Farrelly (McCann 90), Ferguson, Madar (Cadamarteri 48). Subs not used: Gerrard, Bilic and Beagrie.

Coventry City: Hedman, Nilsson, Shaw, Breen (Williams 51), Burrows, Telfer (Hall 89), Solvedt, Boateng, Whelan, Dublin, Huckerby (Howarth 68). Subs not used: Ogrizovic and Boland.

Attendance: 40,109.

Factfile: With another survival campaign behind them, Evertonians prepared for the summer break of 1998 wondering what the future might hold. They had gone through so much in the 1990s, but apart from that one moment of FA Cup glory midway through the decade, there had been nothing but frustration. The fact that the Blues had enjoyed a golden era in the 1980s seemed to add to the pain.

If Kendall thought his feat in plotting a successful survival course would give him further breathing space to rebuild, he was mistaken. The pressure on the chairman saw Kendall depart for the third and last time. It is enough to say Kendall was gone, but he would never be forgotten.

Johnson now set about on his search for his fourth Everton manager. This time, he would not make the mistake of claiming he was in the market for "a world class replacement," having been caught out once before and held to account when the chase became a saga. Manchester United assistant boss Brian Kidd, a former Everton player, was linked with the job, but he was untried and unproven. Leicester's highly rated Martin O'Neill was approached and looked on the verge of accepting. His Filbert Street chairman improved his contract and Johnson seemed to have a major problem.

Then it emerged that Sheffield Wednesday were on the brink of capturing former Glasgow Rangers boss Walter Smith, admired for his success north of the border. Johnson moved in to upstage the Hillsborough club. Disciplinarian Smith could see the potential at Goodison Park. He had left one soccer hotbed and he relished the thought of heading into another along with his respected assistant Archie Knox.

Johnson, having pulled off this coup, suddenly got caught up in the moment and sanctioned a host of big money deals. Smith signed French midfield Olivier Dacourt,

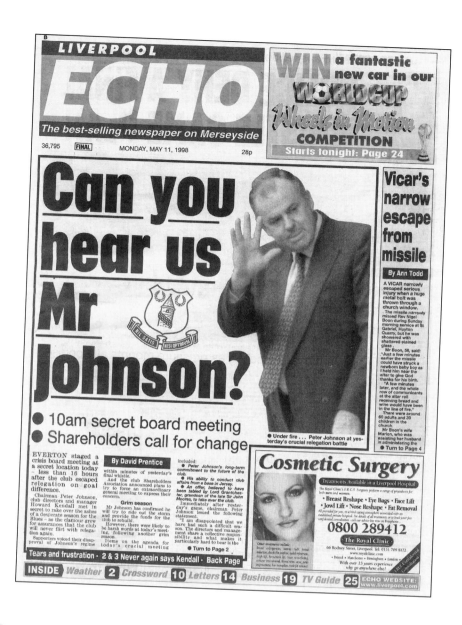

It is Monday, May 11, 1998 and Everton have just survived another relegation nightmare. The fans and shareholders called for change. The *Liverpool Echo* asked a simple question: "Can you hear us Mr Johnson?.

Italian central defender Marco Materazzi, African star Ibrahima Bakayoko, Scottish midfielder John Collins and Tranmere's highly-rated goalkeeper Steve Simonsen. The outlay was in the region of £20 million. The new manager had no idea that he was spending money that the club simply could not afford. Dark clouds were gathering in those blue skies and in November1998, the bank put so much pressure on the club to reduce their overdraft that the unthinkable happened.

Everton accepted a £7 million offer from Newcastle for the fans greatest hero, skipper and centre forward Duncan Ferguson.

Ironically, the deal was pushed though on the day the Geordies played a League game at Goodison. The 1-0 scoreline in Everton's favour was a total irrelevance. An icon had gone. It emerged that the deal was done over the head of the manager and it sparked a showdown that would finally bring Johnson's controversial reign to an end.

Smith, as honest and up front as they come, refused to say that he had sanctioned the deal. With the pressure now white hot, the chairman and majority shareholder quit. Once again, Everton Football Club was up for grabs. What no one realised was that the search for a new owner would literally stretch out into the wide blue yonder. It would take a whole year before the saga was settled and during that time Dacourt, Bakayoko and Materatzzi all departed, good news for the bank manager but bad news for Smith who found himself operating with a painfully thin squad.

The manager would use every ounce of experience to keep the club on and even keel. There were signs that the Blues had arrested the slide and that the club could finally move forward, but under whose stewardship. Bill Kenwright would now run a marathon to fulfil a royal blue dream

Kenwright's Blue Blood Brothers Take Centre Stage

PETER Johnson's Goodison Park reign was balancing on a knife edge in November 1998. The decision to sell Duncan Ferguson to Newcastle United to appease the bank had set off a tidal wave that would ultimately swamp the club's majority shareholder, although the writing had been on the wall long before that controversial news rocked the blue half of Merseyside.

As manager Walter Smith considered his own position, director Bill Kenwright prepared for the second time to embark on a True Blue fight for control of the club.

Little did we know at that point in time that the takeover battle would become a complicated saga, lasting a year.

The real frustration for both manager and fans was that not a penny of the £7 million fee for Ferguson would be available for new signings. Instead it would be used to eat into a massive £20 million plus bank overdraft which had left Everton in a dire financial position.

In the December, Kenwright declared that he and Sir Philip Carter would join forces as the Blue Blood Brothers who could lead Everton into an exciting new era. Of course, Blood Brothers was and is one of the theatre impresario's most successful shows. Could the magic rub off in a football sense?

With Johnson operating his own business from Jersey, the respected Carter had returned to the chairman's seat. Now, with Johnson gone, Kenwright was named as Deputy Chairman and he was the first to show his hand on the ownership front, confirming that he wanted to buy the majority shareholding.

He said: "I made an offer for Everton Football Club four years ago, but at that time I wasn't sure if I was the man to take Everton into the future. Now I am pretty sure that the right people are in place. If I can put together a consortium that is successful then Sir Philip will continue as chairman for as long as he wants because as far as I am concerned the breakdown in Everton's fortunes happened in 1991 when Sir Philip was deposed as chairman – a move I tried to block at the time."

Kenwright revealed that his bid four years earlier included his house, demonstrating just how desperate he had been at that time to claim the royal blue prize.

"I take risks and I can't think of anything in life that I'd rather risk more on than Everton Football Club," he declared. "This is a great day in my life as I once again try to buy the club, but I have to be realistic. It's a big job. There might be other people out there who will pay fortunes for the club, but I still believe they will come through me anyway from what I've heard over the past 12 months."

Carter was asked if more players would be sold to further appease the bank. He smiled and said: "That's not my style."

Clearly, the Kenwright-Carter camp was fighting back and the fans hoped for a swift resolution. However, three months later – in February 1999 – there was still no news of significant progress. Johnson was adamant that he would not give the club away, as he saw it. A fans' group organised a petition, urging him to sell at a sensible price.

I spoke to Kenwright who was anxious to calm the fans' fears. It was a game of cat and mouse with the new vice-chairman keen to keep the communication lines open with the old chairman. Kenwright clarified a number of important points, saying: "It would not be right to discuss in public the actual size of any offer and what Peter Johnson might require to step aside, but I have always been hopeful that we can reach an agreement."

Behind this brave front was an uncertainty stemming from Kenwright's bitter 1994 experience when he had a signed agreement with the controlling Moores family in his hand, only to see it snatched from him at the last possible moment by Johnson's late bid

Kenwright didn't want to have to face such a body blow again and his new film had a fitting title: *Don't Go Breaking My Heart.*

The vice chairman explained his mixed emotions. He said: "On the one hand I am thrilled that I am even talking about a takeover again. On the other I am sad that things have not worked out because it means the club has not progressed in the way all Evertonians like myself hoped it would.

"Yes, I'm thrilled that my dream of leading the club is still alive, but it is a double edged sword. The new leader of Everton will face a bigger challenge now than when Peter Johnson took the chair. It's a whole new ball game because of the vast investment in other leading clubs, not least those in London."

There were three key challenges. The complicated task of securing the major shareholding, the battle to stabilise the club financially and the need to ensure that manager Smith still had enough funds to strengthen should he so desire. Smith had been encouraged to spend as if there was no tomorrow the previous summer when £20 million captured the likes of Olivier Dacourt and John Collins, to name but two.

He would never have gone down that route if he had known the true extent of the club's finances. Now Smith would show that he was not just a good manager, but a realist who would work with the board to achieve stability while not forgetting that fans remain ambitious, regardless of bank overdrafts. There would still have to be measured progress and in this respect Smith achieved miracles with a painfully thin squad.

Sir Philip Carter recognised the manager's special qualities when he said: "He has a total grasp of the situation. Despite speculation about his future, he is in the place he wants to be, doing the job he wants to do. He is under no pressure

from the board. He knows what the score is. I have huge confidence in him that he will lead us forward on the field."

Kenwright picked up on the shock sale of Ferguson, saying: "I was one of those fans who had written angrily to the board 40 years earlier when Everton got rid of my hero Dave Hickson. I told them they didn't understand us. I therefore had every sympathy with those people who were totally bemused about the sale of Duncan to Newcastle. It was history repeating itself. However, we have had a serious financial situation and the board is now trying to deal with it."

Kenwright was still the only one who had come forward publicly to try and buy the club. He had no idea if Johnson was talking to a third party or a variety of possible bidders. This uncertainty further angered the fans who had previously waged war against Johnson's regime and his style of management.

Kenwright assessed the situation with an intriguing quote. he said: "Do I think Peter Johnson made mistakes? Yes, definitely. Is he the devil some fans would like to paint him? No. Do I in any way condone the threats and talk of violence against him? Definitely not. Do I think it is right that he cannot feel comfortable in his home city? Definitely not. Whoever takes over from him just has to get it right."

This was an honest appraisal of a mounting crisis. Kenwright still had to play the public relations game, but then this came naturally to him.

Deep down, his frustration was mounting, but he remained resolute and told the fans: "I believe that every player, whether at youth, reserve, first team or international level, need to know that there is a real future for this club and that everyone is pulling in the same direction."

He didn't add, everyone but the majority shareholder. Johnson was still playing his cards close to his chest and the supporters were becoming increasingly edgy.

Walter Smith now stepped into the debate – putting his faith firmly in the

Kenwright bid. The man who famously had stood up against the former chairman after the Ferguson debacle and effectively forced his resignation, said: "The situation the club finds itself in has gone on long enough. It's time it was resolved, one way or the other. It is not doing the club any good at all to have this uncertainty hanging over us all the time.

"Since Peter Johnson took a back step, I have had to work more closely with different people – Sir Philip, Michael Dunford and obviously Bill.

"I know just how deep his affection is for this club. It makes him a natural to have overall ownership of and responsibility for Everton."

It was now March 1999 and Kenwright finally appeared to be making progress as representatives of the Hong Kong and Shanghai Banking Corporation arrived on Merseyside to tour Goodison Park and the Bellefield training headquarters. More importantly, these potential financial backers were taking a long hard look at the club's troubled financial affairs. The suggestion was that this could takes months and with Everton's Premiership status still in doubt, optimism was guarded.

April didn't just bring showers. Once again the clouds of uncertainty were gathering on the field of play, two wins in 15 League games plunging the Blues into the relegation frame with the future ownership of the club still months from being decided.

A suicidal home 2-1 home defeat against Sheffield Wednesday dropped the club into the bottom three for the first time since August. Kenwright admitted that the Blues need to win three, maybe more of the last six games and made it clear that there would be no resolution regarding the takeover situation before the end of the season.

It was clear that HSBC wanted to know which division the Blues would be playing in before they showed the colour of their money. Kenwright had always admitted that he didn't have the money himself to put together a package capable of meeting Johnson's demands.

The tough six game run-in that the vice chairman had spoken of included away games with Newcastle (and potentially Duncan Ferguson) and Chelsea as well as collisions with fellow strugglers Coventry and Charlton. Would it go to the very last game, a trip to Southampton?

With the ownership battle in apparent deadlock, it was inevitable that speculation – some of it informed and some of it downright misleading – would now cloud the Goodison cocktail. A South African company, fittingly called Spirit, were said to be ready to hijack Kenwright's plans with a £60 million bid for Johnson's 68 per cent shareholding.

Kenwright vowed to continue his fight, but as the crucial month of May loomed, the full extent of the club's nightmare financial situation was revealed. It threatened to force manager Smith to sell more top players as a report by leading merchant bank Rothschild projected the club's overdraft would top £20 million by the summer.

This naturally cast further doubt on any HSBC backing for Kenwright who had been hoping to put in a reported bid of £43 million. "I have not withdrawn from anything and I am still in there fighting," he declared.

On May 5, 1999, with just eleven days of a tortuous season remaining, the inevitable happened. HSBC said it would not finance the theatre impresario's purchase of Peter Johnson's two thirds stake in the club and that discussions had now been terminated. Clearly, the overdraft was frightening off big city institutions.

Most people would have thrown in the towel at this stage. Kenwright's incredible resolve was demonstrated yet again when he said: "It has been a 24 hour a day mission to succeed and will continue to be so."

If only Everton could ensure safety in the top flight, there might still be a silver lining.

Super Kev's A Hat-trick Hero and Everton Are Safe

Saturday, 8 May 1999
Everton 6 West Ham 0

ONE of the real pluses for Everton had been Walter Smith's loan capture of Trabzonspor striker Kevin Campbell. Super Kev, as the fans christened him, was an immediate success. His arrival had coincided with a mini revival. Now West Ham came to Goodison and everyone was dreaming of safety.

Frenchman Olivier Dacourt had stated his desire to leave, claiming that the club had not lived up to its promises to invest in further star talent. He was booed when his name was read out. This was clearly a time for togetherness and the fans were only interested in those ready to fight for Everton's future. One of those men was Campbell.

Aston Villa were said to be ready to table a bid, but Campbell had warmed to the Goodison faithful and they in turn had taken him to their hearts. A second successive capacity crowd packed Goodison and revelled in a storming six goal victory. By the 57th minute a chant went up around the famous old ground: "Stand up if you love the Blues." Almost the entire stadium responded.

It's amazing how a thrilling day of football could suddenly help everyone to forget those ownership worries. Kenwright, for one, was beaming as the team stormed to their biggest win of the season.

Campbell would secure a hat-trick. He opened the scoring with a tap-in after 13 minutes, grabbed his second with a superb chip from a David Weir through ball after the interval and made sure he would be going home with the match ball with a solid drive after 77 minutes. It took his tally to nine in seven starts in a blue jersey. All the complaints and bitterness about Duncan Ferguson's departure seemed a thing of the past.

Michael Ball had added to Campbell's opener from the penalty spot after great work from Scot Gemmill earned the kick. Don Hutchison lashed in the third on 38 minutes to give the Blues a solid interval lead.

Enter Super Kev to bring the house down, Francis Jeffers also getting on the mark four minutes from time after Hutchison's corner was flicked on by Weir.

The problems off the pitch had still to be resolved. On it, Walter Smith had sparked that late season revival with Campbell a key element. It would win him the Merseyside Footballer of the Year award, voted for by *Liverpool Echo* readers.

It would also increase Bill Kenwright's resolve to keep fighting for the ownership of his beloved Blues.

Everton: Myhre, Short, Watson, Unsworth, Weir, Gemmill, Dacourt, Hutchison, Ball, Jeffers, Campbell. Subs: Simonsen, Degn, Ward, Bakayoko, Barmby.
West Ham United: Hislop, Sinclair, Minto, Lomas, Ferdinand, Ruddock, Lampard, Barkovic, Di Canio, Wright (Keller), Foe.
Attendance: 40,049.

Kevin Campbell pounces against West Ham.

The Marathon Man With A Royal Blue Dream

THE close season is normally a time for football fans to wind down, take stock and go on holiday. In the summer of '99 Bill Kenwright was still running the marathon that was the Everton Takeover Saga. Minority shareholders had raised the stakes with a letter to Goodison Park demanding to know if any official bid had been tabled.

Five supporters actually took it on themselves to go to the Waldorf Hotel in London to try and raise the profile of the club. It was a wildly ambitious venture, but it demonstrated how the whole saga was getting to everyone with a love of the Mersey Blues.

There was a certain assumption that nothing was happening behind the scenes and that both Sir Philip Carter and Kenwright were sitting on their hands.

This was not the case. The vice-chairman continued to court giant financial institutions in the City and remained buoyant that everything would ultimately be resolved.

The one thing that Everton needed at that time was unity. Many people recognised the irony of Carter and Kenwright working tirelessly to try and reduce the club's massive overdraft – ultimately for the benefit of Peter Johnson. The more effort the Goodison board put in to reduce the crippling debt, the easier it would be for Johnson to attract a buyer, possibly a rival to Kenwright's dream. It meant the whole exercise was a double edged sword, but Carter and Kenwright had no option but to press ahead with their blueprint for an Everton revival.

The one positive in all of this was that the board had never been more united. Where previously it had been one faction against another, there was now a consensus to work together for the benefit of the club. This was emphasised when the money was found to to complete the transfer of Kevin Campbell.

It was now August and close on nine months since Johnson had walked away from Goodison while retaining his majority shareholding. There was still no information coming from the Johnson camp and because club chairman Carter was seen to be backing Kenwright's bid, he was being kept in the dark as to any rival offers. It was an unusual state of affairs for a company about to be sold to the highest bidder. Some of Kenwright's close aides were advising him to walk away.

Set against this was his dream to take control of the club.

Wirral businessman Gerry White was named as a possible rival. He would emerge as a middle man, looking to broker a solution from the Johnson side. It was stated that there were four interested parties, but who were they and how much were they offering?

Kenwright's bid remained the only one on the table as the club's annual meeting loomed on October 21. Would Johnson actually turn up as the majority shareholder? Would it be a sporting confrontation of the magnitude of Ali v Frazier, Ali v Foreman, England v Germany, Borg v McEnroe? The shareholders were certainly ready to come out fighting from the first bell.

The simple fact was that you can't have a "Rumble In The Jungle" without two combatants prepared to lock horns. Kenwright was there. Johnson did not show. But the fans still wanted answers.

They had read stories of Bernie Ecclestone, the Formula One motor racing giant being interested in pumping millions into the club. Richard Branson had been another name plucked out of the air. A Beverly Hills-based diamond merchant had been mentioned, a Manhattan finance house, a Wirral businessman, a multi-millionaire shipping magnate, not to mention a South African link.

Then there was the leader of the Popular People's Front. Yes, Bill Kenwright was still the only one out in the open. And after mentioning Ali v Frazier and Ali v Foreman to highlight the fighting mood of this historic Goodison AGM, it is fitting that the end to this story should come on Boxing Day 1999.

Fittingly, the team would set up a memorable Christmas party...

Five Star Blues Celebrate The End Of The Ownership Saga In Style

Sunday, 26 December 1999
Everton 5 Sunderland 0

WHEN news broke that Bill Kenwright had finally been successful in his year-long bid to become the new owner of Everton, relief swept over the whole club.

It was the worst possible moment for in-form Sunderland to arrive on a Goodison Park stage. Peter Reid's men began the afternoon in third place in the Premiership and seeking a club record of unbeaten away games.

They finished the game punch-drunk and on the ropes as Don Hutchison inspired a magnificent victory that left Kenwright with a smile as wide as the Mersey Tunnel. Hutchison pounced for the first after 15 minutes following a miscue by Mark Pembridge. He doubled the lead after 25 minutes with a thundering volley.

At the other end, 37 year old Richard Gough marshalled the home defence superbly and even had the legs to get forward and slip a pass to Francis Jeffers to give Everton a 3-0 half-time lead.

Where there had been a pantomime at times, there was now a fairy story. Kenwright Productions raised the curtain for an equally inspiring second half. Mark Pembridge tapped in his first goal for the club to make it 4-0 after good work by Hutchison, Campbell and Jeffers.

Nick Barmby clipped the ball over Sorenson, only to see it cleared off the line. Hutchison then opened up the creaking Sunderland defence again for Campbell to clip a ball into the Gwladys Street net for the fifth.

Bill Kenwright stood in the Directors Box to lead the standing ovation as the players left the pitch. It was a truly an historic day in the life of Goodison Park.

Everton: Gerrard, Dunne, Weir, Gough, Unsworth, Barmby (Cleland 74), Hutchison, Collins, Pembridge, Campbell, Jeffers (Moore). Unused subs: Watson, Cadamarteri, Simonsen.
Sunderland: Sorensen, Gray (Reddy), Bould, Butler, Makin, Schwarz, Roy (Williams), McCann, Summerbee, Kilbane, Quinn.
Attendance: 40,017

Francis Jeffers celebrates his goal against Sunderland.

Kenwright's Agony And Ecstasy On The Finishing Line

AS the seconds ticked away prior to Everton's Boxing Day clash with Sunderland, all eyes had been on the Directors Box where Bill Kenwright, successful at last in his bid for the club's majority shareholding, had been expected to take his seat before the kick-off.

Even his fellow directors were bemused when the match started without the man

The smile hides the agony Bill Kenwright had endured en route to Goodison.

of the moment. Some even wondered if there had been a late hitch regarding his £30m bid for the club. The truth was that Kenwright had been struck down with a stomach bug which he put down to a week of non-stop negotiating.

He was actually advised not to travel up from Sunderland for the game, but nothing was going to stop him on this day of days. He said: "I felt rough but I just had to be there. A journey from London that should have taken three hours stretched out to five and a half. The motorway was manic, the cars were bumper to bumper, but that was only the half of it. I had to keep making emergency stops at every service station. My stomach was churning and I can only think that it was as a result of the intense negotiations."

The vice chairman and new owner finally made it and witnessed a remarkable celebratory 5-0 victory. Minutes later, as he was updating the media on the final moments of his takeover success, he also announced that Walter Smith had accepted an extension to his contract.

The new millennium dawned with a new owner in place, with the manager committed to continuing his process of continuous improvement and with a familiar story edging back into the headlines. Once again, a stadium move for Everton was back on the agenda. Wasn't this where we came in 108 years earlier? The Goodison Story will continue to enthral us for the next hundred years.

Servants Of Everton

Everton were promoted at the first attempt in 1930-31 and also reached the semi-final of the FA Cup before losing to West Brom. The *Liverpool Echo* published this outstanding drawing of chairman Will Cuff, one of the club's finest servants.

DOWN the years, Everton have been lucky enough to have men of rare dedication guiding their fortunes. George Mahon, the Goodison Park visionary, has been given much prominence along with Dr James Clement Baxter, who held the record for official service until his death in 1928. Dr Baxter, whose generosity eased the club's financial worries during those early months at Goodison in 1892, clocked up 39 years service on the board, many of them as chairman.

In 1895, following a major board upheaval, the name of Mr Will Cuff came to the fore. He would become a Goodison Park marathon man, exerting his strong will on the club until he resigned from the board in May 1948 after an internal wrangle with fellow directors.

Cuff had links with the St Domingo Church from which Everton emanated. He became an Everton member in 1890 and supported the club through the difficult times of 1892 when the move from Anfield to Goodison was completed. In 1901, he stepped down from the board to become club secretary, succeeding Mr Richard Molyneux.

He held this office until 1918, when he resigned because it was affecting his work as a solicitor (his Everton work was unpaid). But Cuff returned to the board in 1921, became chairman a year later and retained that high office until 1938. He continued as a director for a further ten years. It meant that, apart from his three year break, he had powerful connections with the Blues for over half a century.

Cuff also worked tirelessly for the Football League, becoming president in 1940. He joined the Management Committee in 1925, taking 42 out of a possible 43 votes. In 1929, he successfully campaigned for the automatic election of Management Committee members on to the FA Council. On the home front, he was at the helm as Everton suffered relegation for the first time, bounced back to gain promotion, won the League Championship and then the FA Cup.

Dixie Dean called him 'The Master'. One or two of his rivals called him other things. Cuff was a man who did not sit on the fence and he was never scared to ruffle feathers. He was largely responsible for selling Everton's original training ground to a brewery for £60,000 and then buying

In November 1934, Everton vice-chairman Mr Ernest Green received a gold wristlet watch from chairman Mr W.C.Cuff to mark his 21 years service. To Mr Cuff's right (arms folded) is former player Jack Sharp, who by now was a director. Second from right is Dr C.Baxter (son of Goodison pioneer Dr J.C.Baxter).

the present Bellefield site in West Derby from the Co-op for £30,000.

Much earlier, in 1911, he had realised the importance of having a strong supplementary League to bring players through and give experienced players out of favour the opportunity to retain their match fitness. Hence, the Central League was born containing the reserve teams of many of the top clubs, including Everton.

As League president, he handled the sometimes bitter negotiations with the Players' Union over wages. He got players'

shirts numbered, helped to introduce the transfer system and then fought hard, but without success, to limit the fees which he felt were getting totally out of hand. He helped to devise the offside law and the methods of promotion and relegation. In other words, he was a man who got things done.

But in his later years, Cuff began to fall out with his fellow Everton directors. Some of them accused him of wrongful use of proxy votes at a shareholders' meeting. He denied this totally. They also complained that he was critical of club

policy, or as he called it, lack of policy. The man himself, now 76, felt his vast experience gave him the right to express his opinions, even if contrary to the views of fellow directors.

There was an uneasy peace for three years, intermingled with spells of bitterness, before Cuff finally resigned in May 1948. He died soon after, on 6 February 1949. His epitaph was not as a troublemaker, but as a troubleshooter, a real leader of men, and most of all a dedicated Evertonian.

He was the loudest and most influential voice Everton have ever had on the Football League Management Committee. It's worth charting other Goodison 'League' men:

R.Molyneux served the Management Committee 1893-95; Dr J.C.Baxter 1904-19; Cuff 1925-36, also being vice-president 1936-39, president 1939-49 and life member 1945-49; P.D.Carter was president from 1986-89. Sir Philip Carter, of course, remains an Everton board member, having been chairman through the most successful spell in the club's history when the League Championship (twice), FA Cup and European Cup-winners' Cup came to Goodison Park in the 1980s.

The members of the Everton board in Goodison Park's Centenary year were: Dr David M.Marsh (chairman), Desmond Pitcher (deputy chairman), Alan Waterworth, Keith Tamlin, Sir Philip Carter, David Newton, Bill Kenwright. Secretary and chief executive as the Blues headed into a bold new era in the newly-formed Premier League was Jim Greenwood. He joined the club in 1975 when he replaced Chris Hassell as secretary. Greenwood served the Blues for over 20 years before announcing his retirement prior to the 1996 European Championships. He had accepted an offer from the Football Association to become Centre Director for the North-West during Euro 96, a prestigious and deserving way to sign off a lifetime's service to football. Michael Dunford would arrive from Derby County to become the new Everton secretary.

Of course, no chapter concerning Everton's greatest servants would be complete without special reference to goalkeeper Neville Southall who would play his 750th game for the club on Saturday, 29 November 1997, when Tottenham visited Goodison Park.

The Welsh international had already broken every appearance record available to him, but this milestone was particularly significant because it was clear that his great Everton career, which had started with a 2-1 win against Ipswich Town on 17 October 1981, was now drawing to a close. The Blues had signed

Thomas Myhre from Viking Stavanger of Norway and it was clear that manager Howard Kendall was considering giving him his big chance.

However, when the teams were announced at Goodison Park shortly before kick-off, Southall was still in his familiar position between the posts. The side was: Southall, Short, Bilic, Tiler, Ward, Williamson, Speed, Farrelly, Phelan, Ferguson and Barmby. It is interesting to compare it with the team he joined in 1981: Southall, G.Stevens, Bailey, Walsh, Lyons, M.Thomas, McMahon, O'Keefe, M.Ferguson, Ross, McBride. It highlights the remarkable road that Southall travelled, enjoying Championship, FA Cup and European Cup-winners' Cup glory along the way.

The fans saluted him in familiar fashion against Tottenham without fully realising that they were witnessing a little piece of Everton history.

That Everton lost this vital game 2-0 is no reflection on Southall. He was beaten in the 71st minute when Sinton's cross was flicked on by Fox to the unmarked Ramon Vega at the far post. The great goalkeeper had no chance as the Spurs player headed home.

Four minutes later David Ginola broke down the left and brushed aside a challenge from Ward before firing an unstoppable rising shot into the roof of the net. Everton were beaten and the crowd vented their anger on the team, the management and the board in a show of understandable frustration. After 16 games, the Blues had managed to secure just 12 points – a clear signal that another worrying relegation campaign was on the cards.

In some respects, it was a sad way for Neville Southall's glorious Goodison Park career to end. His 750th appearance was completely overshadowed by the events of the day. But his contribution to the Everton cause has been so immense that

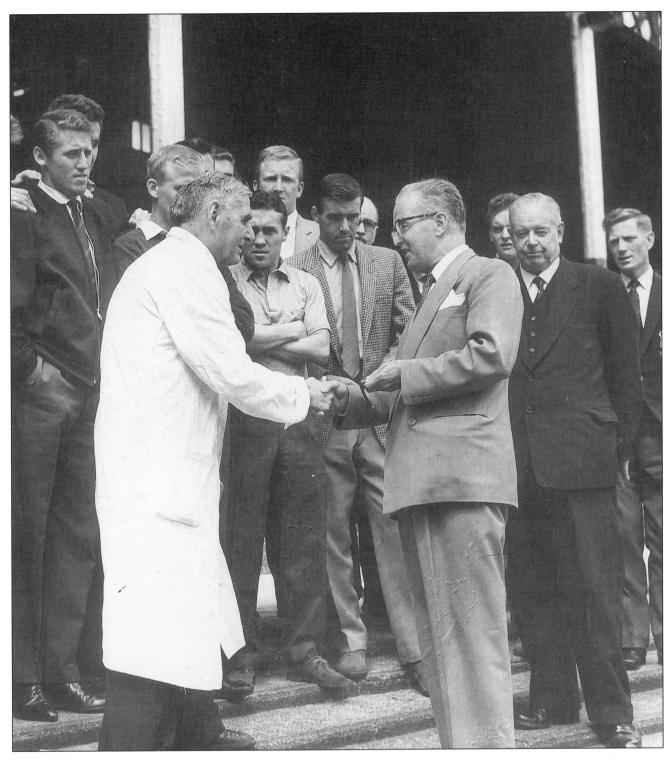

we will remember him only for being the finest goalkeeper in Britain at his peak, a dedicated Evertonian and possibly the most honest professional the game has seen.

He was a tremendous character whose 750 game appearance record, like Dixie Dean's 60 League goals, will never be beaten.

Southall left for Stoke City with a final word for the Evertonians who had supported him for so long. He said: "You look at their faces and you can see how the game frustrates them when things are not going very well, how disappointed they are when you lose and how happy they are when you win. It's a demonstration of how much the game means to them, how much a part it plays in their lives, and what made it even more of an honour to play for those Everton supporters.

"It is a sad day for me to leave Everton after so long, but it comes to everyone and

It's the end of a Goodison Park era. Everton chairman John Moores presents a gold wristlet watch to Harry Cooke on 28 July 1961 to mark the famous old trainer's retirement after 58 years service to the club. The Cooke link continued when grandson Harry Cooke became chief scout.

this time it's me. But I do not believe for a minute that it is the end of the world to be leaving the club. I've had a great career and I've left an awful lot of people I would count as friends behind, but I've got a new challenge and a fresh start at Stoke City. I still believe I am capable of first team football.

"Everton Football Club will always be special to me. Now it is time to start a new chapter in my career."

As a final aside, Neville revealed his greatest dream – to one day return to Goodison Park as team manager. It reflected his love of the club and his admiration for the supporters who had backed him for so long. Everton have had some wonderful servants.

Neville Southall is up there with the very best of them – officially installed in the Millennium Giants Hall of Fame along with Jack Sharp, Sam Chedgzoy, Dixie

Dean, Ted Sagar, T. G. Jones, Dave Hickson, Alex Young, Bob Latchford, and Dave Watson.

What a century it was for Evertonians who revelled in *Goodison Glory*.

Equally, what a century it had been for Goodison Park itself.

The famous old ground had witnessed many changes, staged countless epic clashes and seen legends come and go.

Always a stage for change and challenge, Goodison would now witness a remarkable summer of transfer activity as the first year of the new millennium unfolded.

Walter Smith would part company with Scottish international midfielders Don Hutchison and John Collins to Sunderland and Fulham respectively. More significantly, England's Nick Barmby became the first major Everton player since Dave Hickson in 1958 to leave the Blues for arch rivals Liverpool. This controversial departure would soon be overshadowed by ...the Gazza Factor.

A flurry of close-season activity saw Walter Smith bring in seven new faces.

Allesandro Pistone, Steve Watson, Alex Nyarko, Niclas Alexandersson and Tom Graveson all boosted Walter Smith's squad, but one deal claimed national and international headlines and put everything else in the shade, including the Barmby defection.

Paul Gascoigne, one of the British game's most colourful characters, breezed into

Neville was able to parade the FA Cup prior to his testimonial following a memorable victory over Manchester United. Eleven years earlier, in 1984, the famous 'keeper had held the trophy aloft for the first time after the Blues beat Watford at Wembley.

town. Goodison Park was dubbed 'The Last Chance Saloon' for this remarkable character whose career had been littered with controversy, but whose skill and natural ability still marked him out as one of this country's greatest ever talents.

The Gazza Factor would then be replaced by the Goodison Factor when, in July 2000, a feasibility study commissioned by the club revealed that Everton Football Club would have to leave its historic home of 108 years if it was to realise its 21st-century dream of achieving a 55,000 capacity with state-of-the-art facilities, capable of sustaining the Mersey giants throughout another eventful century.

It was finally countdown time for the Stadium of Royal Blue Legends.

Happy to be a Blue... Paul Gascoigne with Sir Philip Carter and Bill Kenwright after completing his shock move to Goodison Park.

The Gwladys Street End were convinced that Liverpool's Bruce Grobbelaar was a clown and so a couple of Goodison jesters decided to keep the Liverpool 'keeper company during the derby clash of March, 1982. Bruce saw the funny side and had the last laugh. Everton lost 3-1.

The old clock at the Gwladys Street End, long since gone, offered an unusual, if somewhat dangerous vantage point for this young fan when Manchester United were the visitors in December 1975. He saw Bob Latchford score in a 1-1 draw.

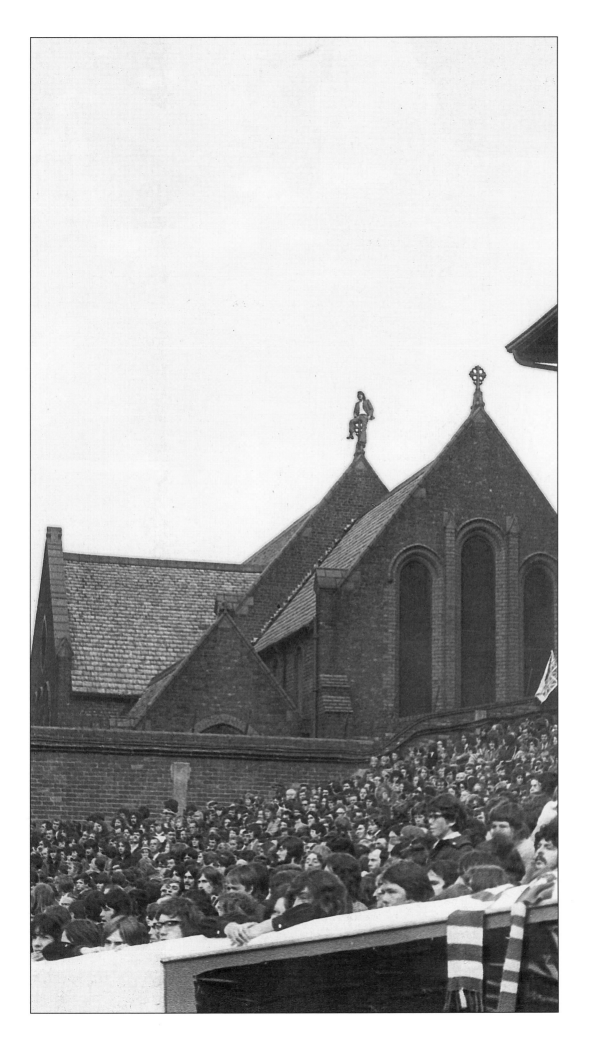

Evertonians have gone to remarkable lengths to watch their team down the years. In 1973, one fan took up a precarious position on the church roof at the Gwladys Street End.

Above: Screen heroes …Everton experimented with big screen action at Goodison in early 1995 to provide fans with an opportunity to watch key away games. Here is a fan's eye view of the action from the Stanley Park End as the Blues lose in controversial circumstances to Newcastle United.

Left: Thousands turned up to scream at the screen and the Geordies with the Blues under fire for being over physical.

Opposite page: The other Goodison Park. Everton daft Harold Boswell painted his Birkenhead house blue and white in 1977 and named it after his favourite ground. It included the club crest, pennants, posters and a flag run up the nearest lamp post. While his wife Lynne was still in hospital after having a baby son, Harold nipped off to register the birth, naming the boy after the entire Everton team. A furious mum stuck to her original choice, Jason.

Bibliography

Everton: The Official Centenary History by John Roberts (Granada).

Everton: The Complete Record by Ian Ross and Gordon Smailes (Breedon Books).

History of Everton Football Club 1878-79 to 1928-29 by Thomas Keates (Thomas Brakell Ltd). Library availability only.

Liverpool Daily Post & Echo archives.

The Football Grounds of Great Britain by Simon Inglis (Collins Willow).

The World Cup: A Complete Record by Ian Morrison (Breedon Books).

The Breedon Book of Football League Records by Gordon Smailes (Breedon Books).

Rothmans Football Year Book (Queen Anne Press).

Liverpool Review (Central Library archives).

League Football and The Men Who Made It by Simon Inglis (Collins Willow).

Football on Merseyside by Percy M.Young (Soccer Book Club).

Barclays League Directory 1992 (Burlington).

The Book of Football (Amalgamated Press, 1906).